ISRAEL
and the
ARABS

ISRAEL
and the
ARABS

Maxime Rodinson

Translated from the French by Michael Perl

Pantheon Books
A Division of Random House
New York

CONTENTS

MAR 17 '69

1 JEWISH NATIONALISM AND ARAB NATIONALISM

Once again in the course of human history, events in a tiny Middle Eastern province (in area about the size of Wales or of three French départements) have shaken the world and unleashed fierce passions from San Francisco to Karachi. The province is that little patch of Palestinian soil, barren and inhospitable, in which only the imaginations of half-starved nomads could see 'a land flowing with milk and honey'. But it is from here that a sizeable proportion of mankind have chosen to derive their God, their ideas, and everything that governs their life, customs, loves and hates.

A new epoch in the history of this land opened less than a century ago. This new phase, strange as it seems, was heralded by events and situations which arose in territories far removed from that land in distance, customs, social structure and ideas. Just as at the time of the Crusades almost a thousand years ago, Palestine's tribulations stemmed from the fact that far away men and women longed for her, and were ready to die for her, like lovers pining for an absent mistress.

In the eleventh century, Palestine's lovers were Western Christians moved by the memory of their God and the danger threatening his tomb. In the nineteenth century, they were Eastern European Jews. For almost two thousand years, Jews all over the world had dreamt of their old homeland as the land in which God would reign in their midst, a dream-world where the wolf would lie down with the lamb and a little child would lead them. But then God discreetly disappeared from the vision, and a very terrestrial kingdom emerged instead. Far from any Messianic prophecy, it was hoped that this would be an 'ordinary' kingdom where the rulers and the ruled, the rich and the poor, wise men and fools would live side by side, just as anywhere else.

7

There would even be, like everywhere else, murderers, thieves and prostitutes – from which no anti-Jewish inference should be drawn.

The Jews, once inhabitants of Palestine, had emigrated and scattered over almost the whole of the earth's surface – like their Syrian neighbours and many other peoples. The independence of their national home, again like many others, was destroyed by the Romans. But the cult of their national god Yahweh had certain characteristics which rendered it peculiarly attractive to many people. Their prophets had proclaimed that he was not only their God but the God of all peoples, although he had conferred a special privilege on the people of Israel, as they called themselves. One of their heresies, Christianity, had conquered the Roman world and spread beyond it. Many Jews were converted to pagan cults, then to Christianity, and later still, in the East, to Islam, a new religion born in the heart of the Arabian peninsula, which also drew its authority from their god, their laws and their prophets.

But as predicted by its prophets, a 'remnant' of the Jewish people was left, scattered over a multitude of different communities, remaining faithful to the old law, to the old scriptures, to ancient, complicated, archaic and cumbersome rituals. These, Jews in the true sense of the word, practising a minority religion, had been tolerated by the Christian states, but came to be viewed with increasing mistrust and hostility. Their failure to recognize the divine nature of one of themselves, Jesus of Nazareth, appeared more and more scandalous. After centuries of more or less grudging tolerance came the era of violent persecutions, of torture and the stake. Again, many became Christians. But as before, a 'remnant' was left, and multiplied in Eastern Europe where the Jews were at first welcomed. In the territory of Islam they were, like their Christian rivals, tolerated and 'protected', at the price of certain special taxes and discriminatory measures, and at the price also, from time to time and under special circumstances, of outbreaks of intolerance on the part of the Muslim mob – the 'poor white' reaction of those who cling to the last vestige of their superiority, their membership of the dominant community.

Within this network of self-contained minority communities,

interpolated like cysts in states professing a rival ideology, the hope of salvation survived. This salvation was to be prepared by God on behalf of his chosen people, whom in his mysterious but infinite love he had allowed to suffer, no doubt so that the happiness they were to inherit should be all the more splendid. The old homeland, Palestine, the land of Israel as they called it, together with its centre the Holy City of Jerusalem, were still worshipped as the place appointed for the final victory, the kingdom of peace and plenty at the end of time. The Jews visited it whenever possible; they hoped to die there; they had themselves buried there. But the task of preparing their return to the promised land was left to God.

After the fall of the Jewish State of Palestine and the last struggles for Jewish independence from the Romans in the years 70 and 135, up to the fateful day of 1948, only two Jewish states were ever formed. The first appeared in the Yemen at the beginning of the sixth century, and took the form of a core of original Jews ruled by South Arabian Arabs converted to Judaism. The other was likewise an Empire of the converted: the Khazars, a people of turco-mongoloid stock dwelling on the lower Volga. It lasted from about the eighth to the tenth century. For nineteen centuries these were the only instances when Judaism was anything other than a group of minority communities, and became itself a state religion.

The new spirit running through Western Europe in the eighteenth century was to change all this. Terrestrial communities were no longer built up around a god, but only within the framework of a state. The world of religious communities began to disappear, to be replaced by the world of nations. And for many men and women, God himself gradually receded from the earthly scene, to the point of disappearing altogether. The French Revolution drew the logical conclusions from these new conditions and new ideas. It proclaimed aloud and carried through to the end the abolition of every act of discrimination – a change already accepted by the enlightened despot Joseph II and by the young American Republic. Faith in a system of dogmas, the practice of certain rites, adherence to one or other religious community were no longer relevant criteria by which citizens of the same nation could be isolated from one another. Jews became Frenchmen like any other. They worshipped their own God after their own fashion, within the framework, if they so desired, of their own religious association, just as did the Catholics.

The logic of the French solution conformed so well with the social and ideological conditions of the time that Western Europe and America gradually came to accept it. The consequences for the Jewish situation were enormous. In this new world, religious communities no longer formed nations or quasi-nations to which the individual was bound, whether by choice or by force, but had become hardly more than free associations much like political parties or chess clubs. In this situation, a Jew who lost faith in the religion of his ancestors was no longer obliged either to be converted to another religion or somehow to sidestep the innumerable practical and moral problems with which he was faced as the subject of a community whose creed he did not accept. He became a Frenchman, an Englishman or a Belgian, of Jewish origin, and even this fact would probably fade from men's memories. No one could hold him to account for his religious opinions. No bond tied him to Judaism. And in conformity with the general tendencies at work in European society, such cases occurred with increasing frequency.

Of course not all Jews went as far as this. But cultural assimilation, which had always existed, became much greater. The notion of a 'Jewish people' had now become outdated. It had some justification when Jewish communities were universally regarded as foreign bodies encapsulated in the different nations, or as minority groups with no right of participation in the government of their states, when a multiple network of common interests united them wherever they might happen to be. Under the new order, all were full citizens of the various states; some of them happened to practise a certain religion, while others were descendants of practitioners of that religion. Even if their common religion created a bond between the Jews of different countries, the example of the Catholics and others showed that this common membership was easily reconciled with total commitment to each separate fatherland, a commitment which extended as far as mutual bloodletting without a trace of remorse or bad conscience.

Thus assimilation triumphed, to a greater or lesser degree. This is not to say that it was accepted and recognized by all non-Jews. For too long the Jews had been denounced as God's murderers and the servants of Satan. The Catholic Church and reactionary elements in every Christian confession smelt the hand of the Jew in every enterprise which undermined, to a degree increasingly dangerous to them, their ideological monopoly and the many advantages they drew from it. It is a commonplace of conservative ideological conventions to refuse to recognize that a progressive movement which attacks acquired privilege is the normal reaction of those classes in society who are discriminated against and oppressed. To denounce the motives of such a movement as a dark conspiracy of the forces of evil is much more convenient for the conscience of the privileged and much better propaganda material to direct at the ignorant masses. And who better to represent these forces than the Jews, to whom liberalization opened the doors of Christian society?

Moreover, it was true that the Jews detached themselves more easily than others from traditions in flagrant discord with the spirit of modern civilization; they were anxious to escape from the stigma of their underprivileged minority position to become a part of a larger society, and found themselves still the object of ancestral enmities. Hence in proportion to their numbers they always provided a very large contingent of liberals, reformers, even revolutionaries.

From time to time – and this is especially evident in the history of British Jewry – almost total assimilation would be freshly imperilled by the arrival of immigrants from parts of the world where the old order still persisted. These immigrants came from communities closed in upon themselves, cysts in the body politic of states in whose life they played no part, and hence having developed, in differing degrees, their own peculiar cultural characteristics. This was true of the Russia of the Tsars and of the whole of Eastern Europe, where the Jews (who had mostly come from the western parts of Germany in the Middle Ages) even spoke their own special language, Yiddish, a Germanic dialect with its own literature, existing in the midst of Slav populations. And then the Jews from Eastern Europe would appear in the West, repopulate the deserted synagogues, and once again build up their own community life until they, in their turn, were assimilated.

In 1879 a fateful event took place. Bismarck, personally devoid of any prejudice against the Jews, found it expedient for his internal policy to launch a campaign of 'anti-Semitism', to use the term which had recently become popular in Germany, where certain writers of small influence had been developing this theme as a stick with which to beat liberalism. The weapon proved effective, and it was taken up to meet similar political circumstances in Austria, France and Russia in the years which followed. As James Parkes very rightly says,

Political antisemitism had extremely little to do with the Jews as such. . . . The enemy was 'liberalism', 'industrialism', 'secularism' – anything the reactionaries disliked; and they found by experience that there was no better way of persuading their electors to dislike these things also than to label them 'Jewish'.*

Extremely violent verbally, political anti-Semitism provoked relatively little physical violence in Western Europe until the victory of Nazism. But in Russia, where Jewish communities of the medieval type still survived in large numbers, the reactionary Tsar Alexander III decided to avenge the death of his father on the Jews (Alexander II was killed by revolutionaries in 1881; the assassins happened to be Jewish). The Tsarist administration likewise deliberately developed anti-Semitism as a political weapon against liberal ideas, and used it with great success among the more backward classes of the population, who were unleashed on the defenceless Jewish communities. The Russian pogroms filled the civilized world with horror.

The Jews reacted in various ways. Many of them gritted their teeth and waited for the storm to pass, remembering that similar persecutions had in the past struck at the French Protestants and the English Catholics. Some emphasized their assimilation, changed their name, and broadcast their attachment to the religion and cultural values of their adoptive homeland, in an effort to obliterate their origins. Others fought with intensified fury, side

*James Parkes, *An Enemy of the People : Anti-Semitism*, Penguin Books, Harmondsworth, 1945, pp. 10–11.

by side with liberals or revolutionaries of Christian origin, for a society from which anti-Semitism would be extirpated root and branch. In Eastern Europe, where the Jews still formed almost a nation of their own with its own Yiddish language and culture, a local cultural nationalism grew up, broadly socialist in spirit. This was the ideology of the Bund, the Jewish Socialist Party of the Russian Empire, founded in 1897.

Another reaction was openly nationalistic in spirit: this was political Zionism, created by a thoroughly assimilated Jew, the Viennese journalist Theodor Herzl. Appalled by the demonstrations of the French mob against Dreyfus, Herzl feverishly wrote his *A Jewish State* in 1896. In it, he showed himself converted to nationalism and in agreement with the anti-Semites on the diagnosis that the European Jews were an alien element, unassimilated for the most part, and in the long run inassimilable. They constituted a people, a nation. The remedy to the situation lay in departure, in the possession of a homeland, such as other nations had. Somewhere a Jewish State, purely Jewish, autonomous and independent, had to be created. But where? A number of possible solutions were canvassed, including the Argentine. But the clear preference was for the ancient homeland, Palestine, abandoned by most Jews for almost two millennia. The messianic fervour of religious Jews, the emotions aroused by Biblical texts, and traditions which retained their power even over Jews who had ceased to identify with Judaism, all contributed to an effective mobilization of Jewish opinion towards this end.

Palestine was at that time an Arab province of the Ottoman Empire. This did not appear a great obstacle. Around 1900 colonization projects did not have the unfavourable aura that surrounds them today. More or less backward populations were being introduced to progress and civilization, even at the cost of being displaced or somewhat subordinated. It is hardly surprising, therefore, that this Europe-originated project showed little concern for the fate of the inhabitants of the one-time promised land. Likewise, as was normal in the atmosphere of the times, the only strategy considered was a pact with some power or group of powers in exchange for favours which the would-be settlers might be in a position to bestow. The terms 'colonization' and 'colony' were used quite without inhibitions by the pioneers of political Zionism. Herzl wrote of Palestine: 'We should there form a portion of the rampart of Europe against Asia, an outpost of civilization as opposed to barbarism.' *

Small Jewish colonies did exist within Palestine. Jews of many different origins had come to settle in the Holy Land, side by side with an already motley population. In 1880 they numbered some 24,000 of a total of perhaps 500,000 inhabitants. After the new wave of anti-Semitism had begun in Russia in 1881, great numbers of Russian Jews fled to Western Europe or the United States, but some directed their steps towards Palestine. A movement had sprung up among the Russian Jews advocating the establishment of Jewish agricultural settlements in Palestine or Syria. Agricultural labour was supposed to regenerate the Jewish people, degraded or at least denatured by centuries in the ghetto. A variety of Tolstoyan socialism became manifest in the movement of the 'Lovers of Zion'. It was possible that a true Jewish socialist society might grow up in Palestine. But the Jewish settlements in Palestine were not numerous, and before the advent of Herzl the prospect of a Jewish State was ignored or considered to be extremely far off. Then came Herzl, and the first Congress of the Zionist Movement held in Basle in 1897 marked a new departure.

Throughout all this, the actual inhabitants of Palestine were ignored by practically everybody. The philosophy prevailing in the European world at the time was without any doubt responsible for this. Every territory situated outside that world was considered empty – not of inhabitants of course, but constituting a kind of cultural vacuum, and therefore suitable for colonization. And in fact the European nations were able to impose their will in most parts of the world without too much difficulty.

It was unfortunate for the form of Jewish nationalism represented by Zionism that just at the moment when it decided to direct its efforts towards achieving a Jewish State in Palestine, the natives of that country began to be affected by a similar ideological movement, namely Arab nationalism.

The Arabs were an ancient people from the near East, whose

* Theodor Herzl, *A Jewish State*, London, 1896, p. 29.

language, like that of the ancient Hebrews, was a branch of the family known as 'Semitic'. Ancient Hebrew mythology recognized them as close relatives of the Hebrews, together with all the other neighbouring peoples, and it is certainly true that the same ethnic or racial characteristics appeared, perhaps in slightly varying degrees, in all these peoples of the ancient Middle East. Of course this by no means prevented bitter rivalries, sometimes going as far as outright hostility. The Arabs, inhabitants of the Arabian peninsula, began at a very early date to make frequent incursions into neighbouring territories. At the beginning of the seventh century they were politically and ideologically united by their prophet Muhammad (or Mahomet), who preached a new religion, Islam, which drew heavily for its inspiration on Judaism and Christianity. The Arabs subsequently conquered an enormous area of the earth's surface, extending from India and the fringes of China to Spain and Southern France. They did not force their religion on the conquered Jews and Christians, since they granted that these religions were in possession of a certain element of the truth. Religious minorities were 'protected', though obliged to pay special taxes. However, the political and social conditions of the state ruled by the Muslim Arabs (soon to become fragmented) gradually induced the majority of its subjects to embrace the Islamic faith. Some of these subjects, between Mesopotamia and Morocco, were gradually 'Arabized' and became indistinguishable from their Arab conquerors.

Arab domination was brief among those peoples – principally the Persians and the Turks – who, although they had become Muslims, had not been Arabized. Native Persian and Turkish dynasties very soon came to power and before long dominated the Arabs and their Arabized subjects. National feeling certainly existed at that time, in that part of the world as elsewhere, but had not as yet acquired an ideology. To be ruled by sovereigns of foreign origin was a perfectly normal phenomenon, in many cases accepted for thousands of years. Co-religionism between rulers and ruled (except for some minority groups) seemed a far more important characteristic.

From the fourteenth century a Muslim state, that of the Ottoman Turks, began to show its strength in Anatolia. By the sixteenth and seventeenth centuries it had subjugated most of the territories with Arab populations, in particular Egypt, Palestine and Syria, which had for two or three centuries been under the suzerainty of the Mamelukes, rulers who were themselves of Turkish origin. The Ottoman Empire was an immense structure, governed from Istanbul (previously Constantinople). The Sultan who resided there ruled over a tremendously varied population, extending from Belgrade and Bucharest to Algeria and the Yemen. His power was, of course, sanctified by Islam. The minority religions, Christianity and Judaism in particular, were allowed considerable autonomy; but the governors of the various provinces of the Empire made their authority felt by all their subjects through their highly arbitrary rule, and above all by extracting the maximum tribute in taxes, dues and rents.

Towards the end of the eighteenth century the preponderance of Europe began to make itself felt. The economic, technological and military superiority of this part of the world, which had for some time been foreshadowed by increasingly spectacular scientific advances, became more and more overwhelming. European merchants who had long had a foothold in the Muslim countries enjoyed an increasingly privileged position. European ambassadors who had earlier had little status were now admitted to the Sultan's counsels and even began to dictate policy. They were frequently aided and abetted by the local Christian community, their common ideology providing a means of mutual understanding, and also by the local Jews, many of whom came from Europe, and who in any case maintained close relations with their European co-religionists. The Ottomans, who as recently as 1683 had stood before the gates of Vienna, now retreated through the Balkans before the Christian powers. The Balkan subject peoples revolted one by one, with European encouragement, eroding the frontiers of the Empire. The French took Algiers in 1830, the English Aden in 1839, thus beginning the movement of direct colonization. After a pause during which the European powers consolidated their indirect but terribly effective hold over the whole of the Ottoman Empire, Anglo-French colonial expansion moved inexorably forwards: Tunisia in 1881, Egypt in 1882, the Sudan in 1899, Libya and Morocco in 1912. At the same time, the cultural influence of Europe grew everywhere stronger. Its values, its forms of organization, even its fashions had increasing impact, penetrating first the rich and cultured elite, then gradually the poverty-stricken masses. Europe brought domination and humiliation; but at the same time she introduced a new style of political and cultural life. She showed that a political structure was possible in which the state's subjects could also have their say in its government, and that a culture was conceivable in which the masses could be educated to a degree enabling them in principle to understand and participate in decisions taken at the topmost level. Moreover it was these organizational forms which appeared to express European superiority, enabling an advance along the path of infinite progress towards greater liberty and greater welfare. Slowly new aspirations, new loyalties, new ideas began to appear and to spread.

This new mentality, the new horizons which Europe had revealed, only served to make European domination, whether direct or indirect, even harder to bear. The most universal sentiment was an immense humiliation, shared by an entire people, from sultan to the humblest peasant. Moreover those who were most determined to learn European ways and share the secret of her power usually did so as a first step on the road towards an implacable revenge.

The Muslim rulers, who had to make decisions from one day to the next, reacted as best they could, according to the pressures acting on them and their different temperaments. Some clung to the old forms and structures on which their power was based, and resisted all change except under duress. Others attempted to introduce reforms, in a more or less consistent manner. In a society in which the old order of things largely persisted, under the watchful eye of the European powers who made sure that such reforms would in no way threaten their dominant position, these measures usually came to nought, or resulted in deadlock or crisis.

The future was being forged elsewhere. Intellectuals of a new type were gradually beginning to appear, who although educated in the traditional disciplines of the old culture were sensitive to the new situation, open to new ideas, and convinced of the need to lead their peoples out of the dark tunnel of backwardness and humiliation. Their level of culture was uneven and frequently superficial, they varied greatly in intellectual power and moral standards; it would be easy to highlight the unscrupulousness of some of them, the deficiencies of others, the defects of all. Nevertheless, it was their function as intellectuals to create dynamic and appealing ideologies; and they fulfilled this function. This was not done as an abstract exercise but with direct reference to the objective situation as they saw it. Their ideas, inasmuch as they reflected the situation accurately and held out some hope of a solution to universal problems, evoked an increasingly powerful response.

The men who won influence over increasingly wide sections of society and ultimately left their mark upon history were the prophets of immediate or eventual liberation. They expected a more or less Utopian breakthrough towards a new set of values: the suppression of privilege; liberty; welfare; in short, happiness. Naturally enough, this liberating upsurge was at first conceived within the old framework of society. The existing frameworks were the Muslim religious community, the *oumma*; and the political structures – the Ottoman Empire, Iran and the state of Egypt. The first great mobilizer of opinion was Jemâl ad-dîn al-Afghâni (1839 – 1897). He belonged to the select line of great nineteenth century nationalist and liberal revolutionaries. Like them, he was a conspirator, and a secularist freemason. By plots, expedients and lies, he dedicated his life to the cause which he hoped to lead to victory. Actually a Persian Shiite, he posed as an Afghan Sunnite in order to gain greater influence over the orthodox Mohammedan world (hence his pseudonymous surname, al-Afghâni, the Afghan). At some point in his career he had decided that religion was still a powerful force and not to be despised. He hoped, indeed, to exploit it in arousing the masses to revolt against reactionary despotism, allied in his view with foreign domination. He thus assumed the character of a Muslim Holy Man, not without revealing quite different features to his European friends. He attempted to play off one European power against others, frequently changing his tactics and running the risk of being himself more exploited than able to exploit these powers. But he sowed ideas; simple and sometimes wrong but always dynamic ideas. They were to fall on fertile ground.

He won many disciples, in Iran, in the Ottoman Empire and throughout the Muslim world. Their attitudes towards Islam, towards the modernization of their society and social progress, and towards the use of violence differed considerably. But they were united by one fundamental aspiration, the most common characteristic of that mass of society which they represented: the recapture of national independence from the European colonial powers.

This central theme was argued on different grounds and with different emphasis by the various ideologies. But it was always present. And around these ideologies there grew up very gradually small and at first insignificant groups of men dedicated to putting the programme of liberation into effect.

Who was to be liberated? The Muslim community, the Ottoman Empire, the Egyptian nation, the Arab people? It mattered little at first, since the enemy was in every case the same – the European imperialist powers, and especially the most dynamic of them at that time and the most actively interested in the area, Great Britain.

Nevertheless, European nationalist ideas infected all the political ideologues of the Muslim world; and they based themselves on a European model – the nation-state built up around a people defined by a common language. This alien model, which ultimately captured the imagination first of the elite and then of the masses, must have struck a chord in pre-national feelings of identification – inhibited no doubt by community of religion, but nonetheless always present in more or less repressed form.

The Turks were the first to be affected by this type of nationalism. The 'Ottomanists' had originally wanted merely to create an Ottoman nation of the modern, liberal type in an atmosphere of romanticism. But because most of the members of this group were Turks, it was soon guided by feelings of specifically Turkish national pride. This found expression in increased interest in Turkish national origins, and a love for historic monuments to the ancient grandeur of the Turks. The Young Turk movement overthrew the despot Abdul Hamid in 1908, and replaced him by a regime which appealed to all the different national elements in the Ottoman Empire, but increasingly tended to maintain and reinforce the supremacy of the Turks in that Empire. This was bound to provoke a reaction among the other nationalities and favour the crystallization of Arab and other nationalist ideologies.

The broad outlines of such an ideology had already been drawn. Not surprisingly, a considerable number of the new ideologues were Christian Arabs from the Lebanon, who were not bound by any ties of religion to the Turks. After 1908, resistance to Turkish supremacy reinforced the movement in this direction. The minimum demand was for the decentralization of the Ottoman Empire; the maximum was Arab independence. But support for these demands was still hesitant. Most Arabs had not forgotten that 'the principal contradiction' (as Mao Tse-Tung was to say half a century later) was the struggle against European imperialism, even if some did not hesitate to court the aid of, say, France against Great Britain. Moreover the Muslim Arabs shrank from conducting a ruthless struggle against the Turks.

In Palestine, which had an Arab majority, the situation was complicated by the gradual growth of the Jewish settlements. These had now generally accepted Herzl's doctrine of political Zionism. Herzl (who died in 1904) had attempted to win the support of various European powers and of the Sultan Abdul Hamid for the establishment of his Jewish State in Palestine. At first this was to take the relatively innocuous form of an autonomous territory under Ottoman suzerainty, on the pattern of the Lebanon. This scheme was unsuccessful. Herzl's successors then put off the achievement of the final objective for a more auspicious time, but never lost sight of it. Meanwhile they continued to found Jewish settlements in Palestine to help reinforce their claims. By 1914 the Jews comprised 85,000 out of a total population of 739,000.

The Palestinian Arabs, in direct contact with the Jewish settlers, had realized the danger of having a foreign community isolated from the life of the local inhabitants grafted on to them. It did not require great perspicacity to understand the aspirations of this alien community to form a new national entity, and hence to subjugate or displace the native peoples. They had protested vigorously in the Ottoman Parliament. However, the virile nationalism of the Young Turks made any early cession of territory seem extremely unlikely. Jewish immigration was restricted by the Ottoman state, although bureaucratic corruption made the restrictions easy to circumvent. Some Arab nationalist leaders, especially non-Palestinians, contemplated an alliance with the Zionist movement against Turkish supremacy. Contributions from the Diaspora put considerable funds at the disposal of the Jews, who were far more advanced both technologically and economically, and were culturally on a level with Europe. They would therefore have been a formidable ally to the young Arab movement, which was poor and inexperienced, with a thoroughly underdeveloped social basis, to express it in fashionable terminology. And some negotiations towards an Arab-Zionist alliance did in fact take place.

But on 2 November 1914, the Ottoman Empire under the rule of the Young Turks entered the world war on the side of Germany and Austria-Hungary against Great Britain, France and Russia. A new era had opened.

2 FROM NATIONALISM TO NATIONS

War is said to be the midwife of revolution. It is also the midwife of nations. The world war of 1914–18 was a turning point in the destinies of both the Arab and Jewish nations.

No-one can say what would have happened if the Ottoman Empire had not been the ally of the Central Powers. But it was, and any weapon could be used against it. In April and May 1916, Great Britain, France and Tsarist Russia drew up a plan of partition for the greater part of the Empire in the secret Sykes-Picot Agreement. At the same time Great Britain incited Hussein, Sherif of Mecca, to revolt and proclaim a Holy War against the Turks. The Arab nationalist secret societies of Syria-Palestine and Iraq vacillated, torn between hostility to Turkish supremacy and their awareness of the European threat. Many Maronite Christians in the Lebanon, followed by Muslim Arab nationalists, looked towards France. The Turks got wind of these secret dealings, and were aware of a certain diffuse hostility. They thought that the Arabs' tentative plans were on the point of fruition. The Young Turk proconsul Jemâl fired the powder-keg by hanging for treason some Muslim and Christian Arab nationalists at Beirut and Damascus. This precipitated Hussein's decision, and he began the revolt on 5 June 1916, proclaiming himself King of the Arabs on 29 October. Britain, France and Italy, however, only recognized him as King of the Hejaz. The exploits of the Bedouin forces led by his son Feisal and T.E. Lawrence, fighting side by side with English troops commanded by Allenby, have passed into legend.

The imminent collapse of the Ottoman Empire was now obvious even to the most short-sighted. It seemed a huge, inexhaustible cake, and every claimant promised portions to those whom they wished to attract to their cause. Great Britain wooed the Jews, many of whom sympathized with Germany out of hatred of anti-Semitic Tsarist Russia. The pacifist tendencies of the American Jews, who played such a major role in American industry, had somehow to be overcome; Russian Jews, said to be influential in the revolutionary movement, a: 1 Jews from all over the world had to be won over to the Allied cause. The British Zionists, led by Chaim Weizmann, persuaded the British Cabinet, in the face of opposition from anti-Zionist Jewry, that favours bestowed on the Zionist movement would win Jewish approval and gain powerful support for the Allies. The strong Biblical leanings characteristic of Protestants, the desire to counterbalance French claims on Syria and the Lebanon, the need to establish a base closely connected with Britain by ties of gratitude and interest (and, moreover, flanking the Suez Canal and the route to India) all helped to sway the British mind. On 2 November 1917 the Balfour Declaration promised the establishment of a Jewish national home in Palestine.

The Ottoman Empire crumbled, as predicted. As might also have been predicted, the ordering of its succession proved an extremely difficult task, in view of the multiplicity of contradictory promises made as to the distribution of its former lands. The Syrian National Congress meeting at Damascus in July 1919 claimed political independence for a united Syrian state (covering what is now Syria, the Lebanon, Jordan and Israel). The new state was to be a constitutional monarchy, with Feisal as king. French and Zionist pretensions were to be rejected and no mandate system could be accepted unless restricted to technical aid. On 8 March 1920 the Congress did in fact proclaim independence of Syria-Palestine with Feisal as king, and a programme of decentralization, the Lebanon being guaranteed a certain degree of autonomy. At the same moment, a meeting of Iraqi Arab nationalists was choosing Feisal's brother Abdullah as first King of Iraq under similar conditions.

On 5 May the conference of the Allied powers meeting at San Remo announced very different decisions. Without waiting for the meeting of the League of Nations, which was in theory supposed to 'bestow' the mandates (a new and hypocritical formula for colonization disguised as benevolent aid), the powers shared the mandates out amongst themselves. Two separate states of Syria and Lebanon were to be formed and placed under French tutelage. Iraq and Palestine (including Transjordan) were to come under British mandate, with a clause inserted providing for the application of the Balfour Declaration.

This announcement was a betrayal of all the promises made to the Arabs, and that betrayal was to condition subsequent events. At once it aroused a chorus of protests. In the Middle East as elsewhere, great faith had been placed in President Wilson's Fourteen Points containing the principle of the self-determination of peoples. Great Britain had made specific promises to the Arabs in order to gain and retain their support. They might have been couched in somewhat vague and equivocal terms; but they had been understood to guarantee the Arabs of the old Ottoman Empire freedom to decide their own destinies and also, to some extent, the right to form a unified state. They had indeed been so formulated as to be understood in this way. An American commission sent by Wilson to Asia Minor to sound out the wishes and complaints of the inhabitants had returned with recommendations based on their findings. All was in vain – given the intransigent claims of France, based on the secret Sykes-Picot agreement, and the strength of the Zionist pressure group. Instead of independence and unity came division and the subjection of the native peoples to the control of the great powers under the hypocritical form of the mandate. The disappointment, frustration and indignation were immense, and their effects were felt long afterwards. They have indeed lasted to the present day. The political situation in this area cannot be understood without reference to this background of profound and general resentment.

The year 1920 was called by the Arabs *âm an-nakba* – the year of the catastrophe. On 14 July General Gouraud, stationed in Beirut, sent an ultimatum to King Feisal of Syria in Damascus. The ultimatum was accepted; in spite of this, French troops marched on Damascus and occupied it. Feisal fled. Anti-Zionist riots had broken out in Palestine; Iraq was in the throes of insurrection. This did not prevent the San Remo decisions from being gradually brought into effect. Great Britain alone did make some attempt to limit Arab resentment against her, and made especially strenuous efforts to turn the fury away from herself on to others. She made some 'prestige' concessions by giving Feisal the throne of Iraq and recognizing his brother Abdullah as Emir of Transjordan. Transjordan was separated from Palestine and therefore placed beyond the scope of Jewish colonization. The French accentuated the division of the territories placed under their mandate. Gouraud created a State of the Lebanon, where France had many sympathizers among the Maronite Christians, by enlarging it to the north, south and east with additions of predominantly Muslim territory. This was Greater Lebanon, founded on 1 September 1920, which was to become later (May 1926) the Republic of Lebanon. The rest of French Syria was divided into three states: Damascus, Aleppo and the Alawi territory. In addition, two separate administrative areas were created: the autonomous territory of the Jebel Druse and, to the north-east, the Sanjak of Alexandretta (Iskenderun), with its partly Turkish population. In 1925 Damascus and Aleppo were joined to form the state of Syria.

The fate of the other Arab countries was rather different. In Arabia Sherif Hussein, whose sons now reigned over Iraq and Transjordan, was supplanted in 1924 by a chieftain from the interior named Ibn Saud. This Ibn Saud had had dealings during the war with the British Viceroy of India. In 1930, at Mecca, he had himself crowned King of Hejaz and Nejd, later to be called Saudi Arabia, a region still largely populated by nomads untouched by the ideological storms of the outside world. The Yemen continued its remote, archaic existence under the rule of the Zaydi Imamate, freed in 1918 of Turkish tutelage, which had in any case been somewhat hypothetical. The Emirates of the Persian Gulf, peopled by scattered tribes of nomads and fishermen, remained under British influence.

The ideology of Arab nationalism had at this time hardly touched the Arab countries to the west of the Suez Canal. Egypt, a British protectorate, rebelled in 1919 under the leadership of the Wafd party and claimed independence. On 28 February 1922 Britain declared Egypt a sovereign nation, and on 15 March the Khedive Fuad took the title of King of Egypt. Italian Libya, the French Maghreb and the Sudan, to all intents and purposes

British, remained under colonial administration; only a few squalls foreshadowed the coming storm.

At the heart of the Arab countries of Asia lay Palestine, where the British vainly tried to reconcile their contradictory promises. During the war the Jewish population had fallen to some 60,000 souls. In the autumn of 1919 it began once again to increase. Between 1919 and 1923, 35,000 Jews entered Palestine. Jewish settlers flocked in from all parts of the world, encouraged by the hope that Zionist dreams might now be near realization; after all, they were now embodied in documents of international law. The Jewish community set up a sort of Parliament and an Executive Council. The British military administration had given way to a civil government. But the first British High Commissioner to occupy the seat made famous in earlier times by Pontius Pilate was an English Jew, Sir Herbert Samuel, who had distinctly Zionist leanings and who remained in office until 1925.

Arab hostility was not slow to show itself in Palestine, and in the most violent fashion. In the spring of 1920 the first explosion of rioting against the Jewish immigrants broke out. Arabs in other countries gave increasingly clear indications of their hostility to the Zionist project of making Palestine Jewish. British governors gradually became aware of the enormous difficulties that Jewish colonization would cause. But the British had gone too far along the road of support for Zionist ambitions to retreat. The Zionist lobby was still extremely powerful; the British tried therefore to moderate Jewish ambitions so as to make them acceptable to the Arabs, whom they were in danger of alienating once and for all.

These considerations resulted in the British statement of policy known as the Churchill Memorandum, published on 3 June 1922. The Balfour Declaration, upheld in principle, was fairly subtly but unmistakably reinterpreted. What was to be the nature of the promised Jewish national home? Not, as some had been led to believe, a Palestine as Jewish as England was English. The intention had been simply 'the further development of the existing Jewish community with the assistance of Jews in other parts of the world in order that it may become a centre in which the Jewish people as a whole may take, on grounds of religion and race, an interest and pride.' Immigration would be limited according to the 'economic capacity of the country at the time to absorb new arrivals'. There was no intention to bring about the 'disappearance or the subordination of the Arabic population, language or culture in Palestine'. *

The British government gave the Zionist organization to understand that it would have to declare its official approval of this interpretation of the Balfour undertaking if it wished the British mandate over Palestine to become official. The organization's executive acceded, thus officially repudiating the project for a Jewish State, and hoping, as Weizmann put it, for 'a framework for building up a Jewish majority in Palestine'. † When such a majority had been established, the Jewish State would come about through force of circumstances. Hence it was with official Zionist endorsement of the reinterpretation of the Balfour Declaration excluding a Jewish State that the draft resolution according the Palestine mandate to Great Britain was presented to the League of Nations, and ratified by it on 24 July 1922.

The basis for future developments had now been created. The new situation had received the official seal, and now dictated the areas of political choice open to the various protagonists. Great Britain and France were now concerned to preserve and consolidate the dominant position in the Middle East given to them by the war. The frustrated Arabs fought for independence and unity. The Jewish Zionist colony in Palestine (the *Yishuv* in Hebrew) sought to consolidate its gains and to swell its numbers by immigration. The majority of the settlers remained faithful to their final goal – the Jewish State. Their preparatory measures, moreover, could not fail to bring this objective about.

In every Arab country resistance to direct or indirect foreign domination manifested itself in strikes, demonstrations and innumerable riots. Repression only reinforced the feeling of frustration and revolt. In some instances the population went as far as full-scale insurrection – witness Syria in 1925 to 1927 and

*Correspondence of Colonial Office with Palestine Arab Delegation and the Zionist Organization. Cmnd. Paper 1700, H.M.S.O., 1922.

†Chaim Weizmann, *Trial and Error* (illustrated edition), London, East and West Library, 1950, p. 361.

Palestine in 1936. Even the revolt led by Abd-el-Krim (1921 – 1926), in distant Morocco, which arose out of local conditions, might possibly be included in this category. In any case it appeared to the Eastern Arabs as another manifestation of the Arab revolt. In the East especially, the struggle against Zionism was on every programme. No matter which ideology happened to be leading the revolt, this projected foreign colonization of an Arab country, with the ultimate aim of amputating that country from the rest of the Arab world, was an affront to Arab nationalism, to Islam and to anti-colonialism alike.

The two colonizing powers, faced with this ever-present smouldering revolt, vacillated between two contrasting attitudes – as would any power in such a situation. Sometimes the policy would be to bestow power on well-trained puppet regimes, suppressing nationalist conspiracies by force. At other times, moderate nationalists with an impeccable record of loyalty to the Arab nation would be chosen as spokesmen for the Arab case. The colonial power would then enter into negotiations with these men in order to find a way of giving some satisfaction to the aspirations of the people without abandoning their foothold in the country concerned. Leaders contacted under these conditions shortly found themselves faced with an agonizing choice. Either they would have to agree to make concessions, and then proceed to suppress more intransigent elements, thus condemning themselves in the eyes of the masses as foreign agents. Or they would have to go back into opposition.

A common tactic on the part of the colonizing powers was to apply the policy of 'divide and rule'. They would give support to minority interests and ethnic groups to counterbalance the unifying and assimilatory tendency of the Arab nationalist movement. The French, for instance, attempted to exploit in this way the Druses and the Alawi in Syria, and the Berbers in the Maghreb. The British did the same in Iraq with the Assyrians, Nestorian Christians speaking an Aramaic dialect.

Similarly minority religious communities such as the Jews and, above all, the various denominations of Christians were supported against Islam, the majority religion, itself historically linked with Arab nationalism. This was the key to French policy in the

Lebanon, in particular. The unsurprising result of this policy was to compromise in the eyes of the masses – who tended to be profoundly nationalistic – all who agreed to play the colonialists' game. *Some* members of minority groups were of course quite eager to do this. At times when concessions to Arab nationalism were being made, these found themselves suddenly abandoned by their protectors, and suffered retaliation for their earlier apparent complicity. Retribution was sometimes terrible. In 1933 for example, the Assyrians paid by wholesale massacre for their earlier enrolment as 'levies' in the British armies of repression. It often happened that members of minority groups became hyper-nationalist so as to avoid this kind of consequence of the suspicions to which they were vulnerable.

The intensity of national feeling, manifested in a thousand everyday incidents, finally drove the colonial powers to grant independence to all the Eastern Arab countries under mandate or protectorate – except Palestine. This formal independence was supposed to satisfy national feeling, but care was taken not to make it full and comprehensive. The European patron states often retained very extensive powers, particularly in military matters and foreign policy. 'Treaties of alliance' signed after independence were sometimes used to restrict or camouflage these limitations to independence, in an attempt to appease general discontent. Thus Great Britain recognized Egypt's independence in 1922, while the mandates were in theory independent anyway. Treaties were signed with Iraq in 1922 and 1932, with Transjordan in 1928, with Egypt in 1936. France made the Lebanon an 'independent' republic in 1926, and in 1936 signed a treaty with Syria which the French Senate refused to ratify.

The Republican leaders of the French mandated territories and the kings of the countries under British influence had to steer a difficult course between their own peoples and the colonial powers. They frequently shared the aspirations of their own peoples, and they could not afford to become too alienated from them; yet at the same time they mistrusted them. On the other hand, they were dependent on the colonialists for their own authority. The Hashemites (sons and descendants of Sherif Hussein) had been deceived by the British, but nonetheless continued to throw in their lot with them, hoping to extract increasingly important concessions which would justify them in the eyes of their peoples. Above all, they could exploit British support against third parties, notably France and the Zionists. The British Secret Service and a host of officials in British pay, varying in number according to the vagaries of British policy, viewed France as an enemy power, and attempted to direct all the hostility of the Arab nationalists on to her. These same circles represented British support for the Zionists as an unfortunate side-effect of the war, destined gradually to disappear; and, indeed, a powerful pro-Arab lobby in London was working in this direction. This did not prevent the contempt and hatred felt for 'collaborator' governments from steadily increasing and spreading to ever-wider sections of the population. The fine past record of some Arab leaders in the struggle for independence and unity did not save them from their countrymen's resentment. The only ones to escape contumely were Feisal (who died in 1933), who charmed the populace by his romantic personality and was always felt to be the victim of the English rather than their accomplice; and his son Ghâzi, himself fiercely nationalistic, who was killed in a motor accident in April 1939 – public rumour seeing in his death the hand of the British Intelligence Service.

The mass of the population remained oppressed by feelings of disillusion, humiliation, frustration and anger. The Arab people itself had been cheated, used as a pawn; promises had been made and immediately broken, once the desired end had been achieved. The Arab world as a whole burned with the desire for revenge, to throw off the yoke of foreign occupation and achieve independence. Vague feelings of identity among the Arabic-speaking peoples, based on their common tongue, cultural heritage and history, were now reinforced by their struggle to free themselves from their common plight, a struggle directed against a common enemy. Upheavals in one country had major repercussions in all the others, whatever their outcome. The ideology of Arab nationalism, born in the Asian part of the Arab world, gradually spread.

Social conditions assisted this development. The growth of a modern economy, the creation of bureaucracies to sustain the new states, the wants of the occupying powers, all accompanied or followed by a widening of education, combined to expand and develop the tertiary sector, producing a new and numerous middle class. The new intelligentsia in particular were closer to the people and hence more militant and uncompromising than the old leaders of the nationalist movement, who tended to be large landowners and merchants with their own intellectual coterie, with international connexions and a cosmopolitan culture. Leadership of the nationalist movement gradually passed into the hands of these new elements, who had no strong ties with traditional intellectual culture and subscribed to a new ideology.

The influence of international ideologies was also felt. Marxism had only limited influence, although some of its ideas were taken up subsequently in a very general form. Only the Syrian-Lebanese Communist Party, after 1936, achieved anything significant. Fascism, on the other hand, especially in the form of Nazism, won considerable success after 1933 in the Eastern Arab world. Seen from a distance, it represented the ideal of a strong and unified state from which all internal dissensions had been eradicated, founded on the nation's will to autonomy and strength. This corresponded exactly with the current phase of the Arab national struggle. Added to this identity of aim was the coincidence of a common enemy. The principal enemies of Germany, and subsequently of the Axis, were the ensconced colonial powers, Britain and France; and, artificially, the Jews. These were the very enemies of the Arabs. Sympathy between the two movements was therefore inevitable. However, the Arabs were not blind to the darker side of the Fascist regimes and were mistrustful of their promises. After all, they too were European states, and if they had no colonies at the moment, this was only because the others had taken them away, a fact of which the Axis powers never ceased to complain. It was wiser not to trust interested allies too far; in any case, they gave little assistance. But a common enemy has always tended to move political groupings closer together, and the Arabs had at any rate nothing to lose from an upheaval bringing about the collapse and humiliation of the colonial powers.

Centrifugal forces also existed. However artificial the new

frontiers may have been, they had created regional networks of economic and political interests. Local patriotisms had grown up – Iraqi, Lebanese etc. Some of the more realistic leaders had appreciated the need for flexibility and manoeuvre.

By and large however, the most striking feature of the situation was the Arabs' hatred for the occupying powers, especially Great Britain. This was stirred up by very skilful German and Italian propaganda. The idea of Arab unity was an additional factor; Egypt espoused the cause in 1936, and it spread westward. The role of the press, radio and books gained in importance as the level of education rose, exerting a markedly unifying influence. It was at this stage that the war of 1939 broke out.

In Palestine, the *Yishuv* had increased in strength and level of organization, while Arab opposition to it became increasingly violent. The British were forced to take serious account of this Arab opposition.

British protection had enabled the *Yishuv* to increase its numerical strength through Jewish immigration. At the end of the Great War, there were some 60,000 Jews in Palestine, out of a total population of 700,000. A further 117,000 Jews entered the country between 1919 and 1931. But political crisis and unemployment forced many to leave again. From 1924 to 1931, 29 out of every 100 immigrants left the country after a brief stay. In 1927 there were more departures than arrivals – 5,000 as against 3,000. Nevertheless, in 1931 the Jews constituted 175,000 of the 1,036,000 inhabitants, or 17.7 per cent. Hitler's persecutions unleashed a new flood of immigrants, which saved the *Yishuv*. Numbers more than doubled. Between 1932 and 1938, 217,000 Jews entered Palestine, mainly from Poland and Central Europe. Many of them had some capital. 1,250 'capitalists', each possessing more than £500 sterling, arrived between 1926 and 1930; from 1931 to 1939 inclusive, immigrants owning more than 1,000 pounds numbered 24,247. In 1939 the Jews numbered 429,605 out of an estimated population of 1,500,000, i.e. 28 per cent.

The Jewish *Yishuv* was a thoroughly well organized force, practically autonomous, progressive and dynamic. Jewish agriculture was partly organized in settlements with a collectivized internal structure, and was geared to the production of high-quality, profitable and readily marketable produce. Every effort was made to use the most up-to-date techniques. Products were marketed through a network of cooperatives. A large-scale industry, by the standards of the country, had grown up. Practically all the electricity in the region was supplied by a Jewish company, the Palestine Electric Corporation. As mentioned earlier, the *Yishuv* was self-governing, through an elected Representative Assembly which controlled various social activities such as the organization of education. The Assembly could levy taxes on its own authority. Purely Jewish trade unions were united in the powerful *Histadruth* (trades union confederation), which as well as its trade union activities fulfilled the functions of capitalist entrepreneur, banker, insurance company, landowner and social security service. The *Yishuv* was divided into several political parties, and at its fringes some extremist religious Jews declared themselves anti-Zionist and refused to recognize the authority of its institutions. Nonetheless it formed a coherent bloc, a quasi-state, ready to take over full power in part or the whole of Palestine if occasion should offer. The majority, it is true, did not at this time place great hope in the objective of a purely Jewish State, and tended rather to explore the possibility of some kind of bi-national state. This meant negotiation with the Arabs, but these negotiations always came up against the question of immigration. Unrestricted immigration must necessarily one day lead to Jewish preponderance in a bi-national Palestine, and this the Arabs were not prepared to accept. An extremist wing within the *Yishuv*, the Revisionists, reproached the majority for its indecision, its dealings with the English, its consideration for the existence of the Arabs. It demanded a revision of the mandate, the extension of Jewish colonization to Transjordan, and the formation of a Jewish army which would establish the Jewish State by force.

The Arabs were divided into clans and factions, and found it difficult to achieve unity, despite the fact that the religious differences between Muslims and Christians counted for little, and that all agreed on the main issue: the need to prevent the *Yishuv* from creating, by whatever means, a Palestinian State dominated by the Jews in which the Arabs would be forced to choose between a position of inferiority and exile. One by one, they used every means of opposition open to them: political action, strikes, demonstrations which degenerated into brawls, and sometimes terrorism. Some were in favour of moderate tactics, leaving open the channels of communication with the British authorities, and even attempting to reach a basis for agreement with the Zionists. Others pressed for violent action, some turning hopeful eyes towards the Fascist powers. These, however, had more taste for inflammatory propaganda than for specific promises or concrete assistance. Hitler Germany even favoured the emigration of German Jews to Palestine. By 1936 tension in Palestine had risen to such a degree that the increasing spate of minor incidents finally erupted into a state of war. Armed bands of Palestinian Arabs supplemented by Syrian, Iraqi and other volunteers took to the hills, defying a British force of several tens of thousands of men (including Jewish auxiliaries) armed with tanks and aeroplanes. Strikes, street-fights and assassinations followed thick and fast upon one another's heels. The Arab rebels were divided into all kinds of different factions. In the countryside, full-scale peasant revolts took place, just as dangerous to the big Arab landowners as to the Zionists. Thanks to the Haganah, the illegal but tolerated Jewish secret army, the Jews were able to defend themselves. Some even undertook reprisals. On the other side, the Mufti of Jerusalem, an extreme nationalist leader, had Arab moderates executed. Just as a large number of wealthy Jews from Germany and Austria were entering the country, the Palestinian economy was in a state of paralysis, social life was disrupted, and the British army was fully occupied in obscure and dangerous missions.

The British themselves were divided into several different factions, in varying degrees sympathetic or hostile to one or other of the warring parties, and interested to a greater or lesser degree in the protection of the Suez Canal and the route to India. The Labour Party tended to support the Zionist cause, presented by the Zionist lobby as being in keeping with socialist ideals. Another major factor was hostility to Nazi anti-Semitism. On the spot, in Palestine itself, British officials and the military were frequently hostile to the Jews; but in any case, all attempts on their part to give objective consideration to the claims of one race was immediately interpreted by the other as shameful collusion with its enemy. By and large, however, the English were beginning to appreciate the substance of the Arab grievances and the dangers inherent in ignoring Arab public opinion in the current state of world crisis, when the conviction was growing that war was now inevitable. Various commissions were sent to the area to inquire into the causes of the difficulties and strife, and to suggest possible solutions. In 1937 the report of the Peel Commission first proposed the partition of Palestine into an Arab State and a Jewish State, with a third small state containing Jerusalem and a corridor to the sea to remain under British mandate. To the great astonishment of the English and the Arabs, it was the Jewish population, conditioned by Messianic propaganda proclaiming an all-Jewish Palestine, which forced its leaders to reject the plan. In 1938, when the civil war in Palestine broke out with renewed violence and the British had practically to reconquer the country, the Woodhead Technical Commission concluded that the Peel plan could never be put into effect. A round-table meeting held in February 1939 broke down in deadlock.

War was approaching. London was deeply preoccupied with the Anglophobia and pro-German sympathies of the Eastern Arab world. In May 1939, the question was brusquely settled by the British White Paper, which dictated the following terms: Palestine was to continue to be ruled by Britain. Negotiations for a constitution were to take place after five years, and for independence after ten years. 75,000 more Jews would be allowed to immigrate within the next five years, but after that the level of immigration would be conditional on the consent of the Arab majority. Sales of land to Jews were restricted in certain areas, and prohibited in others. Palestine was to be neither an Arab state nor a Jewish state. In fact, in the bi-national state envisaged, the Jews would be kept down to a level of one third of the population. Zionist indignation reached its highest pitch.

War broke out three months later. The White Paper did much to convert most Arab leaders from their policy of declared hostility to Great Britain. The Arabs' favourite policy was 'wait-and-see'. At first they hoped for an Allied defeat, which promised to liberate them from Anglo-French tutelage. The anti-British insurrection in Iraq in April and May 1941, led by Rashîd Alî Kaylânî, was motivated more by anger at Britain's Arab and Palestinian policies than by any great love for the Axis powers. The revolt failed. The Grand Mufti of Jerusalem, who had played a part in it, fled to Germany, there to assist the Nazi propaganda machine. The British made strenuous efforts to win back Arab friendship. In May 1941, Anthony Eder announced that Britain's attitude towards Arab unity was 'sympathetic' England played a decisive role in putting an end to the French protectorate over the Lebanon (1943) and Syria (1945), thus contributing to the achievement of full independence by these countries. On 22 March 1945 the founding charter of the Arab League was signed in Cairo under the aegis of the British.

In Palestine, the Jews were in general committed to assist the struggle against Hitler in every way possible. Many held important positions in the British Near-Eastern armies. They nevertheless continued to protest vigorously against the White Paper. Militant minorities among them, right-wing extremist groups, soon decided to begin terrorist activities against Britain, which they regarded as a colonial oppressor. Those most attracted to this form of action were, naturally enough, the young, who had not known the period when the English were primarily the protectors of the Jews – ill-disposed and harsh at times, no doubt, but protectors nonetheless. These youthful elements soon carried with them increasing numbers of adults, embittered especially by the restrictions on immigration imposed at a time when European Jews were being massacred wholesale. The organization which gave the first signal for terrorist action was the *Irgun Zvai Leumi* (National Military Organization), a splinter-group of the Revisionist party, from which in turn emerged the Stern Gang (or *Lehi*, for *Lohamei heruth Yisrael*, 'Fighters for the Freedom of Israel'). The latter rejected the truce the former had accorded the British at the outbreak of war. But the Stern Gang broke up on the death (probably by assassination) of its leader. The struggle started again in earnest at the beginning of 1944. It was condemned by the Jewish Agency and the Haganah, but supported by an uncompromising Jewish public opinion, outraged by the British refusal to allow free entry into Palestine to European Jews fleeing Nazi persecution. At the end of 1945, with the world war over, the Haganah also entered the war against the British, who continued to maintain restrictions on immigration. A deadly round-dance of terrorist raids, assassinations and blind reprisals followed. The situation soon became untenable for the British. The Arabs desired the victory of neither of the two antagonists and therefore remained passive spectators.

On 14 February 1947 Bevin capitulated. He announced that Great Britain would withdraw from Palestine, and handed over responsibility for deciding the country's future to the United Nations. Discussions then began at international level. The strength shown by the *Yishuv*, the solidarity of its local base, its single-mindedness and will to independence, and the efficiency with which it had conducted the 'war' against the English had convinced the great powers that peaceful coexistence with the Arabs was a pipe-dream. On 29 November 1947, the United Nations passed a resolution prescribing the partition of Palestine into an Arab State and a Jewish State, the internationalization of Jerusalem, and economic union of all three parts.

But the U.N. proved incapable of putting the plan into practice. The British refused to supervise its implementation, stating only that their troops, the only force capable of maintaining peace, would evacuate the country on 15 May 1948. From that moment, a bloody head-on collision between the two races became inevitable. The day after the U.N. decision was announced the Arabs launched a guerilla war, repudiating the international resolution. The Jews, who had become wiser since their rejection of the Peel plan, accepted a Jewish State far below their expectations; one which, nonetheless, might provide them with a firm base and, perhaps, a nucleus for further gains. The Arabs indignantly rejected what they regarded as an amputation of their territory and a confirmation that they were to be sacrificed to a project of colonization.

Guerrilla warfare raged throughout the months preceding the fateful day of 15 May 1948. Each side attempted to seize as much territory as possible in preparation for the departure of the English. The British troops who were gradually being concen-

trated in the major centres ready for evacuation observed an
ambiguous neutrality tending, if anything, to favour the Arabs.
The only truly military engagements in which they were involved were in an unsuccessful move to prevent the Jews from
conquering points attributed by the U.N. to the Arab zone,
notably Jaffa. The volunteers of the Arab Liberation Army,
numbering several thousands under the leadership of Fawzi al
Kawakji (who had earlier commanded a similar force from 1936
to 1939), entered Palestine in January 1948 and launched several
abortive attacks against the Jewish settlements. The daring raids,
skirmishes and street-fights in which this Army engaged provoked
Jewish reprisals on an even greater scale. These were at first led
by the right-wing extremist groups, the *Irgun* and the *Lehi*. The
official Zionist leaders who controlled the Haganah, the semi-
clandestine official army of the Jewish Agency, took a more sober
view of the recourse to arms, and still entertained some hope of
effective international intercession. But the response which
nationalist extremism evoked among the Jewish populace forced
them also into the attack. The flames of this nationalist fervour
were fanned by the *Irgun* and the *Lehi*, and ample fuel provided
by the havoc wrought by the Arab irregulars, who began more
systematic attacks, notably the blockade of the Jewish quarter of
Jerusalem. Reprisals became increasingly indiscriminate, spectacular 'warnings' to discourage further Arab attacks and to win
as much territory as possible before the British left. Some also
hoped that the Arabs too would be driven to leave, thus ensuring
a homogeneous Jewish population of the future Jewish State.
Terror against the Arabs was carried to its logical conclusion by
the *Irgun*. On the night of 9 to 10 April, a commando detachment
systematically massacred all 254 inhabitants, men, women and
children, of the Arab village of Deir Yassin. A full-scale military
campaign was conducted to take Jaffa, an Arab island in the
middle of Jewish territory according to the U.N. plan; in fact it
constituted a major military threat to Tel Aviv. Similar campaigns
were mounted to relieve the Jewish quarter of Jerusalem (international territory according to the same plan) and to clear the
road connecting the Holy City with the Jewish areas.

On 14 May 1948 the British High Commissioner left Palestine

and the evacuation of British troops was begun. On the same day, David Ben Gurion proclaimed the foundation of the Jewish State at Tel Aviv. The next day the regular armies of the neighbouring Arab countries moved into Palestine. They had prepared far-reaching plans of campaign, but in the end they were only able, with one or two exceptions, to occupy part of the areas granted to the Arabs by the U.N. plan. They were defeated by the Jews on every front. The Jewish troops were well-trained, their morale was extremely high, and they were totally dedicated to their cause. Their numbers were at first about equal to those of the Arab forces, but their lines of communication were much less extended. In the final phase of the war, there were 60,000 Jewish soldiers facing 40,000 Arabs. The Haganah networks in Europe and America had excellent connexions, and organized the purchase of arms, the recruitment of volunteers and mercenaries and their shipment to Palestine with tremendous efficiency and panache. The Arabs were handicapped by military inexperience, the uneven morale of their soldiers, the slackness of many of their officers, the corruption and incompetence of their bureacracies, and above all perhaps by the rivalry between states supposedly acting in concert who never communicated to one another their respective plans of campaign. The two cease-fires imposed by the U.N. seem to have served chiefly to allow the Jews to rearm and gather reinforcements. In order to maximize his advantages, Ben Gurion broke the truce and the various partial cease-fires on several occasions. The last time this was done, the operation code-word was, significantly, 'Fait accompli'. Only an Anglo-American ultimatum prevented him from pressing on into the Sinai Desert, beyond the Egyptian frontier.

The U.N. finally secured a prolonged cessation of hostilities on 7 January 1949. The last cease-fire dates from 11 March. Between February and April, a series of armistices were concluded between Israel and the various Arab states. The war was over, but peace had not been made.

The Zionists had achieved their aims. A Jewish State now existed. While its territory did not cover the whole of the mandate of Palestine, still less the lands of ancient Israel (which extended eastwards beyond the River Jordan), most Jews were content with the substantial platform they had won. As for the Arabs, a foreign colony had succeeded in seizing a part of their territory and driving out a number of its Arab inhabitants – and this with the support of the entire Western world, regardless of ideology, from the capitalist United States to the socialist U.S.S.R. The British mandate, imposed by force, had prevented them from taking any political or police action to halt the immigration of this new population. Once this population had achieved a firm base and sufficient strength in numbers it demanded its independence, first from its erstwhile patron, then from the native population which it hoped to dispossess or dominate. It had achieved this autonomy by force of arms, with the blessing of the whole of Europe and America, represented by the United Nations. Virtually all its violations of the decisions and 'orders' of the U.N. had been crowned with success. Even the murder of the U.N. mediator, Count Bernadotte, by Jewish terrorists was not allowed to count against it. The policy of the *fait accompli* never failed. The Arabs, full of bitterness and rancour, refused to recognize this European *Diktat*, this colonial amputation which had been imposed on them. Hostilities were only broken off because of their own impotence, which they hoped would be temporary. One way or another, for them the war would go on.

3 ISRAEL'S
FIRST DECADE

Israel was founded by a group symbolized by one man: David
Ben Gurion. The secret of Ben Gurion's success was that his
militant attitude was in perfect harmony with the logic of the
Zionist movement. He had made his choice as a young man, and
he was always able to see which actions accorded with the general
direction of Zionist policy and which drew their inspiration from
some other source. Like all great leaders of ideological movements, he held firmly to his central idea and was able at any point
in history to understand its implications in terms of action. Again
like many such leaders, there were times when he may have suspected that the chosen course itself might one day prove a dead
end. But men of action cannot retrace their steps or allow themselves any doubts. They will pursue their ends through fire and
water; it is left to history to make the final decision.

David Ben Gurion, like others in his group, was a non-Marxist
socialist. But socialism was for them a means, not an end. Their
dream was not to create a more just and freer society for all men,
but to regenerate the Jewish people within its own state. Those
among the Jews most deserving of sympathy and most capable of
realizing such a project were the workers. Jewish society of the
future was to be a hard, pure society of workers not ruled by any
leisure class, a society which they alone were capable of sustaining
just as they alone had been capable of creating it.

Ben Gurion's impatience, even hatred, for middle-class Zionists who were usually careful not to soil their hands in Palestine is
thus understandable. In all their decisions he saw a dangerous
leaning towards solutions which endangered the realization of
Zionist aims. This was his opinion of Chaim Weizmann himself.
In recognition of his historic services, Weizmann was offered the
Presidency of the new state. But he was not allowed the right to

append his signature to the declaration of independence of 14 May 1948 (he was in New York at the time) and it was made clear that his functions would be purely honorary.

There were at the outset 21 parties in Israel, but the state centred on Ben Gurion and his party, the Mapai. The first elections, held in January 1949, gave the Mapai 35 per cent of the votes, 20 per cent more than its nearest rival. But the majority was not absolute, and has never become so. Attacks on the Mapai from both the Right and the Left were numerous, violent and venomous. Since only a coalition government was possible every party haggled long and skilfully before granting its support. None failed to take advantage of the opportunities for political blackmail. Nevertheless, the Mapai always came out on top.

Despite the violence and aggressiveness of the internal jealousies and struggle for power, the instinct for unity always prevailed. Israel was a besieged fortress, and no-one could afford to forget it. The frontiers, defined merely by the front lines on the last day of hostilities, were tortuous. At its narrowest point the country was less than ten miles across.

The state began to take shape. Essential institutions were set up. Israel became a parliamentary democracy. Instead of a written constitution, it had a series of fundamental laws voted by the Assembly, or *Knesset*.

Administrative questions were, however, less important than the fulfilment of the Zionist dream. To make this dream a reality was the State of Israel's first priority. It was made plain from the beginning that Israel did not wish to be a Levantine state among others, but the setting in which the destiny of the Jews was to be accomplished, the place where the exiles were to be reunited, the true home of all the Jews of the world. All restrictions on immigration were lifted, and a solemn appeal was sent out to all members of the 'Jewish people' to come and settle in Israel. A law, regarded as fundamental, and without parallel in any other legislation, was promulgated in July 1950. This is the famous Law of the Return: 'Every Jew has the right to come to this country as an '*oleh*.' '*Oleh* is a Hebrew expression, not strictly translatable, literally 'One who ascends', a Jew who comes to settle in the land of Palestine. It was found impossible (or dangerous) to define the term 'Jew'. A law of nationality, adopted after years of discussion in April 1952, emphasized the special nature of the state. Israeli nationality belonged to every *'oleh* by right, whether or not he renounced his original nationality. The same applied to every person residing in Israeli territory on the day on which the state was proclaimed, or who had legally entered that territory before the date on which the law was promulgated. It applied to Arabs who had remained in their homes or who had legally been accepted into the country since. By contrast, every Palestinian Arab who left his home at the time of the war and had not since been able to return had to apply for naturalization, and swear an oath of loyalty to the State of Israel like any other foreigner. Acceptance of the application would then depend on the result of inquiries and on the good will of the Minister of the Interior. His only privilege by comparison with other foreigners was that he was not obliged (in principle) to know Hebrew. A similar fundamental law accorded official status to the world Zionist Organization.

Under these conditions, Jewish immigration began again in earnest. Just before the war there were 650,000 Jews on Israeli territory compared with 740,000 Arabs. Only 160,000 Arabs remained. Between 1948 and 1951, 687,000 new Jewish immigrants arrived, more than the original number. Among the first to arrive were 70,000 survivors of Nazi concentration camps and 300,000 from the Peoples' Democracies (especially Rumania and Poland, whose governments at that time left the door open to Jewish emigration). But above all, between 1948 and 1951, 330,000 Asian and African Jews 'ascended' to Israel. On the one hand, the conditions under which the State of Israel had been created rendered the Jewish minority in Arab countries (from which came 247,000 of the 330,000 immigrants) suspect of being sympathetic to the Arabs' enemy. This led to hostility, and in some cases (witness Morocco and Libya) full-scale pogroms. On the other hand, these events appeared to the pious Jews of the Third World, usually grouped into orthodox communities, to presage the coming of the Messiah and to demand their return to Zion. Between 1952 and 1954 the flow thinned considerably, and in 1953 Jewish departures from Israel even surpassed the arrivals. But the wave was swollen once again at the end of 1954 by the influx of some 100,000 Jews, mainly from North Africa; these came mainly out of fear of the rabid nationalism which had exploded in the Algerian War. By 1956, there were 1,667,500 Jews in Israel, as against 200,000 Arabs. The composition of the Jewish population changed markedly in favour of Orientals. In 1948, 54.8 per cent of Israeli Jews were of European birth, 35.4 per cent had been born in Palestine and 8.8 per cent in the rest of the Middle East. In 1956, 37.7 per cent were born in Europe, 29.4 per cent in the Middle East and 32.9 per cent in the country itself. The European Jews were from then on in the minority.

This enormous flood of immigrants more than doubled the population, and naturally caused considerable economic difficulties. Even in the period of the mandate the *Yishuv* had subsisted largely on foreign aid. The trade deficit of Palestine under the mandate was very large. In the period from 1933 to 1937, exports paid on average for only 29 per cent of imports. The young State of Israel was in an even worse position. The rupture with the Arab countries forced it to trade mostly with distant countries: England, Canada, the United States, Germany. Furthermore, it was an uphill struggle for Israeli products to compete in these markets with the local products of a better equipped and better organized local agriculture and industry. In 1952 exports were only 11 per cent of the value of imports. Integration of the immigrants was very costly. From the proclamation of independence to the end of 1952, the cost of bringing them to Israel, receiving them and housing them was 2,250 dollars per head.

The usual sources of funds proved inadequate to cope with this situation. At the time of the mandate they had been composed chiefly of a flood of voluntary contributions from the Jews of the Diaspora, especially American Jews. Between 1917 and 1942, 86.8 per cent of the £22,535,000 sterling total receipts of Jewish institutions and national funds came from such contributions. The means of conducting the war of 1948 were secured largely thanks to the eloquence of Golda Myerson, who managed to extract 50 million dollars from the American Jews. Eighteen months later she returned to the United States to appeal for funds for construction. On 27 April 1949, Ben Gurion said in announcing his austerity programme to the Knesset:

It would be a cruel illusion to imagine that the absorption and housing of the immigrants is an undertaking which can be quickly and easily accomplished. We believe that despite the enormous financial, technical and administrative problems, the State will be able to absorb this immense flood of immigrants if it succeeds in obtaining every possible assistance from Jews abroad.*

Thus was the Zionist programme to be carried out, in spite of the enormous economic problems to which it gave rise, and at the cost of a heavy dependence on the outside world.

Massive immigration, however, was not the only burden which the young state's situation and programme obliged it to bear. Surrounded by a hostile world, it had to have arms. The Haganah had proved its strength in the war against the Arabs. In its new role of the National Army, it now needed to be strengthened, provided with superior equipment, and kept in a constant state of readiness for immediate mobilization. Military expenditure and special budgets in 1950 and 1951 amounted to 44 per cent and 42 per cent respectively of the whole of government expenditure. This proportion then fell to 30 per cent in 1953, then rose once more to 37 per cent in 1955. The state was threatened with financial collapse when, in January 1952, Ben Gurion proposed the acceptance of reparations payments from Germany. This proposal had to overcome opposition from a wide spectrum of public opinion, from Right to Left, outraged that the debt to millions of victims of Nazism should be considered atoned for by this means. Ben Gurion won the assent of Parliament by only 61 votes to 50, after having had to suppress a popular uprising in Jerusalem.

Militarization did not exclude democracy, and in a sense was one aspect of it. Hence the contrast between Israel as seen by the Arabs and the vision of her cherished by Europeans. To the former, Israel was a colonial offshoot of the Western world, imposed on the Oriental world by force and therefore the very epitome of injustice and oppression. The word 'Zionism' has acquired in Arabic a meaning sinister in itself, evocative of evil, like the words 'imperialism', 'colonialism' and, for many people

* Quoted in *Cahiers de l'Orient contemporain*, nos. 18–19, Paris, 1949, p. 148.

nowadays, 'capitalism'. For them, seen on the world scale, Israel is an armed camp peopled by aggressive conquerors. Indeed, Israel is an armed camp set in the midst of hostile territory, like the makeshift forts surrounded by palisades which European pioneers erected feverishly, Western-style, in every alien territory to which they penetrated, posting lookouts to scan the prairie anxiously for the movements of unfriendly tribes. But the West had solemnly endorsed the legitimacy of this island transplanted from the Western world, and no longer questioned it; what interested Westerners was the internal structure of the state. To admit and even exalt its virtues helped to eradicate, retrospectively, all the wrongs which had been done to the European Jews. It helped Westerners to forget the religious persecutions of old, the hatred and contempt still contained in many religious books, the massacres carried out by some while others looked on and did nothing, the repugnance felt for an alien people. This repugnance had become almost instinctive over a thousand years of history and was aggravated by intellectual, cultural and social cleavages which assimilation had not yet succeeded in effacing. The Jews of Europe and America had not on the whole been very eager to emigrate to this barren land, a country foreign to them and speaking a strange tongue. But they could not help feeling a thrill of pride at the success of those, their own cousins and brothers, who had shared their humiliation, and at seeing in them the resurgence of the Maccabean virtues. While before the war Zionism had been only a minority cult among the Jewish masses, now, after the holocaust which had devoured so many of their people, they felt uneasy about refusing their support to an independent community where so many had found refuge. Sometimes discreetly, sometimes with militant ostentation, they therefore became highly effective propaganda agents. For them, any attack or criticism of Israel smacked of the furies of Nazism, and they would at the least brush it aside, with secret unease, or else passionately denounce it. Films showing the action of the war of 1948 from the Israeli point of view were vigorously applauded all over the world. The showing of a film shot from the Arab point of view was inconceivable. The only Jews who (apparently) did not share such sentiments were either the fervent adherents of militant anti-Zionist ideologies such as Communism, or the admittedly very large number who had opted for assimilation and had taken to it with such enthusiasm that they were well on the way to breaking all links with Judaism. The latter group tended to take refuge in silence, however, and therefore passed unnoticed – especially since they had merged with widely differing peoples and nationalities.

Europe was also led to idealize Israel and to see in her the image of its own aspirations. Paradoxically, some saw a parliamentary, pluralistic democracy, with a capitalist free-enterprise economy; while others saw at least the beginnings of an egalitarian socialist society, free of the privilege conferred by wealth, allowing to all the free development of their potentialities in their own chosen direction. Both of these opposite schools were able to adduce facts to support their conflicting analyses.

The Palestinian *Yishuv* was largely founded by settlers from Tsarist Russia strongly influenced by socialist or progressive ideologies of the Marxist or Tolstoyan variety. Indeed it was this class of settlers which furnished a large number of the leaders and chief administrators of the new state. Some set up agricultural colonies on the collectivist principle, the famous *kibbutzim*. Other settlements quickly sprang up representing a transitional form of small peasant ownership. For the distribution of their products these production units were then interconnected by networks of cooperatives. This sector is undeniably socialist in character. As far as the collective settlements are concerned, there is a great deal of truth in G. Friedmann's assertion that 'the *kibbutzim* seem to us . . . the most successful attempt so far to replace the individual's own private interest by community principles as the basis for social existence'*. It is hardly surprising, therefore, that a major section of European intellectuals should have viewed this socialistic sector with admiration and hope, particularly since it is free of the unpleasant associations which the Stalinist system has given to other existing forms of socialism.

* G. Friedmann, *The End of the Jewish People?*, London, Hutchinson, 1967.

On the other hand, both under the British mandate and to an even greater extent in the young State of Israel, this socialist sector within the Palestinian *Yishuv* formed part of a social structure dominated by economic considerations which had nothing specifically socialist about them; the market economy was paramount. The *kibbutzim* float in a mixed-economy capitalist environment, to which they have to adapt. The apologists of private enterprise need therefore have nothing to fear from this kind of micro-socialism. As a certain Israeli banker has stated:

> To the outside world, the *kibbutz* behaves exactly like a capitalist enterprise, and keeps to its contracts better than an individual. If the *kibbutz* is internally composed of people who renounce private property, who bring up their children collectively or who . . . crawl about on all fours, that is none of our concern.*

As for the workings of Israel's parliamentary democracy, it may well live up to all the (theoretical) principles of liberalism. Elections to the Knesset are surrounded by a network of precautions guaranteeing maximum electoral freedom. Seats are distributed by a system of proportional representation. In 1959 as many as 24 lists of candidates were submitted to the electorate. 75 to 83 per cent of electors actually go to the polls. The seats are distributed among about 10 parties, all with a fairly stable representation. Coalitions form and re-form. As mentioned before, the Mapai (Labour) party generally polled 40 to 47 per cent of the votes. It was therefore never able to govern alone. Government coalitions have usually been between the Mapai and the religious parties, which obtain about 12 to 15 per cent of the votes and of the seats. The result is that these religious parties have a permanent lever for blackmail, and only give their support at the price of further concessions to clericalism. The alternatives – support from the Left or the Right – also present problems. Ben Gurion has been campaigning for a long time for the adoption of the simple majority system, on the pattern of the Anglo-Saxon countries, but so far without success. Simple-majority

* B. Goriely, *Cette année à Jerusalem*, Paris–Lausanne–Bâle, Ed. Vineta, 1951, p. 69.

voting would lead to a simpler and more stable two-party system which would ensure greater security of office for the government.

Clerical influence is an embarrassment to the pro-Israeli Left in the outside world. It is more difficult to idealize than the micro-socialism of the *kibbutzim* or political democracy. It does not only stem from the unique position of the religious parties, but also from the expectations of American Jewish organizations who would be unwilling to finance bodies exhibiting anti-clerical tendencies. Thus the salvation of the American Jews is conveniently assured by the strict religious observance imposed on Israeli Jews, while their consciences are assuaged and their supposed duty as Zionists fulfilled at the price of certain financial sacrifices. Also, Israel inherited from before the time of the British mandate the community structure of the Ottoman Empire. Every religious community is self-governing and is empowered to regulate legally the personal status of its members. Hence the impossibility of mixed marriages in Israel, as in the Lebanon, which has a comparable structure in this respect. The fear of a purely secular constitution has driven the religious parties to oppose the introduction of any constitution whatsoever. Thanks to the support of the Mapai and against opposition from all the other parties, they have succeeded in their aim, because the Mapai was not prepared to go against the express wishes of its political allies. As a result of these political junketings the Israeli people is obliged to conform to strict religious observance which it finds repugnant, or at least irritating: cessation of all transport on the Sabbath, the imposition of Kosher food, etc. In several cases, clerical tyranny has actually harmed the national interest.

A deeper consequence, and one no doubt more serious in its long-term implications, nas been the growth of a common ideology, which was deeply rooted in many minds though not always made explicit. This ideology is a rather incoherent mixture of nationalism with racialist overtones, and religion. Ancient Israel has the great distinction that it developed, at the time of the prophets, one of the very first universalist ideologies in the world. This transcended the old ethnic religion of the national god Yahweh fighting against the gods of other peoples. At a certain stage in social evolution, this ideology corresponded so closely to a real human need that it conquered, in the shape of the Christian and Islamic 'heresies', a large part of mankind. This universalist beginning has now been practically abandoned. God is with His people Israel in work and in battle. Those who do not believe see in their religion primarily a national value, and are externally all the more faithful to it. For many, nationalism has been one step on the road to faith. To believe in dogmas about the universe and man in general merely because they are the ones which your race or nation has adopted many years since is an affront to reason and morality. It is, indeed, a common phenomenon; but in Israel it has been developed into a State theology to an extent which is fairly uncommon in the modern world. The reading, veneration, meditation and teaching of the Old Testament has had the most deplorable effects, as it has in some Puritan Christian communities devoted to the imitation of Israel. In Israel's present situation, what most minds, and especially children's minds, retain most easily are the battles fought by the ancient nation against its neighbours, Moabites, Amalekites, Philistines and others, the exaltation of carnage, the wrath called down by God on the heads of Israel's enemies, the supreme value accorded to the nation. Next to these tendencies, the universalist values emerging from the tradition of the great prophets do have some influence, but it is (not surprisingly) small by comparison.

The State of Israel is only a purely Jewish State in its leadership and in its official ideology. Several hundred thousand Arabs fled their homes in the territory later to become Israel at the time of the war of 1948. The official line is that they were incited to leave by the Arab leaders themselves. This theory is accepted by most foreign commentators, but except in a few limited cases without any historical evidence. There were many causes for the Arab exodus, the main one being simply that which operated in Spain during the Civil War or in France in 1940: to get away from the theatre of military operations. The fear of Jewish terrorism also played a major part, even though the terror was sporadic and restricted. The massacre of Deir Yassin, despite the condemnation of it by the ruling Jewish bodies, was fearfully effective as an act of terror. Many leading Jews were glad to see the departure of a population which by its very presence presented an obstacle to the realization of the Jewish State projected by the Zionists. At all events, most of the refugees hoped to return to their towns and villages when hostilities had ended, but could no longer cross the front lines, now congealed into the new frontiers.

There were about 580,000 refugees. 160,000 Arabs remained in Israel, their number eventually increasing to 380,000. About one third of these are Christians. Israel was greatly embarrassed by this minority which never wanted to become integrated into a Jewish State, and which prevented that state from being purely Jewish. Should it be treated as a Trojan horse, a danger to the security of the state? Or as a bridge to the hostile Arab states, providing a model example of coexistence between the two races? It was doubtless impossible to take up an unequivocal position between the two policies. Clearly nothing would entirely disarm the hostility of the Arabs inside the country, while those outside would remain irreconcilable. The Israeli Arabs were excused military service – any other course would have been unthinkable. Many of them lived in frontier areas – or rather, in view of the small size of the country, one should perhaps say areas closer to the frontier than others. 80 per cent were under military administration. Army passes were required in order to travel short distances. Since it is not always possible to tell an Arab from a Jew at first sight, special identity cards carrying the letter 'B' were issued to Arabs. All this was done for reasons of security, and followed logically from the way in which the state had been constituted. Moreover, thanks to the Arab exodus, 80 per cent of Israeli territory after the war consisted of abandoned land, one quarter of which was cultivable. Israeli land laws settled the question by massive confiscations with offers of monetary compensation, which many people thought inadequate. But in any case, the vast majority of Israeli Arabs refused to give their consent to the confiscation. It has been estimated that they lost 40 to 50 per cent of their land.

Seen from another angle, however, it is certainly true that the Israeli Arabs benefited from the general rise in the standard of living compared with that of neighbouring Arab countries. They enjoyed political rights, and entered to some extent into the internal political game. They joined various parties, usually of the opposition, the Communist Party in particular. Arab deputies sat in the Knesset (and still do). This did not help them to forget their status as second-class citizens, the discrimination from which they suffered in the allocation of administrative posts and all positions of responsibility, and the natural mistrust with which Jewish society regarded them. Consequently they could hardly be expected to accept completely the new state which had been imposed on them. This led to many incidents, which the Arab states outside seized upon, to denounce the oppression to which their Arab brothers in Israel were subjected.

Naturally enough, the Palestine refugees left outside the country gave even greater cause for denouncing the Israelis. They had a high birth rate, and their numbers increased. In June 1956 there were estimated to be 922,000 refugees in all, of which 512,000 were in Jordan, 216,000 in the Gaza Strip, 102,000 in the Lebanon and 90,000 in Syria. At the end of 1949 the United Nations created U.N.R.W.A. – the United Nations Relief and Works Agency for Palestine Refugees in the Near East, with headquarters in Beirut. The aim of this body was to provide minimum rations (which always proved insufficient), shelter, medical services, education and professional training to all those who had not been integrated in the economies of the various countries. Because financial resources were limited, the aid was wholly inadequate. In 1964–5 U.N.R.W.A. aid came to 37 dollars per refugee per annum. Many Palestine refugees did, however, find employment in the country to which they had emigrated. In the Lebanon, for instance, they actually acquired a reputation as an active and industrious minority, with considerable achievements to its credit. But the great mass of unskilled labourers and landless, destitute peasants stayed in the U.N.R.W.A. camps with their wives and children. There they lived in conditions of extreme privation, frustrated, bitter and vengeful, clinging to the hope that they would one day be able to return to their villages and win back their land. They represent for the Arabs the living evidence, the symbol of the great injustice which has been collectively perpetrated on them.

The consequences of the Israeli victory in the Arab countries were enormous, but it was some time before they were fully felt.

Their defeat was a rude shock to the Arabs, an unprecedented humiliation. At the very moment when they had a real hope of liberation from the Western yoke, a Western colony gave the Arabs a brutal reminder of how weak they were, and how easily vanquished. They were then preached at by the whole world and told that their defeat was just.

> They were attacked both ways [writes Michael Ionides]. It was morally wicked of them to fight to prevent the Zionists enjoying what was theirs; they were weak and incompetent to fight and fail. As aggressors they had no right to win; for their military incompetence they deserved to lose. They should have been loyal to the United Nations' decision to partition, for the rule of law must be honoured; they must accept the consequences of defeat, for victory goes to those who are strong. The Jews were there as of right; anyway, they had beaten the Arabs in war. It was right for the Jews to fight to acquire; wrong for the Arabs to fight to hold.*

The old political groupings in power in the Arab countries found defeat as mortifying as any of their subjects. But they were incapable of conducting policy in any other way than the familiar, traditional fashion. Out of the universal indignation new forces arose which attacked their policies, remorselessly unmasking the internal vices of these regimes. Furthermore, these very policies and vices were seen as the real reasons for failure. The sociologically minded probed the endemic vices of Arab society and the mentality which they engendered, seeking the 'Meaning of the Disaster', to quote the title of a book on the subject by the Lebanese historian Constantine Zurayq. But these new forces, especially young people belonging to social classes so far excluded from power, were impatient and had no time for distant reforms laboriously prepared for by a long-term educational programme. In any case, how was it possible for such reforms to be carried out within the framework of a decayed political structure? The time was ripe for an attack on that structure to be launched.

The old ruling classes had fought for independence and against

* M. Ionides, *Divide and Lose: The Arab Revolt 1955 to 1958*, London, Geoffrey Bles, 1960, p. 79.

Zionist encroachment. But their internal weaknesses were only too apparent. This band of kings, aristocrats, large landed proprietors and wealthy merchants were concerned above all with sectional and personal interests. They had been unable to make the sacrifices necessary to achieve unity. They had no conception of technology, which is the key to power in the modern age. Absorbed in their court intrigues, they failed to consider wider social alternatives, they were incapable of effective mobilization of the masses. They were corrupt and incompetent. They had put their trust in the support of the European world, especially Great Britain. Great Britain did indeed help them to get rid of the French, but only in order to take their place. Under the provisions of treaties signed by the dynasties, British troops were stationed everywhere except Syria and the Lebanon, ready to intervene if necessary in any part of the Eastern Arab world. But Great Britain had not even succeeded in preventing the Israeli victory – if one can assume that that was her object. And the entire Western world had actively assisted this victory. The first priority was to get rid of these ill-starred regimes, identified with policies which had failed so spectacularly.

Only one of the Arab rulers, a survivor from the period of the revolt against the Turks, was so preoccupied with the realization of his personal ambitions that he failed, despite his adroitness, to appreciate the profound social transformation that was taking place. This was Feisal's brother Abdullah, Emir of Transjordan, who had himself proclaimed king in April 1946. He had made several attempts to reach an understanding with the Zionists over the partition of Palestine, and even looked beyond this. While the talks which he had with Golda Myerson on the eve of the outbreak of war may not have resulted in a signed pact, the strategy followed by his troops could easily be interpreted as dictated by a tacit agreement with Ben Gurion. At all events, in December 1948 he seized the available portion of the cake by annexing unilaterally all the Arab territory remaining to the west of the River Jordan, ignoring the protests of the Palestinians and the other Arab states. In April 1949 he made his action irreversible by renaming his state the Hashemite Kingdom of Jordan. In 1949 and 1950 he entered into top-secret discussions with Ben

Gurion's special envoy, Moshe Dayan. He agreed to sign a peace with Israel, in return for a corridor to Haifa. His cabinet opposed the project, however, unless a proper Jordanian corridor several miles wide were accorded. Ben Gurion only wanted to allow a free road, with a few hundred feet on each side. Abdullah beat a retreat, but continued to seek agreement despite his cabinet. Rumours of these secret discussions leaked out, and Abdullah, who had for some time been regarded as a puppet of the British, became increasingly unpopular. On 20 July 1951 he was assassinated by a Palestinian Arab in the mosque of al-Aksa in Jerusalem.

Agitation against the regimes responsible for the conduct of the Palestine war combined with the violent anti-Western movements which had grown up in response to British domination and the Western support for Zionism. Everyone not already corrupted by the existing regime by sumptuous gifts and favours spoke out against domination by Europe, joining either Right-wing or Left-wing organizations according to their predilections. The U.N. vote in November 1947 in favour of partition of Palestine inflamed the anger of the Arabs. In December 1947 the Egyptian prime minister Nokrashi Pasha, who had outlawed the Muslim Brotherhood, a Right-wing extremist organization, and suppressed the Communist Party, was assassinated by a student, a member of the Muslim Brotherhood. The prime minister of Iraq, Saleh Jabr, signed a treaty with Bevin at Portsmouth on 16 January 1948 which provided for the evacuation of British troops, but allowed Great Britain the right to bring them back in case of the threat of war, to use military airfields, and to train the Iraqi army. The riots which greeted the announcement of the treaty were so violent that the Crown Prince, who was intensely pro-British, was forced to declare that the treaty would not be ratified. The prime minister resigned and fled to Jordan, fearing assassination.

Once the defeat had occurred, of course, matters only became worse. Discontent showed itself most openly in Syria. This was the first centre of Arab nationalism, deeply wounded by the defeat because of its geographical proximity. Until 1918 no frontier had divided Syria from Palestine. Syria was a republic with a more open political structure than the Arab kingdoms, with no foreign troops on its territory, and without the Lebanese pre-occupation with holding the balance between Muslims and Christians. Syrian intellectuals had added the influence of the French Left to the ideology of Arab nationalism. Popular anger could be more easily expressed there than elsewhere, and after December 1948 violent demonstrations broke out against the old ruling clique of Shukry Kuwatly. The situation became so troubled that the army was called in to restore order, and became immediately aware of its own strong position. On 30 March 1949 Colonel Husni Zaim seized power. This was the first Arab military coup to take place since the war. It was not to be the last.

Radicalism made great strides in every part of the Arab world in the years which followed. Syria was, beset with intractable problems. Torn between the Saudi-Egyptian alliance and the possibility of union with Iraq, and between American, English and French factions, the country was subjected to two successive military dictatorships: Hinnawi (August – December 1949) and Shishakli (December 1949 – February 1954). The latter had fought in Palestine. But the military rulers had to take account of their public opinion, of clandestine and legal parties, of pressure-groups of every description. By 1950 it was clear that in foreign policy the neutralist school had overwhelming popular support. The Communist Party's following was stronger than in any other part of the Arab world. There was also a new force emerging: the Ba'ath party (Socialist Party of Arab Resurgence). This party set out to re-formulate the ideology of pan-Arab nationalism on a strictly secular basis, with a seasoning of socialism. In September 1954, in the first elections after Shishakli's downfall, 22 Ba'athists were elected to the Parliament, together with the Communist leader Khaled Begdash. This was the Left's first great success in the Arab world.

In Iraq, the old pro-British politician Nuri es-Said, a survivor from the times of King Feisal, seemed to have the situation well under control, despite popular unrest. But his authority was only apparent. The opposition parties attracted more and more attention. Neutralism and socialism increased in strength, and so, despite brutal repression, did Communism. The elections of June 1954 saw the appearance of a block of 26 opponents of Nuri's policy, while his party lost seats. He dissolved Parliament, suppressed 18 newspapers, took repressive measures against the Communist Party, and searched and closed down the offices of the main opposition party. After this, the September elections naturally produced more satisfactory results. It was however a Pyrrhic victory.

In Egypt the king had been forced, in July 1949, to admit into his coalition cabinet the Wafd, the old bourgeois anti-British party. The Wafd had fallen into disrepute to some extent, because the British had imposed it on the king during the second world war, needing a popular government capable of maintaining peace. Its social policy (or rather its absence of a social policy) had been a disappointment. But there had been no other party available capable of expressing the popular will. In the elections of January 1950 the Wafd won 228 seats out of a total of 319. This victory unseated the team held directly responsible for the defeat in Palestine. Driven forward by public opinion and the Left-wing of his party, Nahas Pasha, leader of the Wafd, demanded from Britain the revision of the Anglo-Egyptian Treaty of 1936. This move was designed to eliminate British influence in the Sudan and expel British troops from the Suez Canal Zone. The British refused. The Wafd became all the more intransigent. The government began to move towards a neutralist position. In October 1951 Nahas unilaterally renounced the treaty, anti-British riots broke out, and detachments of volunteers and auxiliary police attacked British troops guarding the Canal. British reprisals further antagonized public opinion. On 26 January 1952 groups of terrorist incendiaries began burning and looting in the streets of Cairo. 277 fires were started. The police and the public fraternized with the rioters. The army restored order, and the king dismissed Nahas. But a clandestine group of young officers, most of whom had fought in the Palestine war, had formed within the army. United by their common resentment against those responsible for and profiting from the defeat, they seized power and drove out King Farouk, symbol of a corrupt and unrepresentative hierarchy. This was on 23 July 1952.

It is true that the Egyptian revolution only represented a danger to Israel in the long term. The nationalist officers undoubtedly desired a free and strong Egypt, able in case of need to settle all accounts with its rivals. But up until March 1954 they were primarily occupied with their internal struggle against the forces of the old society—including the Communists and the Muslim Brotherhood—who had combined behind the figure of General Neguib to demand a return to pluralist Parliamentary rule, in which they might stand a chance of gaining power. The Palestine problem, while it served to illuminate the depths of corruption of the old regime, was far from being first on the list of priorities. The younger officers were at the time particularly attracted by the prestige and wealth of the United States, which meant that they would have to put off to a later date any project of revenge against Israel. On the other hand, they wanted to liberate their country once and for all from the remains of British tutelage. They effected a compromise with Great Britain over the Sudan in February 1953, and signed a treaty on the Suez Canal on 27 July 1954. Though this treaty did promise the evacuation of the Canal Zone, it also committed Egypt fairly deeply to a pro-Western policy: the English were to be allowed to return in the event of an attack on Egypt, the members of the Arab League, or Turkey. This last provision was no doubt directed against the Soviet Union. These pro-Western measures certainly helped to secure British good will. At the same time, the barrier of British troops between Egypt and Israel was now removed.

The Western powers were at this time completely blind to the strength of Arab aspirations. The Eastern specialists and others who advised Western politicians only pushed them further towards monumental errors of judgement, which the experts proceeded to justify. The burning desire for complete independence and the irreconcilable hostility towards Israel were seen as minor infantile complaints which greater political maturity, coupled with the wise counsels of the great powers and backed by their wealth and military strength, would quickly cure. The rise of new forces attacking the old structures was seen as the product of the machinations of Moscow, which also explained the demonstrations against the Western presence. Broadly speaking, the Atlantic powers were incapable of viewing Middle Eastern problems in any other light than that of the cold War. Their only interest in the area was a barrier against possible Soviet attack. They totally failed to appreciate that the world struggle on this level was not of the slightest interest either to the peoples or the politicians of the Arab world. Nobody in the Middle East felt remotely threatened by any Soviet danger. What they feared, rightly or wrongly, was Israeli expansionism, and what they wanted was to get rid of the last vestiges of Western occupation. Arab politicians who wished to retain their connexions with the West were acutely aware of the danger of an internal upheaval, even if they did not consider the danger immediate. Thus Nuri es-Said, the most important pro-Western politician, begged the British to provide him with some moral capital to help disarm his own public opinion, either by forcing Israel to make major concessions, or at least by coming down firmly on the Arab side. His efforts were in vain. Similarly fruitless were Nasser's public declarations in August and September 1955, to the effect that Arab public opinion would be prepared to align with the West as long as the Arab states were not bound by any treaties making provision for a military presence, even conditional. This would be unacceptable to peoples who had already suffered too long from the West and had become profoundly suspicious of Western intentions.

These problems, which to the Arabs were crucial, were seen by the Western powers as rather small flies in the ointment. They were only interested in them to the extent that they interfered with the great cause of the 'Defence of the Free World'. They were irritated by requests for arms from the Middle Eastern countries, arms which the Western powers needed for the struggle against the 'Communist menace'. On 25 May 1950 the United States, Great Britain and France published a joint declaration expressing opposition to the use of force in this area. Arms would only be sold to those who promised not to embark on any act of aggression. If any danger of this arose, 'The three Governments . . . would . . . immediately take action, both within and outside the United Nations, to prevent such violation.' The states concerned finally agreed to declare that the arms would be used purely for defensive purposes. But the Tripartite Declaration was widely interpreted as a guarantee of the status quo favouring

Israel and as a threat of direct intervention. Shortly after this, the Korean War broke out. The United Nations claimed to be giving military support to the victim of aggression – South Korea – and thus punishing a violation of the international organization's decisions. The Arab states, whose attitudes to the war varied, did not fail to notice that not so long before the three powers had expressed their 'unshakable opposition' to the use of force, and that Israel's violations of United Nations decisions had not provoked any similar action.

The Western powers were profoundly disturbed by the Korean War, and they redoubled their efforts to gain the support of the Arab countries in the Cold War. The Soviet threat was gradually transformed in Western minds to a danger of internal subversion, against which the Middle East had to be supported by economic aid and the supply of arms, and bound to the West by military treaties. But the Arab reaction to this viewpoint was the same as ever, to the great astonishment of the Americans, who found it difficult to understand that such a conservative, religious people should have so little enthusiasm for defending themselves against the insidious menace of Communism. The missions of the English General Brian Robertson and the American Secretary of State McGhee in 1951 met with little success so far as the Arab governments were concerned, and excited violent popular reaction. J. Foster Dulles' trip in 1953 had the same effect. Dulles took note of the setback, and resorted to a different plan: to create a shield (or a launching-base) against the Soviet Union by means of a 'Northern Tier' of sincerely anti-Communist, Muslim nations: Turkey, Iran and Pakistan. Turkey had been a member of N.A.T.O. since February 1952, and had sent troops to Korea. In Iran, a coup d'état organized by the C.I.A. had overthrown Mossadeq in August 1953. A pact was signed between Turkey and Pakistan on 2 April 1954, followed by a military aid agreement between the United States and Pakistan on 19 May. In April the United States announced a military aid programme to Iraq.

Britain was shocked by this American intrusion into the Middle East, which it regarded as its own sphere of influence. The Arab governments were still divided. Egypt pleaded for a policy of non-alignment sympathetic to the West, but with no pacts entailing any automatic obligations. It would have been absurd for them to place themselves once again in a position of inferiority in an alliance with powers whose only concern was the defence of their interests against the U.S.S.R., and who paid not the slightest attention to Arab grievances over Israel and the needs of Arab defence against Israel. The Western powers had shown nothing but indulgence towards Israel; Turkey had good relations with her. Most Arabs were sympathetic to the Egyptian standpoint. At the very least, any agreement with the West should be conditional upon some kind of bargain. Benefits would have to be mutual. If the Arabs were to throw in their lot with the West, it would have to be in return for Western pressure on Israel to negotiate her frontiers on the basis of the U.N. partition plan of November 1947. There seemed, moreover, to be signs of a more conciliatory attitude in Israel itself in this respect. But Nuri es-Said and Abdulilah Crown Prince of Iraq were not primarily concerned with Israel. A settlement could in any case not be imposed on the West by Arab weakness, and would depend on the friendship of the Western powers. These rulers were much more afraid of Communist and nationalist subversion. They were attached to the alliance with Britain and sought Turkish and Iranian support against the claims of the Kurds. Iraqi rivalry with Egypt for supremacy over the Arab world made them suspicious of the plans of the young and inexperienced officers in Cairo. Attempts to reconcile the two opposing viewpoints failed. On 24 February 1955 Nuri signed a pact with Turkey in Baghdad, and on 4 April an agreement with Great Britain endorsing the Iraqi-Turkish pact. Shortly afterwards Pakistan and Iran also joined the pact. In November the Baghdad Pact, as it was called, was consolidated by the establishment of a joint secretariat.

The first pact had been signed on 24 February. On 21 February Ben Gurion returned from retirement on the *kibbutz* to become Israel's Minister of Defence. On the 28th he launched a massive reprisal raid on Gaza and destroyed the Egyptian headquarters there, killing 38 Egyptian soldiers and wounding 31. These events were connected in Arab eyes. The Arab revolution against the Western alliance, which had proved incapable of dealing with the Israeli threat, was about to erupt.

In 1948, the primal choice in international politics was that between the Western power bloc and the Soviet Union, flanked by its socialist satellites. The policy of cooperation between the Big Three, an extension of the wartime alliance, was dying. The Cold War began in earnest in the autumn of 1947. In October, Zhdanov laid down the principle that 'All those who are not with us are against us'.

One of the few points on which the leaders of the two blocs, the United States and the Soviet Union, were in agreement was the decision to partition Palestine, taken in November 1947, and to recognize the new State of Israel in May 1948. The newborn state had had to face British hostility, but was greatly aided by the United States, both as a state ('Truman is incontestably one of the principle architects of the State of Israel',* writes M. Bar-Zohar, the Zionist historiographer) and through the numerous and influential American Jewish community. Truman did have a passing moment of indecision, in March 1948, when the gravity of the situation in Europe and the outcry raised by the American Ambassadors in the Arab countries moved him to renounce the partition plan and propose international control over Palestine. This was also due in part to the fears for the safety of the new state entertained by friends of the Jews, forseeing the imminent Arab attack. Israel also possessed highly influential supporters in the West, especially in France. On the other side, she very opportunely acquired a consignment of Czech arms, a deal in which the Yugoslavs were also involved. This combination of both blocs in Israel's favour made the subsequent choice between them doubly difficult.

A policy of non-alignment was theoretically possible, and naturally enough this was the policy officially announced by the Israeli government. Moshe Sharett (previously Shertok), first Minister for Foreign Affairs of the new state, was a sincere advocate of this policy, while the Left clamoured for a policy of active friendship with the Soviet Union.

But irresistible forces pushed Israel towards the Western bloc,

* Michel Bar-Zohar, *Ben-Gourion, le prophète armé*, Paris, Fayard, 1966.

a development clearly foreseen by David Ben Gurion from the outset. Neutrality between the blocs was still possible as long as it only needed to be expressed by diplomatic gestures with no great influence on events, but not beyond this. Israel's strength depended in very large measure on money provided by American Jews and by the pressure they were able to exert on the American government. In February 1948 an alert American observer was able to write: 'Without a continuous flow of money and political support from the American Jews, the new Judaea would head for almost certain destruction'.* In January 1949 the Export-Import Bank of Washington, a government agency, granted Israel a loan of 100 million dollars, 35 million of which could be drawn upon at once. The Labour government which ruled the state may in part have considered non-alignment a necessary expedient on the diplomatic plane. But its whole sympathy was with the Western camp. In Palestine as in the second International, to which the Mapai was affiliated, it had always had to fight against the Communists. The brand of socialism represented by the Mapai entailed the defence of working-class interests without excluding the use of capitalist investment. In 1950 an Investment Centre was set up to assist foreign capitalists. Approved companies would benefit from special privileges in taxation, writing-off invested capital, etc. This appeal to foreign capitalists was given wider scope, and the facilities made available to their shareholders were extended.

The U.S.S.R. for its part quickly cooled in its attitude to the new state. The Communist International had always been opposed to Zionism in principle, since it distracted Jewish workers from the struggle to overthrow capitalism in every country. Within the Soviet Union itself, Zionism offered the Jews a second loyalty to a foreign state. While this may be acceptable in a pluralistic society – although difficult for any state to accept openly – it was intolerable for a totalitarian state. Nonetheless, the *Yishuv*'s hostility to Great Britain gave Stalin the idea of exploiting the situation of the Jews in the Middle East. At that time, the Arab states were reactionary and for the most part pro-British, and

* T. W. Van Alstyne, *Current History*, February 1948, p. 80.

seemed hardly likely to be sympathetic to the Soviet cause. Marxism evidently gave the Soviet leaders no better inkling of the revolutionary rumblings within the masses than the capitalist politicians had. Hence the U.S.S.R.'s support for partition (which was to strike a terrible blow at the Communist parties in the Arab countries) and the fleeting support given to the new state.

Disillusionment was not slow to follow. The first steps taken by Israel, seen from close quarters, might have suggested to Stalin the very thoughts expressed above. The demonstration of the Moscow Jews in September 1948 had a profound effect on him. It took place on the day of the Jewish New Year, when the new Israeli ambassador, Golda Myerson, attended the Moscow synagogue. From 30 to 50,000 people invaded the streets to welcome her. Here was clear evidence that many Soviet Jews were attracted to the new state. The Zionist programme continued to call for their emigration to Israel. The elections to the Knesset in January 1949 gave 34.7 per cent of the votes to the Mapai, 14.54 per cent to the neutralist Mapam and 3.44 per cent to the Communists. Israel's orientation now seemed obvious, and Stalin quickly drew his own conclusions. At the beginning of 1949, the Soviet bloc put into effect severe anti-Zionist measures. In the U.S.S.R. itself these soon assumed a more ominous character, leading to decisions which deprived the Yiddish culture of its means of expression, to malignant discrimination against the Jews, to executions and deportations. In short, anti-Zionism had turned into anti-Semitism. The other countries of the Soviet bloc followed Russia's example, and emigration to Israel was made extremely difficult.

This process rapidly accelerated. In 1950 Israel aligned herself with the Western camp over Korea. In 1951 Ben Gurion paid a triumphal visit to the United States. He made advances to Great Britain, then to the United States. In order to give them an interest in Israel's existence, he offered a military alliance, the right to use Israeli ports and aerodromes, service depots, a whole military infrastructure. The Old Man was very farsighted; he knew very well that these were the only means of support on which he could rely to ensure Israel's survival in the long term, permanently threatened as she was by the Arab desire for revenge. In 1955 he offered the United States bases, point-blank, in exchange for a firm guarantee of Israel's frontiers. But after some hesitation the British and the Americans, aware of the importance of the Arab world, refused these offers, which would automatically commit them to support Israel.

What of the Arabs? Surely it was possible to mollify their hostility? Again, there were two schools of thought. Some wished to make concessions to the Arabs to secure peace – Sharett because of his essentially conciliatory temperament, and the Left wing for ideological reasons. Ben Gurion detested the Arabs, but being himself a nationalist, he understood them. He did not believe that it would be possible to neutralize their desire for revenge by any other means than force, although it occurred to him at times that the force would perhaps not always be on the same side. Such a contingency was distant, however, and he left it to his successors to worry about it. Meanwhile, he considered that the territory so far conquered was a minimum. He would not hear of yielding an inch of it. And the Jewish state already had too many Arabs, on the whole more prolific than the Jews. He was not prepared to take one single extra refugee.

This question was bound up with the Israeli attitude to the U.N. Ben Gurion the realist despised the international organization. He knew very well that united action to impose a solution on Israel was inconceivable. He rightly reckoned with disagreement among the great powers and the weight of public opinion in Europe and America working in Israel's favour.

In theory, the United Nations' plan of partition of November 1947 was still valid. The Arabs had rejected it in principle, but in practice they had, willy-nilly, occupied only areas accorded to them by the plan. The Israelis had added considerably to their portion of Palestine by their military successes, and the frontiers won by force of arms were frozen into immobility by the armistice agreements of 1949. On 11 December 1948, during a break in the fighting (which was to prove more or less permanent), the General Assembly of the United Nations adopted a resolution creating a Conciliation Commission for Palestine, comprising representatives of the United States, France and Turkey. The Assembly declined to deal with the question of frontiers, but nonetheless 'resolved' that Jerusalem and its immediate environs would be internationalized, as provided for in the partition plan. It was also decided that 'refugees wishing to return home and live in peace with their neighbours would be allowed to do so as soon as practicable, and that compensation would be paid for the property of those choosing not to return.'* Israel was admitted to the U.N. on 11 May 1949; the Assembly specified its views on the internationalization of the zone around Jerusalem on 7 December, in a resolution sponsored by France, the U.S.S.R. and the Arab countries. Jerusalem was to be governed by the U.N. Trusteeship Council. Ben Gurion, against the advice of Sharett, decided to brave the U.N. and on 13 December he transferred the capital to Jerusalem. Protests by the powers were of no avail.

Defying the proposals of the U.N. mediator Bernadotte and American pressure for the return of the refugees, Ben Gurion had declared in July 1948: 'We must do everything in our power to ensure that they never return.'† In 1949 Israel announced to the Conciliation Commission that she was ready to accept as Israeli citizens the 200,000 refugees in the Gaza Strip, plus the 70,000 native inhabitants of the strip, provided the zone passed under Israeli sovereignty. Naturally the Arabs rejected this offer, emphasizing that priority should be given to the unconditional return of the refugees in accordance with the U.N. resolution, without being subject to the territorial settlement and peace treaty desired by Israel. Sharett then made a major concession. He would allow 100,000 refugees to return. The Arabs did not reject this offer, but demanded first the unconditional return of the refugees originating from the areas conquered by Israel and lying outside the territory accorded her by the U.N. partition plan. This entailed recognition, in some measure, of that plan and hence of the existence of Israel within these limits – already recognized in practice by the armistice agreements of 1949 and by the promise not to resort to force. Israel refused, despite

---

* U.N.G.A. Resolution 194 (III/1), para. 11, 11 December 1948.
† See Michel Bar-Zohar, *Ben-Gourion*, op. cit., p. 207.

American pressure. Israeli public opinion was practically unanimous against Sharett, who gave way. In 1953 the Arab states signed agreements with U.N.R.W.A. for the reintegration of a fairly large number of refugees in their respective countries. Mounting tension led to the abandonment of the agreements. Contacts between Nasser and Sharett, set up in 1954 through the intermediary of the Labour Members of Parliament Richard Crossman and Maurice Orbach, seem to have been cut short. But at the same time, Arab reactions to the Charles T. Main plan were encouraging. This was a plan for the utilization of the waters of the River Jordan by all the countries through which it flows, presented under the auspices of the American government to the various states by Eisenhower's personal representative Eric Johnston.

The Arabs were constantly forced to operate on two different levels. They were accustomed to haggling, in which the speaker's intention is only understood via hints and allusions. This is not merely an Oriental idiosyncracy, but the common practice of international diplomacy. But Zionist activists and their innumerable sympathizers throughout the world caught them in the trap of their own words, pointing to actions which were or might be represented as confirmation of those words. Ideologically, the Arabs could not openly accept the *fait accompli* of colonial encroachment of their territory. Moreover it was in their interest, diplomatically, not to throw away their trump card: non-recognition of Israel, rejection of diplomatic relations and therefore of any possibility of negotiations with Israel. Ideologically again, they could not disavow, in the face of public opinion in their own countries, the raids and incursions of the Palestinian Arabs; on the practical plane, they were unable entirely to prevent them. Neither could they accept Israel's constant encroachments of the status of the demilitarized zones, and had to do something to prevent limitation of their rights.

Something more needs to be said in regard to these latter problems since European opinion is commonly familiar only with the Israeli point of view. The 1948 frontiers, arbitrarily delimited by the front lines reached on the cessation of hostilities, were the cause of much trouble. Villages were cut in two, pastures were separated from the source of drinking water for the animals, farmers were cut off from their fields. Traditional bonds between villages were broken. Large numbers of Palestinians tried to return clandestinely, and many succeeded. The Bedouin always moved about freely in the border areas, ignoring the frontiers. Looters, bandits and smugglers also crossed the frontier. In a population in which the blood-feud was a customary feature of social life, some crossed the border to seek vengeance for wrongs they had suffered.

In addition, the 1949 armistice agreements had made provision for demilitarized zones, which presented serious problems and were variously interpreted. These zones caused a number of incidents, despite the presence of joint armistice commissions presided over by officials of the U.N. truce supervisory body.

Generally speaking, Israel's attitude in the innumerable cases of friction resulting from these fragile frontiers was for the most part roundly condemned by the various military commanders of the U.N. truce supervisory force. With monotonous regularity, the Israelis denounced them as anti-Semites. The repeated accusation led to the recall of some of the commanders, and induced others to take up a conciliatory attitude towards Israel. It seems unlikely that the U.N. should have placed a series of anti-Semites at the head of its mission. In reality, Israel's intransigent and aggressive attitude emerges clearly from all these incidents, and it is an attitude which is readily explicable. The Israelis considered that the Arabs had refused to negotiate a final peace on the basis of the 1948 frontiers, and had therefore, according to them, violated Article 1 of the armistice agreements referring to a gradual transition towards the re-establishment of peace. They in turn, therefore, were not bound to any scrupulous respect for the other provisions of these agreements, they could refuse to cooperate with U.N. representatives, etc.

In Israeli eyes, the neighbouring Arab states were responsible for all infiltrations, lootings, rapes and murders committed within her frontiers, even when police investigation was not able to place the responsibility for the crime outside the country's borders. Israel had no confidence in inquiries carried out by the U.N. officials, even less in those conducted by the Arab police forces, and refused to cooperate in them. In any case, the Arabs were responsible for everything by refusing to negotiate a peace, i.e. to recognize Israel within the frontiers of 1948, and by conducting an unremitting campaign of verbal propaganda against her. Force was the only means of winning respect. Force was all the Arabs understood. The policy of collective reprisals had its roots in this attitude.

The policy was applied with rigorous severity. On 13 October 1953 a grenade attack in a Jewish village killed a woman and two children. The tracks left by the assassins indicated that they had taken refuge in Jordan, and the Jordanian police took up the case, under the direction of Glubb Pasha, the English commander of the Arab legion. On the night of 14 to 15 October a contingent of the Israeli Army bombarded and attacked the Jordanian village of Kibya, blowing up 40 houses, killing 53 villagers, men, women and children, and injuring 15.

Two months later Ben Gurion, who had ordered the attack resigned and withdrew to the *kibbutz* of Sde Boker. Leadership of the government now fell to Sharett.

Moshe Sharett governed from December 1953 to February 1955. He favoured a more flexible policy, and the contacts established with Egyptian officers date from this period. Nasser was well-disposed towards him. The Arabs could not officially give way over non-recognition nor cease their propaganda activities, but they had shown de facto recognition of Israel while still contesting the frontiers, and they waited for feelers to be extended aiming at an agreement based on the U.N. resolutions. It is not impossible that an Israeli declaration of principle in this direction would have resulted in some intimate bargaining. Territorial adjustments and the return of refugees might have been discussed. The outcome of the discussions might well have approximated to an acceptance of the status quo. Israel would have been recognized, and perhaps saved.

It might have been the salvation of Israel. But it would have been the end of Zionism. What neither the Left nor Sharett saw was clearly perceived by the old chief, tucked away in his *kibbutz* in the Negev. An Israel recognized, an Israel become a Levantine state like any other, admitting a certain number of Arab refugees

to her breast, abandoning some of her conquests, conforming to
the decisions of the U.N., was necessarily subject to a certain
limitation, a definite restriction of Jewish immigration. This would
have meant the extinction of the proud dream of reviving the
kingdom of David and Solomon, bridgehead of the Jewish
Diaspora, able to call on the aid of the whole of the world Jewry
for its defence and ultimate victory. The 'normal' progress of
events was fatal for Zionist Israel. Internally, the increasing
number of Levantine Jews would become a majority and gain
the upper hand. Once the external danger had disappeared,
Messianic fervour would decline. The pioneer spirit was in
jeopardy. Ben Gurion's call for the colonization of the Negev had
aroused little response. If Israel was just a country like any other,
why go there, why become attached to it? By 1953 more Jews
were leaving the country than arriving. In external affairs the big
powers would be inclined to ignore this rather awkward little state.
By contrast, Zionist Israel throve on a bellicose atmosphere and
the threat of danger. The world could not allow her to be destroyed,
Jews the world over would rally to the aid of those whom in
times of peril they could not help regarding as their brothers.
Zion's salvation lay in permanent danger.

The shady Lavon affair – based on a programme of provocation
planned by the Israeli Secret Service to force the British to stay
in Egypt by simulating Egyptian outrages against British institutions – brought Ben Gurion back to power on 21 February 1955.
He immediately gave notice to the Arabs that Israeli policy was
now reverting to the hard line, that Israel would react violently
to infiltration, to the non-recognition which justified it and the
propaganda which accompanied it. The powers which had just
formed the Baghdad Pact were shown that Israel was an important
factor, which they ignored at their peril. The immediate pretexts
for this policy were no more urgent than at any other time. The
previous year Egypt had prevented an Israeli ship from passing
through the Suez Canal. On 2 February, three agents of the Israeli
intelligence network in Egypt were found guilty of acts of terrorism and hanged. Sharett had appealed to Nasser for clemency.
But members of the Muslim Brotherhood had earlier been executed on similar charges, and Nasser could not therefore show

favour to Israeli agents. On 28 February Ben Gurion unleashed the massive reprisal raid on Gaza mentioned earlier.

The Gaza raid marked a turning point. The Arabs had been given a severe shock. They realized that Zionist Israel had resumed its traditional policy. They were afraid of its expansionist tendencies. The 1955 elections, in which the Mapai lost five seats, were interpreted as a repudiation of Sharett's policy of appeasement. The Egyptians, together with all politically aware elements in the Arab world, feared that the Baghdad Pact would deprive them of all possibility of independent action, and tie them to the chariot of the West; and Israel was the West's favourite son.

In their eyes, the threat of Israeli expansionism was again taking shape. With Ben Gurion the partisan of unlimited immigration back at the wheel, Ben Gurion the friend of the activist military clique dominated by Dayan and Peres, Ben Gurion who always wanted more, who always imposed his own policy regardless of U.N. decisions, all hope of concessions which might lead to peace faded into the distance. The Arabs therefore had to get arms. The Arab world was aware of its own weakness. According to a military spokesman, Egypt had at this time six serviceable aeroplanes and enough tank ammunition to last through one hour of battle.

Nasser and the ruling officer group in Egypt continued to press the United States for arms. But Foster Dulles kept the carrot too far in front of them, and used the stick too hard: no arms without entry into a regional 'defence pact', i.e. into commitment to the Western military system against the U.S.S.R. Great Britain's attitude was the same. France, who supplied arms to Syria, had become shy of arming the Arabs since the outbreak of the Algerian War. Faced with these pressures and with the threat of a pro-Western military bloc actually protecting Israel, and covering the whole of the Middle East under the leadership of Turkey and Iraq, the Egyptian tendency towards neutralism was accentuated. Nasser drew closer to Nehru, and established links with Tito. In April 1955, at the conference of the 'Third World' held at Bandung, he opened a line of communication with Chou En-Lai. The Third World hesitated, appreciating that the Arabs were in the same boat as the rest of them, while Israel properly belonged in the Western camp. Israel was excluded from the conference. Nasser's requests for arms were transmitted to the Soviet Union by the Chinese. Nasser had got the Americans and the British in a corner. They thought he was bluffing. On 27 September 1955 Nasser announced the conclusion of an agreement with Czechoslovakia for the supply of arms to Egypt. In response to Baghdad in October he concluded pacts with Syria and Saudi Arabia. A wave of neutralist fervour swept over the Arab world. The pro-British regimes were threatened. In Jordan, a popular revolt prevented the government from signing the Baghdad Pact. King Hussein gave way to popular pressure in dismissing Glubb, the British commander of his army, on 1 March 1956. The elections held on 21 October brought a Popular Front government including Ba'athists and Communists to power. On the 25th, Egypt signed a military pact with Jordan and Syria. In Syria likewise a neutralist coalition hostile to the Baghdad Pact was in power. Saudi Arabia supported the movement through fear that her old enemy, Hashemite Iraq, would win hegemony over the Arab world.

After the Gaza raid, Egypt was preoccupied with her potential loss of face in the confrontation with Israel; somehow public dissatisfaction had to be quelled, and Arab claims upheld. So-called death commandos, the *fedayeen*, were organized in Egypt to conduct guerilla raids inside Israel. The Straits of Tiran was closed to ships carrying strategic materials to Israel. Ben Gurion responded to the challenge. In October a raid was conducted on the Syrian frontier; on 2 November the demilitarized zone of al-'Auja on the Egyptian frontier was occupied; in December an attack in force was carried out against Syrian positions – to the anger of Sharett, who was at that moment attempting to obtain arms from Dulles. But Ben Gurion wanted to demonstrate to the Arabs the emptiness of the Egypto-Syrian pact. The Burns plan, providing for local agreements to prevent frontier incidents, with joint Israeli-Egyptian patrols, was accepted by Egypt and rejected by Israel.

At the same time, final attempts at conciliation were made. An American politician of high standing was sent to act as a secret intermediary between Nasser and Ben Gurion. The plan foundered on the question of the return of refugees, which Ben Gurion would not have at any price. An official plan proposed by Dulles, which he rather clumsily tied to the Main-Johnston water allocation plan (which if accepted on a purely technical basis might have had a chance of unfreezing the situation in the long run), suffered the same fate. On 9 November 1955 Sir Anthony Eden, rather more realistically, spoke of a compromise between the Arab demand for a return to the 1947 plan and Israeli insistence on the frontiers of 1949. On the 12th the Israeli government refused any territorial concessions. At the end of November Nasser again mentioned, to Jean Lacouture, the possibility of recognizing Israel on condition that negotiations were held on the basis of the Eden proposals. On the same date, Ben Gurion submitted to the Israeli cabinet Dayan's plan for attacking Egypt and opening the Strait of Tiran to all Israeli shipping by force. The majority of Ministers, including Sharett, rejected the plan. Ben Gurion submitted – for the moment.

Sharett made superhuman efforts to achieve a peaceful solution. Ben Gurion meanwhile prepared for war. Failing to obtain arms from Great Britain and the United States, he approached France. Guy Mollet's Socialist Party, which had come to power in January 1956, was well disposed to Israel's request. The Socialists had capitulated to the Algerian settler lobby, and abandoned all thoughts of bringing peace to Algeria by carrying out far-reaching reforms. Reduced to desperate expedients, they resolved to put an end to the war by bringing about the overthrow of Nasser, who was supposed to be supporting and even directing it. Sentiments of socialist solidarity with the Mapai, the primitive identification of aid to Israel with an anti-racist, and hence anti-Fascist, socialist and 'Left-wing' position, all played a part. The British, for their part, attributed to Egypt the upsurge of Arab nationalist feeling, and hoped also to avenge the rejection of the Baghdad Pact. Eden, who enjoyed good social relations with Nuri es-Said and the youthful King Feisal of Iraq, was scandalized by Nasser's coarse and indelicate competition against them. The British and French governments and the press in both countries launched the myth that Nasser=Hitler, which was to be carried so far and do so much damage.

Alone among the Western countries, the United States tried to maintain contact with the Arabs and to woo Nasser away from neutralist, let alone Communist, influence. The financing of the Aswan High Dam, an essential project if Egypt was to escape from her disastrous economic situation, was projected by Washington on relatively favourable terms. Funds for this purpose were released in December 1955, and a loan from the World Bank was envisaged, but with controls and conditions irksome to the Egyptians, who were suspicious from bitter experience. Great Britain had a finger in the pie. The British, French and Israelis all tried to dissuade Dulles from granting the loan. The American Congress jibbed at voting it. Nasser conducted parallel negotiations with the Soviet Union for the money, but announced to the Americans that he would prefer the aid to come from them.

At the same time Ben Gurion, prevented for the time being from embarking on a full-scale war, continued his campaign of harrassment. He refused to make any concessions to the U.N. on the al-'Auja demilitarized zone, launched a military expedition on the southern frontier, and shelled Gaza. On 18 June he drove Sharett, who opposed his policy, to resign from his post of Foreign Secretary. Ben Gurion's way was now clear.

On 18 July Dulles, learning that the U.S.S.R. was unable to finance the Aswan Dam, announced that the United States was cancelling the offer of aid, adding some disparaging remarks by way of explanation. Great Britain followed suit. Nasser had been taught a good lesson. Egypt and the Arab peoples were humiliated, their backs to the wall. To the Western powers, capitulation seemed certain.

But the Egyptian officers' group refused to take the snub. They bridled, and on 26 July, at Alexandria, Nasser found his answer. He announced the nationalization of the Suez Canal.

There then took place the event which was to engrave the image of Israel in the mind of the Third World (at that time still unsure of its attitude), an event which was to give the final impetus to the radicalization of the Arab world: the Suez expedition, undertaken jointly by Britain, France and Israel after a secret treaty signed at Sèvres on 23 October. Of course the motives of the three partners were very different. For Ben Gurion, who took the lead on the Israeli side, the object was to strike a crippling blow at the Arabs, forcing them to recognize Israel in its present boundaries, to call off the state of virtual war and the now quite serious attacks of the *fedayeen*, together with the blockade of the Strait of Tiran. No doubt the possibility of territorial gains also entered his head. Any upheaval might bring about potentially advantageous changes. But Ben Gurion had in any case long been haunted by the spectre of a united Arab revival. He wondered whether Nasser might not prove the Arab Mustapha Kemal, who would lead his people out of chaos; he watched the development of the Arab alliance with the East, and the influx of arms and munitions. He decided that the time had come to strike, to crush the power that was now arising, or at least gain recognition while Israel held the upper hand, before it was too late. Also, it seemed foolish not to profit from the happy circumstance of finding two major, well-armed Western powers on Israel's side. Such an opportunity might not occur again for a long time.

The French Socialist government, strangely upset by the nationalization of a large capitalist enterprise, were hoping to win in Egypt the war they were incapable of winning in Algeria, both to make peace and to win the war – an illusion analogous to that which makes the Americans bomb Hanoi, through inability to defeat the South Vietnamese guerrillas. For the British Conservative government, the main aim was to overthrow Nasser, the symbol of anti-imperialist radicalism in the Arab world, and the number-one adversary of the faithful Nuri es-Said, whose policy was based on alliance with Britain. The latter had again attempted, on 8 October, with British support, to achieve a peace on the basis of a return in principle to the U.N. partition plan. Israel's response to this was naturally a scornful and vigorous 'no'. The English and French were certain that the slightest setback would set the Egyptian people against Nasser and bring a rival group to power. They were confirmed in their opinion by their own expert advisers, themselves prisoners of the same prejudices.

The situation was eminently favourable to the conspirators. The U.S.S.R. was busy suppressing the Hungarian revolt. Eisenhower was kept in ignorance by the C.I.A., who knew what was afoot. On 29 October the Israeli army invaded Sinai. French aeroplanes kept the Israeli columns supplied, and machine-gunned Egyptian convoys, at the same time protecting Israeli air space. French warships patrolled the coast, by secret agreement behind the backs of the British. On 30 October, as agreed by the three allies, an Anglo-French ultimatum was delivered, masquerading as a peace-keeping manoeuvre; it demanded that Israeli and Egyptian troops should withdraw to a distance of 16 km from each bank of the canal. The Israelis would thus keep the territory they had occupied, except for a strip of 16km, while the Egyptians would retire from a part of their own country which had not even been conquered. It was calculated that this obvious and deliberate partiality would force Nasser to reject the ultimatum.

On 1 November the General Assembly of the U.N. ordered a cease-fire. On the 3rd, once their troops had overrun Sinai, the Israelis agreed to comply, but then withdrew their acceptance to give their allies, who were a little slow in moving, a pretext for military intervention. On the 5th, British and French paratroops were dropped on the Canal Zone. But the Soviet Union threatened atomic reprisals. The U.N. Assembly decided to send an international peace-keeping force. On the 6th Eden capitulated, carrying with him Guy Mollet, who was eager to continue. At midnight on the 6th, a cease-fire was announced in Egypt. Nasser had not fallen, as the British and French had hoped. But Israel was victorious. On 7 November Ben Gurion, intoxicated by success, declared to the Knesset: 'We have created the third Kingdom of Israel!'

4 THE RISE
OF ARAB SOCIALISM

Like most of the manoeuvres of the Western powers, at least during this period and in this area, the Suez campaign achieved precisely the opposite result to that intended. Nasser was supposed to fall. Instead, he achieved the status of an Arab national hero and the stature of a near-legendary figure at the summit of his popularity.

Independence of the West was the consuming passion of the Arab world; no voice dared raise itself, no party dared take its stand against this aspiration. Israel, a Western enclave in Arab territory, appeared in Arab eyes as the living symbol and busy agent of Western imperialism. The Suez campaign was hardly calculated to make the Arabs change this opinion. Nasser had been the first to dare defy the West, and had been the West's first victim. He had emerged victorious – diplomatically if not militarily. His people had put up a spirited resistance to the Anglo-French paratroops in Port Said, chalking up the Arabs' first glorious feat of arms for many years.

In 1952 Nasser had been a nobody; he remained in the background till 1954, while the myth of the Egyptian revolution was symbolized by Neguib. Subsequently his halo was successively brightened by the moves taken in the direction of neutralism, his attack in 1955 on the Baghdad Pact, his presence at Bandung, and his decision to purchase arms from the Eastern bloc. To the West, neutralism meant Communism. To the masses of the East, it meant anti-imperialism. This implied intervention in Arab affairs. The possibility no doubt existed of Egypt standing alone, in isolated neutrality; the politically conscious element in the Egyptian masses had only been aware of the affairs of the Arabs of Asia for perhaps a score of years, while the Egyptian army officers had been very reluctant to commit themselves to the imbroglio of pan-Arab politics. But how was Egypt, the most heavily populated Arab country, and the pole of the cultural, intellectual and social life of the Arab world, to hold aloof from the Arab masses, who all looked up to her in admiration and hope? Had not the enemy powers and Israel themselves nominated Egypt head of the Arab world by making her their principle adversary and directing all their fury on to her? 'Nasserite' movements sprang up in every Arab country. This does not mean that Egypt's internal policy was everywhere approved (in so far as anybody knew what it was). But everywhere there was tremendous enthusiasm for the challenge to Western domination thrown down by Nasser.

The social struggle was a secondary consideration. All Arabs wanted to modernize their countries and raise their desperately low standard of living. Most were undecided on how to set about achieving these ends. Experience had already shown, and was to continue to prove, that every effort in this direction tied to a liberal-style economy and alliance with the West only produced a degree of economic growth wholly dependent on exterior forces and having nothing in common with a healthy and self-sufficient internal development. More important still, this economic dependence carried with it a political dependence. An unmistakable indication of this was the passivity which the more dependent regimes displayed towards Israel, their tendency towards capitulation and the abandonment of Arab claims.

Nasser was the incarnation of the Arab drive towards independence and modernization. From the point of view of the Arab middle class, the most active politically, he had the further merit of standing for independence from Communist ideology too, which had its own recipes for attaining the same ends (a point completely overlooked by Western analysts, blinded by myth and prejudice). The popularity of the U.S.S.R. among the Arab masses did not in the main stem from an enthusiasm for Communism as such. The Soviet Union had merely assumed the popular role played by pre-war Germany. In both instances, the Arab masses saw simply a European power not involved in the colonial dismemberment of the world, and hostile to the two great colonial powers whose domination the Arab countries had had to endure:

Great Britain and France. As for the United States, also apparently a non-colonial power, initial good will towards her had been dissipitated by her friendship for Britain and France, her eagerness to enrol the Eastern countries in the anti-Communist crusade (which seemed to be nothing but a thin disguise for Western domination), her support for Israel and for the more reactionary Arab regimes. Finally, Lenin's idea of imperialism was gaining increasing credence among all sections of the population, and seemed confirmed by the outpourings of American wealth, invariably tied to Foster Dulles' obsessional pact-making schemes.

Immediately after Suez the United States almost managed to win back popularity in the Arab world. Eisenhower was anxious to avoid losing the area entirely, and furious with the French and British for their duplicity towards him. He was eager to cooperate with the U.S.S.R. to prevent a conflict which might snowball beyond the control of the two super-powers, and had played an important part in forcing the British and French to retreat. Again in conjunction with the U.S.S.R., which threatened Israel with atomic retribution, he succeeded in obtaining an Israeli withdrawal from the occupied areas. Ben Gurion struggled furiously in his efforts to avoid this result, only retreating step by step, trying to keep at least some of the fruits of his victory. But Israel's dependence on the United States had a telling effect. American economic pressure proved far more persuasive than Soviet threats, which would have been very difficult to carry out. Ben Gurion knew this from the start. He is said to have declared to the Israeli cabinet on 28 October, on the eve of the attack: 'The Americans will force us to leave. America need send no troops to achieve this result; she need only state that she will break off diplomatic relations, prohibit collections for the Jewish fund, and block Israeli loans. She will ask herself: what is more important to her: Israel or the Arabs?' * Calculations of this kind duly played their part. The result was unfavourable to Israel. The U.N. unanimously condemned the Israeli conquest. An American loan was blocked. Israel feared that the Americans might press West Germany to stop the payment of reparations, they feared inter-

* Michel Bar-Zohar, *Ben Gourion*, op. cit., p. 313.

national economic sanctions, and what might follow from them. France, Israel's last ally, was in favour of a compromise.

Ben Gurion gave in. He would evacuate the conquered territory. All he would get was the presence of U.N. troops in the Strait of Tiran, guaranteeing free passage to Israeli shipping in the Gulf of Aqaba. These troops would also be stationed in the Gaza Strip, providing a barrier between Egypt and Israel to prevent frontier incidents. They would thus be stationed on Egyptian or Arab territory. Because Israel was the victor, she was spared encroachment on her own territory.

The fund of Arab good will which the United States had won by forcing Israel to evacuate was shortly to be dissipated. This was once again due to the Americans' anti-Communist phobia, to their profound lack of comprehension for Middle Eastern problems, and to their backing of Israel in the 1949 frontiers. Suez led to the exclusion of the British and French from the region and weakened the position of Nuri es-Said, Great Britain's staunch friend. The Soviets and the Americans were the only powers left to compete for influence in the Middle East. The Americans were afraid of the force of the neutralist wave, behind which they of course saw the hand of Moscow. They were apprehensive of the 'vacuum' created by the disappearance of British and French influence. On 5 January 1957 Eisenhower put forward a doctrine annotated by Dulles and accepted by Congress. The President was authorized 'to include the employment of the armed forces of the United States to secure and protect the territorial integrity and political independence of such nations requesting such aid against overt armed aggression from any nation controlled by international Communism.*' In March, the Eisenhower Doctrine was approved by Congress, James P. Richards, the Special Assistant for Middle Eastern affairs, left on a tour of the Middle East to exhort the countries of the area to join the Pact, and the United States became a member of the Baghdad Pact's Military Committee.

As usual, the immediate reaction on the part of some Middle

* Text from the *New York Times*, 6 January 1957, quoted by G. Lenczowski, *The Middle East in World Affairs* (3rd ed.), Ithaca, N.Y., Cornell University Press, 1962, pp. 676–7.

Eastern governments was extremely favourable to the United States, while the effect on the masses was disastrous and was to have long-term repercussions. Iraq of course immediately supported the Eisenhower Doctrine, as did the Lebanon, ruled by its pro-Western president Camille Shamoun. In Jordan Hussein officially rejected the Doctrine, but at the same time dismissed his neutralist ministers. Encouraged by the Americans, Saudi Arabia decided to attempt a reconciliation with her old Hashemite enemies, Iraq and Jordan.

But violent riots broke out in Iraq, accompanied by a full-scale peasant revolt. Martial law was proclaimed. In Jordan a wave of strikes and riots also forced the government to resort to martial law, backed up by a general curfew, the suspension of Parliament and the suppression of political parties. Dulles was obliged to put up a show of force by sending the Sixth Fleet into the Eastern Mediterranean, and to take charge of the financial affairs of the little kingdom.

The Egyptian and Syrian governments alone remained faithful to the neutralist line. But they had the support of all the Arab peoples. The hostility of the West only pressed them further. Nasser did not intend to burn all his bridges to the United States, far from it. But he no longer needed to pay any attention at all to the British and French, and in January 1957 all British and French companies in Egypt were 'Egyptianized' (and the Jewish ones too). The State had to intervene in the financing and management of the new Egyptian companies, but the Egyptian bourgeoisie also participated, to its own great profit. A certain degree of political liberalization followed the proclamation of a Constitution in January 1956 and the elections to the Legislative Assembly, held in July. Left-wing detainees were set free. Nasser succeeded in mobilizing the natural Left-wing sympathy for his new foreign policy. He allowed the Left its own press outlet, and made use of its services, especially to reinforce the internal ideological front. But the military clique still kept firm hold of the reins of power.

In Syria, where a neutralist coalition was in control, policy also took a new direction. The government included the Ba'ath party, a socialist and nationalist party committed above all to Arab unity, which at that time was symbolized in the person of Nasser. The Ba'ath saw in him their natural leader, in control of the powerful resources of Egypt, without whom no unity was possible. Sharing power with the Ba'athists was the Communist Party of Syria, the best organized in the whole of the Middle East. It possessed in its leader, Khaled Begdash, an eloquent public speaker, able to move the masses, gifted, intelligent and ambitious, overshadowing bourgeois politicians with his formidable political expertise, yet bound with every fibre of his being to the Communist International in which he was trained, and to the Soviet Union in which he continued to see the torch-bearer of world progress. His strength rested less on the Syrian proletariat, which was small and divided in its loyalties, than on the support of middle-class groupings attracted by an alliance with the Soviet Union. These were primarily represented on the political scene by the millionaire Khaled el-'Azm, scion of an old Damascan aristocratic family. The coalition was led and held together by a skilled politician, Sabri al-'Asali.

The policy of reliance on the Soviet bloc took shape in June 1955. A series of arms contracts, long-term credits, and the construction of an oil refinery bound Syria to the Soviet Union and the other countries of its orbit. Suez reinforced this trend. Washington was horrified to witness, as it thought, the creation in the Middle East of a people's democracy subject to the authority of Moscow. The Americans were the victims of their own ideological mythology. They were quite unable to understand that Syrian policy was primarily conditioned by local factors, and in the final analysis by the popular desire for independence and modernization, not in the very least by the daemonic machinations of international Communism. Nor did they appreciate that the U.S.S.R. had not the slightest desire to burden itself with a Middle Eastern Soviet state, unruly, dangerous to Soviet international policy, and requiring the investment of enormous sums to drag itself out of its material backwardness. The Soviet Union, and Begdash also, only wanted a Parliamentary regime sympathetic to Soviet foreign policy, and guaranteeing this orientation by permitting the existence of a Communist Party able freely to make its own propaganda and exert its influence. In contrast to the Americans, the middle-class Syrians led by Khaled al-'Azm understood this attitude very well.

The Americans behaved in the clumsiest fashion possible in their attempts to exorcize the imaginary menace. Clandestine moves by the American Embassy to achieve the overthrow of the Syrian government resulted in the expulsion, in August 1957, of three American diplomats. This was the first rebuff of its kind to American power in the region, and it was bitterly resented. The Syrian government appointed as Chief of Staff in Damascus 'Afif al-Bizri, denounced in Washington as pro-Communist. From that time on the Syrian government was outlawed by the West. If it was not possible to achieve its overthrow from within, external measures would be tried. At the end of August the American Under-Secretary of State Loy Henderson was sent to Ankara, where he met the democratic President Menderes, loyal to the American alliance, together with the kings of Jordan and Iraq and the Iraqi Chief of Staff. He then went to Beirut for talks with President Shamoun. All were promised arms. Turkey, which had had long-standing territorial disputes with Syria, became an increasing menace. Ben Gurion seized the opportunity to play on American anti-Communist susceptibilities, and wrote to Dulles offering him the benefit of his advice and services, sent Golda Meir on a special mission to Washington, and contacted the friendly French and German governments to try to obtain a N.A.T.O. guarantee of Israel's frontiers in exchange for Israeli cooperation.

Neutralist Syria justifiably felt threatened. Her only recourse was to Soviet aid. American policy, in its habitual fashion, had resulted in creating the very situation which it sought to avoid. The Soviet Union dispatched two warships to the Syrian port of Latakia. The pro-American Arab states were embarrassed by America's antics, which only resulted in condemning them in the eyes of their peoples as accomplices in the suppression of Syrian and Arab aspirations to independence, unity and modernization. King Saud of Arabia intervened; he visited Damascus in September, preached moderation to Washington, and brought Jordan and Iraq round to his point of view. All declared their opposition to any threat to Syrian independence.

Egypt could not stand aside. In October Egyptian troops disembarked at Latakia to take their stand at the side of the Syrians on the Turkish frontier. The successful launching of the first Soviet sputnik was received with enthusiasm by the Arabs. In the face of the American threat, exerted from its bases in Turkey and Israel, the great protector from the North had shown that it, too, was powerful. Patrick Seale writes: 'In short the net effect of America's brusque intervention in Arab affairs in 1957 was to confirm the Soviet Union and Egypt as Syria's twin protectors in the face of Western hostility.'* One might add the two champions not only of Syria but of Arab aspirations in general.

This was not the end of the matter. Soviet influence, up till then a myth, established itself. The Syrian Communist Party was stimulated by these developments, and many Syrians, feeling the way the wind was blowing, joined the party. Others began to share some of the American apprehensions. Begdash's voice was heard increasingly loudly, though he still made no reference to a socialist economy or to political power on the Soviet pattern. In fact, neither he nor the Soviet Union envisaged any such measures. But many could not avoid the fear that they might.

The Ba'ath party was especially nervous of Communist influence, reinforced as it now was by the Soviet alliance. This party had won a considerable following by virtue of the seductive appeal of its immediate programme and rousing slogans, which corresponded closely to the trends and aspirations of the masses. But it lacked a numerous party membership and a stable core of supporters. It was an elite, dominated at the time by a thoroughgoing intellectual, the French-educated Michel Aflaq. Aflaq's ideas of socialist nationalism were developed in Paris before the war. They were largely a reaction against Stalinist Communism, whose world strategy was contemptuous of national claims and accorded them no place in it. He was greatly influenced by André Gide's *Return from the U.S.S.R.*, and feared the Communist Party's organizational ability, however potential.

The Ba'ath saw one hope of salvation, and one only: the Arab nationalist, anti-imperialist state of Egypt, which even exhibited

* Patrick Seale, *The Struggle for Syria*, Oxford University Press, 1965, p. 306.

some socialistic tendencies. Above all, Nasser the national hero was seen as the only man able to marshall all the Arab masses behind himself. His immense popularity alone could woo them away from the seductions of Communism. The Ba'ath's preoccupations were shared by that section of the Syrian middle class which really feared Communism, while remaining ardently nationalist, and by the Syrian army, disillusioned with civilian politicians and envious of the privileged position enjoyed by the Egyptian military caste. There emerged throughout Syria an increasing enthusiasm for the plan of federal union with Egypt, as a first step towards the realization of the dream of Arab unity.

The greatest obstacle was Nasser himself. He certainly favoured strong Egyptian influence over Syrian policy, which would remove the danger of this key country's falling under the domination of a hostile Arab power such as Iraq. But he was loath to become too closely embroiled in Syria's turbulent politics and in the complex rivalries of the Eastern Arabs' multifarious pressure-groups. The problems created by Egypt alone were already quite difficult and complex enough.

The Ba'athists and the Syrian army were insistent. As for the Syrian Communists, they had always been in favour of Arab unity, like everybody else. But like many others, they were afraid of its realization in practice. Egypt, where Communists were persecuted, did not attract them, and their excellent prospects in Syria itself were liable to suffer from the union. Knowing Nasser's reservations, they outbid him in their efforts to abort the scheme. The only effect of this was to encourage the Ba'ath to demand, not federation, but total union with Egypt. Perhaps in the new united Arab state, the Ba'ath would provide the source of the nation's ideology and so come to control its policy while Nasser would be content with the role of symbolic leader.

In the end, Nasser agreed. It was a dangerous gamble, but one from which he intended to extract the maximum advantage. He laid down his conditions. The Syrian army was to withdraw from politics, and the political parties were to be disbanded. The Ba'ath hesitated for the last time. Would they be committing political suicide? The party's leaders considered that although dissolved, the Ba'ath would re-emerge strengthened in the form of the National Union (the sole party according to the Egyptian prescription). Military leaders were sceptical of the practical applicability of the measure directed against them. Khaled Begdash and Khaled el-'Azm tried in vain to avert the danger threatening them by falling back on the old proposal of federal union. The ideological power of the idea of Arab unity swept away all resistance. The Syrians accepted Nasser's conditions. The United Arab Republic was proclaimed on 1 February 1958. The Communist menace had been removed. On the 4th, Khaled Begdash left Damascus, and the Communist Party went underground.

Unity had carried the day. The old-style Arab nationalists were jubilant. In their eyes, the sovereign ideal of Arab unity, which had previously floated somewhere between heaven and earth like some Platonic Idea or Hegelian concept, was finally incarnate upon earth. An initial kernel had been formed. It could only grow – as Germany had grown from Prussia, as Italy had grown from Piedmont. The Arabs were bound to turn to this centre of the Arab nation. Their hour of triumph was at hand.

Actual developments were very different from these dreams. For a few months of 1958, however, circumstances lent them some measure of verisimilitude.

In the Lebanon, the tensions between the faiths usually resulted in driving the Christians – especially the Maronite community – into the arms of the West. For some time, however, this tendency had been balanced by the ideological force of Arab nationalism, especially powerful among the Muslims, but rapidly gaining ground among the Christians as well. It was from them, after all, that the idea had originated. Loyalty to the little homeland of Lebanon was extremely strong in the Christians, but in the case of the Muslims it was less ideological than utilitarian; they accepted it, after 1943, on condition that it remained compatible with allegiance to the larger Arab nation. The Lebanon's endorsement of the Eisenhower Doctrine roused Muslim indignation; but it also offended all pan-Arab sympathizers, not to mention those with special or sectarian interests. Even the

Patriarch of the Maronite Church found himself in the ranks of the so-called 'Nasserites'. This term is rather misleading, since outside of Egypt itself Nasser was primarily a symbol. These people were anti-imperialist Arab nationalists with pan-Arabist leanings, vaguely socialist in inclination, but not partisans of any specific doctrine.

The formation of the United Arab Republic awakened extra-ordinary enthusiasm in this shade of opinion and filled the opposite faction with dismay. The situation became explosive when the pro-Western President, Camille Shamoun, announced his intention of standing for re-election. This would have entailed amendment of the Constitution, which forbade the re-election of a President of the Republic for a second term; Shamoun himself had earlier opposed a similar attempt by his predecessor. The murder on 8 May 1958 of a 'Nasserite' Maronite journalist provoked a general strike against Shamoun, which then exploded into civil war. The war was a very curious one, conducted by scattered armed bands with no central direction, under the command of local gang leaders. The Lebanese army took no part in the affair. The Army chief, General Shehab, regarded the whole business as a violent quarrel between politicians, and his troops only intervened to restore equilibrium between the warring factions when it seemed in danger of being upset. The pro-American rulers of the country, Camille Shamoun and Charles Malik, his Foreign Minister, represented the conflict as foreign aggression, a planned piece of subversion directed by Nasser. They took the matter before the United Nations, hoping for Western intervention to come to their support.

In Iraq, too, the gulf separating neutralist public opinion, sympathetic to the Egyptian and Syrian position, from the country's pro-Western rulers, bitter enemies of Nasser and the Syrians, only widened. Social tensions aggravated the situation. Nuri es-Said and the Regent Abdulilah (who coveted the throne of Syria) had undertaken a programme of public works (mostly large dam projects) financed by the royalties on Iraq's oil revenue. But the masses derived no benefit from these projects, which could only have very long-term effects upon the economy. No money and no technical resources were left over for small improvements whose effects might have been more rapidly felt.

Nuri had taken decisive control of the anti-Nasser party. He saw the formation of the United Arab Republic as a challenge, and as a counterblast he arranged a Federation with Jordan. He had close ties with Great Britain, the United States and Turkey, and by the summer of 1958 dominated the bloc in which Shamoun of the Lebanon and Hussein of Jordan were associated with him in opposition to the Syrian and Egyptian neutralists. This was not all. At the time of the Jordan crisis in April 1957, when Hussein had dismissed his neutralist ministers and stifled a popular revolt, Eisenhower had declared the integrity of Jordan a vital interest, and Israel had reserved freedom of action in the event of any threat to Jordan's status. This could only mean that Israel would occupy the West Bank if Jordan were swallowed up in any Arab union. Objectively, therefore, Israel appeared as the ally of Western imperialism and of the coalition of pro-Western Arab governments.

In May 1958 Moshe Dayan revealed to Field-Marshal Montgomery a plan, supported by Ben Gurion, for an alliance to contain Arab turbulence between all the states on the periphery of the Arab world: Iran, Turkey, Ethiopia and Israel. Dulles continued to emphasize the threat of armed Soviet aggression, which he considered imminent. In June 1958 Nuri arrived in London. On the 27th, in an interview with *The Times*, he made a thinly veiled plea for Anglo-American intervention. On his way home he stopped off for conversations with the Turks, and a meeting of the Baghdad Pact members was announced for 14 July. It was common knowledge in the Arab world that he planned a joint military assault by the United States, Great Britain and Iraq to detach Syria from the U.A.R. and place the Fertile Crescent under the rule of a Hashemite king, who would be a client of the British. He sent troops into Jordan, no doubt as part of this plan, perhaps to start the war with Syria in the hope that the Western powers would follow. But the commanders of these troops, Brigadiers Kassem and Aref, marched instead on Nuri's villa and the Royal Palace. The King and the Crown Prince were killed, and Nuri fled, only to be found the next day disguised as an old woman and lynched. The Baghdad mob ran riot in the streets. On 14 July 1958, to the strains of the *Marseillaise*, the last powerful pro-imperialist regime in the central zone of the Arab world was overthrown. The Arab Revolution was victorious.

Naturally, the Iraqi Revolution was interpreted in the West as the outcome of a cunning Muscovite plot. It is quite certain that the Soviet Union was overjoyed to witness the abrupt collapse of the military edifice erected against her in the South. But the primary responsibility for the revolution must rest with the West, and especially the Americans. Their obstinate insistence on press-ganging the Arab countries into an anti-Soviet crusade in which they had not the slightest interest, and the British preoccupation with bolstering up unpopular monarchs in an attempt to win back their lost sphere of influence, sapped the foundations of their policy. The Western attitude towards Israel, which was looked upon as a firm base in a troubled world, and not as a problem confronting the Arabs and a threat to them, only made matters worse. It resulted in the strengthening of the militant clique in Israel, instead of encouraging conciliation. Behind these attitudes lay total lack of comprehension of the sociological factors. The political games played with chieftains and governments took no account whatsoever of Arab public opinion. Arab nationalism was regarded as the artificial creation of Nasser and the Russians, whereas in fact it was an entirely spontaneous, deeply rooted passion, which forced governments to obey its will, or else swept them away, dragged them down and cut them to ribbons, as happened to Nuri es-Said and Regent Abdulilah.

The Iraqi Revolution naturally filled the Arab nationalists – that is to say the vast majority of the Arab peoples – with exultation and terrified those who stood opposed to the wave: Hussein and Shamoun. They appealed for aid, which was hardly necessary. On 15 July American marines landed at Beirut, and on the 17th British paratroops from Cyprus were flown to Amman, permission having been obtained from Israel to overfly her territory. The Saudi rulers, fearing too much unpopularity, refused to allow American fuel intended for Jordan to pass their borders. It was therefore transported by plane from the Lebanon over Israeli air space, with Israel's consent. 'Where an Arab nation refused', Hussein writes bitterly in his memoirs, 'an enemy agreed.'*

A new pattern was emerging. And it was by no means characterized by the unconditional victory of Nasserism, as the Arab masses hoped and the Western powers feared. The idea of Arab unity was not to carry all before it, as the Arab ideologues had believed. One phase of development had come to an end. New problems were about to arise.

Up until this point, anti-imperialist Arab nationalism had been represented by Nasser. The Ba'ath his only competitor, was comparatively weak, and the formation of the U.A.R., as will be seen, had apparently subordinated it to Egyptian power. A new alternative to Nasserism now arose, a new competitor appeared on the scene: Kassem's Iraq.

Although it was unleashed by a purely military action, the revolution of July 1958 was the first real revolution in the Arab world. In 1952 the Egyptian officers had waited in vain for a positive massive popular reaction to their coup – although as lovers of order, they also did all in their power to prevent such a reaction. In Iraq, from the very first hours of the insurrection the masses came out into the streets, acted on their own initiative, and gave passionate, violent, even cruel vent to their aspirations and hatreds. Scenes which vividly conjured up the France of 1793 were accompanied by singing of the *Marseillaise* and the *Carmagnole*. Kassem, the new Leader (*Za'im*), gave popular spontaneity a free rein, and the attitudes and decisions taken by him manifested a still unaccustomed radicalism. From the start, the nationalist narrow-mindedness typical of so many Arab movements was overruled by a spirit of generosity, exhibited in the recognition of a Kurdish nationality, which was granted equal rights with the Arab race. Diplomatic relations were established with the U.S.S.R. and the Soviet bloc. Political refugees, including Communists, returned. A military tribunal was set up, very revolutionary in tone, which sat in public; sessions were broadcast and televised, and presided over by a Communistic

* Hussein of Jordan, *Uneasy Lies the Head*, London, Heinemann, 1962, p. 168.

colonel of ferocious truculence, Mahdawi, Kassem's cousin. Peoples' Militias were organized.

The Iraqi Communists, ruthlessly persecuted under the old regime, and apparently eliminated from the political scene, re-emerged surrounded by all the glamour of the underground, the prestige of a persecuted but tough and resilient group with a firm, apparently unequivocal political line. Party membership grew, despite the theoretical ban on political parties imposed by the regime. The Party's first objective was to canalize, under Soviet influence seemingly communicated via Khaled Begdash, popular enthusiasm and especially the reactions of the peasantry, which pressed for an extension of the revolution. Without more ado the peasants seized the lands of the big proprietors. Once again the U.S.S.R. stated her preference for a parliamentary regime sympathetic to her own foreign policy. Party pressure was exerted on Kassem with the principal object of obtaining major concessions to relieve the plight and calm the revolutionary fervour of the most poverty-stricken layers of the population. Agrarian reforms were rapidly decreed, but their actual execution was delayed or sabotaged by the civil service and the bourgeoisie, and it was therefore a long time before they took any effect.

On the national level, the regime's protestations of Arab solidarity and the solemn declaration contained in the Provisional Constitution of 27 July 1958, according to which 'The Iraqi State is an integral part of the Arab nation' (Article 2), did not solve all its problems. Kassem was not eager to relinquish the privileges of independence, and supported no doubt by a large section of the army he resisted the pressures towards organic union with the U.A.R. He was also supported by part of the nationalist middle class, which disliked Nasser's military authoritarianism, and by the very numerous racial and religious minorities (together constituting a majority of the population), which were apprehensive of Sunnite Muslim domination in a Greater Arab State. The Communists assumed the role of protector of the minorities, and did not hesitate to enlist the aid of the bourgeoisie. 'The idea of union with the U.A.R.', declared the Political Bureau of the party on 3 September 1958, 'is unwelcome to the people, because such a union would limit the opportunities for growth and development of the national economy and the nation's capital.'* The party and Khaled Begdash proposed simple federal union, which they knew Nasser would refuse. Kassem upheld this point of view, in opposition to the Ba'athists and the Nasserite section of the middle class represented by his team-mate Brigadier Abdul Salem Aref. Aref was excluded from power in September 1958. His conspiracy to stage a come-back resulted in his being condemned to death in January 1959. He was subsequently pardoned by Kassem.

The existence of Kassem as an alternative to Nasserism, the competition between the two movements, and the endemic geopolitical rivalry between Egypt and Iraq led to a number of realignments. As recently as the beginning of 1956, the U.S.S.R. had decided finally to abandon the Zhdanov-Stalin theory of the two blocs, and to recognize the progressive character of the non-Communist regimes in the Third World. She supported Nasser, hero of the anti-imperialist struggle. The general stiffening of the party line after the Hungarian and Polish rebellions in 1956, renewed hostility towards Nasser's friend Tito, the suppression of political parties in Syria, including the Syrian Communist Party, while the Iraqi Communist Party enjoyed a privileged position, all helped to increase Soviet suspicions of Nasser and favour Kassem.

Events in Syria tended towards a similar conclusion. In this 'Northern Province' of the United Arab Republic, Egyptian army officers often behaved as though they were in a conquered country. In every field of activity, Syrians were subordinated to Egyptians. As has already been mentioned, the political parties had been disbanded and replaced by a National Bloc on the Egyptian pattern. The Ba'ath, which had pressed for Union and had hoped to dominate the National Bloc, was undermined by Nasser, who simply dispensed with its services. Meanwhile both Communists and conservatives became increasingly enraged at Egyptian depredations of their economic and other interests, and held the Ba'ath responsible as instigator of the Union. Instead of the Ba'athists, the only Syrian given power and support by Nasser

* Quoted in *France Nouvelle* (weekly of the French Communist Party), 22–28 January 1959, pp. 16–17.

was the sinister Colonel Sarraj, Minister of the Interior for the 'region', who stocked the prisons with his opponents and practised torture on a grand scale. The fall of Nuries-Said removed any danger of annexation by a British-dominated Iraq – one of the hazards which had pushed Syria into the arms of Egypt.

The Communists and a growing proportion of the Syrian middle class, including even some of those who had been appalled at the excesses of the Iraqi Revolution, turned against Nasser. At successive Congresses of Eastern European Communist Parties (and for a time in Syria itself), Khaled Begdash denounced his authoritarianism, which had previously been overlooked; and condemned his 'Titoist' foreign policy as insufficiently attuned to that of the U.S.S.R. This irritated Nasser, and at the beginning of January 1959 he had a large batch of Egyptian Communists arrested. This action further aggravated Egyptian-Soviet relations. On 16 March Khruschev pronounced his verdict: the Iraqi regime was the more progressive. At the same time, the cold war between Egypt and Iraq was intensified. The radio stations of the two countries rained insults on one another. In March 1959 a Nasserite revolt at Mosul was nipped in the bud with the aid of local Communists and Kurds. In July 1959 Kurdish Communists instigated a massacre of 'reactionary' Turkmens in Kirkuk. Kassem shifted his ground, and condemned these excesses. The Iraqi Communist Party was penitent, and Kassem retained the support of the Left and of a section of the middle class. The Nasserites continued to denounce the Red Terror reigning in Iraq, while condemning Iraq's refusal to join the Union. Nasser then outdid himself with public protestations of Muslim piety and inveighed against the atheistic Communism to which Kassem had delivered Iraq. This led him towards a reconciliation with the reactionary Arab states, Jordan and Saudi Arabia. In defiance of the U.S.S.R., which had become hostile, he improved relations with the United States and the Western powers. From October 1958 the U.A.R. once again began to accept American aid.

Despite his slanging match with the U.S.S.R., Nasser did not break with the Soviet Union altogether, and attempted to maintain reasonable relations with both blocs. The economic ties

which he had established with the socialist countries were difficult to undo and replace. But the West was by now also contributing to Egypt's economic effort. Internally, Egyptian business-
men found the Syrian market open to economic penetration, and
were able to realize large returns on their capital by cooperating
in state-controlled enterprises or by taking advantage of other
openings left free to them. However, the nationalization of English,
French and Jewish companies after Suez had caused a considerable loss of confidence in Egyptian business circles, many of
whose members had close financial connexions with these companies. Most of the holders of the nation's capital had, shown little
inclination to invest it where the government considered it most
necessary. Despite all the soothing assurances made to them,
capitalists felt a vague unease, and many looked back with longing
to the old days of the free economy and parliamentary government,
which had guaranteed them their power. The more these reservations made themselves felt, the more the government was forced to
nationalize, in order to ensure that vital functions which private
capital refused to perform were fulfilled. It was then obliged to
justify these actions in speeches which became, perforce, increasingly socialistic in tone, thus arousing yet further alarm among
the capitalist classes. All in all, the State's role thus expanded
considerably, at the expense of the private sector. In February
1960 Egypt's two largest banks were nationalized. The central-
ization of power made rapid strides. The old middle class fell
increasingly under the domination of the military machine.
Nasserite rule remained true to its two great aims: independence
and modernization. But it now took the view that the Western
powers were resigned to abandoning any claims on Egypt's independence and that good relations with these powers could therefore
be resumed without fear, and even to Egypt's advantage. Private
capital had proved incapable of achieving modernization or the
building up of an autonomous industry. The participation of the
Communist Left had proved dangerous, in that it provided a
possible nucleus for an alternative policy. The development of
industry was therefore controlled by the State, in which the
military caste enjoyed a near-monopoly of power and very considerable privileges. A further step was taken in June and July

1961. The entire cotton trade, all banks and insurance companies, and 44 companies in the primary industries were nationalized. State control over foreign trade and over a large number of firms in commerce and light industry became paramount. However, it was made clear that the object of all these measures was merely to ensure economic growth and to raise the standard of living. Capitalism was only condemned for its excesses. No appeal was made to class consciousness or the class struggle. Compensation for expropriated possessions, the inviolable right to private property, the regime's protection of the civil rights of its subjects, its fidelity to Islam, respect for the value and dignity of the human person were strenuously insisted upon. Naturally, opponents of this programme were tortured. When Heykal, Nasser's confidant, published a newspaper article entitled 'A Workers' and Peasants' Revolution', it transpired that he meant a revolution *on behalf of* the workers and peasants.

Egypt's new external policies, especially the *rapprochement* with the United States and the reactionary Arab regimes, caused her sympathizers abroad considerable disquiet. The Ba'athists became increasingly cool in their attitude. Worse followed. At the end of June 1961 Kassem laid claim to the Arab sheikhdom of Kuwait, which had only six days previously been granted full independence by a treaty with Great Britain. Claims to a share in Arabia's oil wealth, monopolized by a handful of despotic rulers while so many heavily populated Arab countries were tragically lacking in resources, was one of the theme songs of Arab nationalism. However, hostility to Kassem drove the U.A.R. to defend the integrity of the sheikhdom, in conjunction with Jordan and Saudi Arabia and even with Great Britain, who dispatched troops to protect the feudal oil magnate's interests, closely bound up with her own. The replacement of British troops by a mixed contingent of Jordanian, Saudi Arabian and Egyptian soldiers did not help much to improve matters.

Egypt's authoritarian rule in Syria, the eclipse of the Ba'ath, the exploitation of Syria to bolster up the Egyptian economy finally became too much for the Syrians. Sarraj himself was dismissed and transferred to Egypt, with some honorary titles but stripped of all power. General discontent finally exploded in a military coup at Damascus. Syrian officers arrested the Egyptian proconsul, Marshal Abdul Hakim Amer, on 28 September 1961 and deported him to Egypt. They proclaimed Syria's secession from the U.A.R. The formation which was to have been the nucleus of Arab unity had blown apart.

Nasser wisely decided against any military campaign to re-conquer Syria. But he was profoundly disturbed, and undertook a painful reappraisal of his policy at every level. This was ex-pressed in a series of self-critical speeches covering the last quarter of 1961, and in one in particular which he made on 16 October. The tenor of these texts throws light on the whole process of the Arab Revolution.

Nasser, with whom the great majority of the Arab masses identified, saw this movement as above all else a national move-ment. In his *The Philosophy of the Revolution*, written at the be-ginning of the Egyptian Revolution, he explains that it (the Revolution) was 'the realization of the hope held by the people of Egypt since they began in modern times to think of self-govern-ment and complete sovereignty'.* The principal object of modernization was to guarantee the nation freedom of decision in its own affairs. The democratization of economic and social life were merely the corollary to these two things. As in every other ideology, the end was seen as possessed of every virtue. An inde-pendent and powerful nation ought automatically to abolish privilege and injustice. In his view, in fact, Egypt's ills were either the result of foreign influence or of the moral turpitude of individuals.

This nationalist outlook, extrapolated from Egypt to apply to all the Arab peoples, resonated with the feelings of the masses. Under conditions of foreign oppression, everything is attributable to that oppression. Likewise, every aim is subordinated to the primary aim of national liberation. Under the influence of Marxist thinking, Nasser had admitted the necessity for a second revolution. This would be a social revolution, bringing into play the class struggle with the object of ensuring 'equity to all the children of the same fatherland'. This, however, was a disagree-

* Gamal Abdul Nasser, *Egypt's Liberation : The Philosophy of the Revolution*, Washington, Public Affairs Press, 1955, p. 18.

able necessity. Significantly, Nasser depicted the national revolution as fostering a host of noble qualities: unity, mutual love, the spirit of sacrifice. By contrast, the social revolution would induce ('despite ourselves' he writes) division, hatred, selfishness. This is the precise opposite of the classical Marxist view, according to which it is the internal struggle which is healthy, which develops the most noble qualities. External struggles on the other hand – however necessary to achieve liberation – are to be deplored, divide the workers who ought to unite ('Proletarians of all lands, unite!'), bring out prehistoric instincts of group interest, and are generally symptoms of retrogression.

Nasser must have admitted to himself that some blame attached to the Egyptians for the way in which they had governed Syria. But he thought it his duty to take a more profound view of the matter. In his eyes, the Syrian secession was a betrayal by the Syrians of the ideal of the Arab nation, united and free. How was he to account for this unnatural phenomenon? Basically he saw in it a reaction on the part of the Syrian privileged classes against the socialist character of the regime, which had been accentuated by the wave of nationalizations in July. The subsequent policy of the secessionist Syrian government was to appear to justify this opinion. These privileged classes had succeeded in misleading the people by taking advantage of Egyptian errors and of grievances against the Egyptians, whether legitimate or not. Therefore the conclusion drawn from this was that not enough had been done to combat privilege, either in Egypt or Syria, and the masses had not been sufficiently enlightened. Nasser thought he detected a universal conspiracy directed against Egyptian socialism – a conspiracy both external and internal.

I have given the matter much thought [he declared on 16 October], and I have made my choice. I have chosen to pursue the revolution begun nine years ago on both the political and the economic plane, whatever the cost. ... We over-estimated our strength and our opportunities by under-estimating those of the reactionaries. We have, as a result, had to make terms with the reactionaries, and we have been thrown off our stroke. ... We have suffered a serious setback in organizing the people by opening the gates of the National Union to reactionary forces. Our efforts to educate the masses have been inadequate . . .*

The Egyptian reaction to Syrian secession therefore expressed itself in the form of a more radical social policy. The revolutionary movement exemplified by Nasser had not at first possessed any specifically socialist ideology. However, the logic of unyielding anti-imperialist nationalism, in continual conflict with the blind reactions of the imperialist powers in order to maintain itself, led Nasser's group through the elimination of the large landed proprietors first into a centralized statist economy controlled by the military caste, and then to an appeal to the revolutionary fervour of the underprivileged classes. This appeal was unquestionably sincere in Nasser's own case, and in that of some of his colleagues. They were also fully aware of the immense difficulties facing Egyptian economic development. The country possessed an extremely limited acreage of usable soil, which the Aswan High Dam had not as yet been able to increase significantly; the mineral resources necessary to build up a prosperous industry were totally lacking; and the population was multiplying at a dizzy rate. A superhuman effort, a Great Leap Forward according to the Chinese prescription, was needed – not to progress, but simply to avoid catastrophe. Who was capable of mobilizing the masses? It would perhaps be possible with the aid of a network of a hundred thousand small, completely dedicated revolutionary cells, capable of enormous sacrifices, to set an example to the millions of peasants who had viewed their rulers with mistrust and scepticism ever since the time of the Pharaohs. It was becoming apparent that the military bureaucracy, whose principal concern was to extract the maximum profit from positions of responsibility, bore not the slightest resemblance to the completely dedicated cells which had carried with them the Chinese and the Vietnamese masses, or those which had earlier ensured the relative success of Soviet economic development. It was now essential to establish militant cells drawn directly from the ranks of the suffering masses. And in order to win their enthusiasm for such a project, it was essential to offer them other prizes than external independence, which had now been assured. They would have to be promised a relentless struggle against

*Quoted in *Cahiers de l'Orient contemporain*, no. 47, Paris, 1961, p. 401.

privilege and the privileged – and not only those of the old society, but also those with whom the masses were in daily conflict. It had become necessary to promise the people liberty and equality – in brief, to have recourse to a socialist ideology.

In the immediate aftermath of the schism, nationalization measures were extended and stepped up. A wave of arrests and confiscations struck the members of the old property-owning classes. Above all, Nasser arranged for a National Congress of People's Forces to be elected, in which farmers, workers and peasants almost formed the majority. The Congress gave rise to a lively debate on the draft of a 'National Charter'.* This spoke of the 'will to revolutionary change, which rejects every tie and every limitation other than the rights and the claims of the masses', of the dangers of bureaucracy, and of liberty, which alone could overcome the passivity of the masses. 'A powerful public sector will direct progress in every field, and will bear the main responsibility for planning development.' The draft was accepted as it stood, with a reference to Islam inserted as the sole concession to the Right. The National Union, Egypt's only party, formed in 1957, was replaced by an Arab Socialist Union, half of whose party officials at every level had to be workers or peasants, except in the very highest ruling body of the party. A Constitutional Proclamation on 27 September 1962 laid down – in theory – that power at the top must be shared.

In his relations with the other Arab states Nasser returned to ideological intransigence. He broke off diplomatic relations with Jordan, denounced the regime in Saudi Arabia and refused to recognize the new Syrian government. He ended the vague confederation he had entered with the ultra-reactionary Yemen. Egypt's effective withdrawal from Arab affairs was accompanied by ringing proclamations of revolutionary Arab unity, and of unyielding hostility to the combined forces of imperialism, among which Zionism figured prominently.

Nasser's diagnosis of the causes of the Syrian secession did have some justification. The Syrians' irritation at Egyptian hegemony in their country was aggravated by the Syrian bour-

* *Mashroû‘ al-Mithâq*, Cairo, Department of Information, 1961, p. 10, 62.

geoisie's hostility to nationalization. Hardly had secession become an accomplished fact than the nationalization measures were reversed, to loud applause from the Communists who laid emphasis on the services performed by Syrian industrialists in the national struggle. Agrarian reforms were largely abolished, and many proprietors regained, sometimes by force, possession of the lands which they had lost.

Nasser's socialist, Arabist and anti-imperialist stand gave a new dynamism to these three guiding principles throughout the Arab world. In Syria the leaders of the Ba'ath had through their hatred of Nasser publicly approved the secession. But faced with the defection of all their supporters, they had to eat their words and go into opposition. Young Ba'athist officers, more Left-wing than their elders and supporters of a truly socialist policy, were appalled by the shiftiness and incompetence of the traditional leaders of the party, and formed their own clandestine breakaway party.

In September 1962 the wave of revolutionary feeling sweeping the Arab world led to the most unexpected developments. A Republic was proclaimed in the medieval Imamate of the Yemen, and recognized by the U.A.R. and the U.S.S.R. But a hard core of royalists regrouped under the leadership of the Imam Badr, with the support of Saudi Arabia; the United States refused to recognize the Republic. In October Nasser sent Egyptian troops to the aid of the threatened Republic. More than ever, he was acclaimed as the hero of revolutionary pan-Arabism.

Kassem's Iraq had also recognized Republican Yemen, but could do no more than this, being entangled in inextricable difficulties of its own. Kassem, a wild and fantastic personality, attempted to steer an even course between the various Iraqi pressure-groups and the international powers, but succeeded only in sowing the greatest mistrust on every side. He had given free rein to a wave of popular demands and claims at the beginning of his rule. The result had been neither a proletarian dictatorship (for which neither Moscow nor the local Communists had the slightest enthusiasm); nor a stable state with a smoothly running institutional machinery for the peaceful and permanent settlement of clashes between different interests, different aims and different

ideologies. Demonstrations, expropriations, the excesses perpetrated by unruly mobs (rendered more severe by the rivalries
between religious and ethnic communities), the televized sessions
of the revolutionary tribunal, all these only succeeded in terrifying
the bourgeoisie and the privileged classes of every sort. In self-
defence they mobilized the forces of religion and of pan-Arab
nationalism, helped from outside by Nasser. He for his part was
only too eager to make use of the tactical weapon placed in his
hands by indignation at Iraqi impiety and Kassem's separatism
(Nasser's propaganda fortuitously gained from the fact that
Kassem's name, in Arabic, can mean 'the Divider'). Kassem
busied himself with appeasing the Right while endeavouring to
retain the support of the Left, to whom he therefore also had to
make concessions. But his attitude towards his competitor Nasser
remained intransigent. His international policy was also one of
maintaining a shifting balance between the Western powers and
the Soviet bloc. Kassem attempted to harness the nation to his
own ends by adopting a policy of repression towards the Kurdish
minority's claims to autonomy, and continually putting off the
promised implementation of administrative and cultural autonomy. The Kurdish revolt broke out in April 1961, and Kassem
had the Kurdish villages shelled. The claiming of Kuwait in June
1961 was also intended to stimulate national unity, but the ridiculous aspects of the claim did not contribute to gaining mass
support for it, especially since the issues dividing the masses
were of much greater consequence.

The Army was united on a programme of pan-Arab nationalism.
Weary of the crazy oscillations of Kassem's policy, the leading
Army officers made a pact with the Ba'ath with the object of
achieving an organized party with mass support. A military coup
on 8 February 1963 (known as the Revolution of the 14th Rama-
dan, after the corresponding date of the Hegiran calendar)
dethroned Kassem, who was killed. Power was taken over by a
coalition of Nasserites and Ba'athists, with the latter at first in the
dominant position. Conservative forces rejoiced at the abrupt
disappearance of the danger of a gradual slide into Communism.
A neo-Ba'athist militia was formed to hunt down suspected
Communists and fellow-travellers; some 5,000 were slaughtered.

This bloody settlement of accounts lanced the boil of five years' accumulated hatred and resentment. From their position of dominance, the Ba'athists then turned to the elimination of their Nasserite allies. Their pan-Arab nationalism caused them to step up the war against the Kurds, which became bitter and frequently horrific. One month after the Iraqi putsch, on 8 March 1963, Syrian army officers brought off a similar military coup at Damascus, overthrowing the weak parliamentary regime which had governed since the secession in 1961 and bringing the Ba'ath to power, in Damascus as in Baghdad.

Thus in the spring of 1963 the Eastern Arab world was dominated by two regimes, both avowedly socialist in spirit and both pan-Arab nationalist: the Ba'ath in Iraq and Syria, and Nasserism in Egypt. The two blocs entered into negotiations at Cairo in March and April 1963 to find a basis for unity. But the two parties, made wary by the Egypto-Syrian experiment in unity of 1958–61, rivalled one another in mistrust and suspicion. Each accused the other of authoritarianism – not without reason in both cases – and each blamed the other for the failure of the earlier experiment. The Ba'ath would have liked to have been able to take advantage of Nasser's prestige without giving up any of its own power. Nasser was not prepared to accept unity unless Egyptian ideas were given precedence. The negotiations ended in an 'agreement' which put off a final solution to a later date.

Relations between the Ba'ath and the Nasserites became extremely strained as a result of the Ba'athists' manoeuvrings to preserve their hegemony on the Syrian political scene, in violation of the Cairo agreements. A purge of Nasserite officers was followed by the bloody repression, on 18 July 1963, of an attempted Nasserite coup in Damascus. Nasser began to denounce Ba'ath 'fascism', pointing to the paucity of the latter's social reforms in respect of the Egyptian Charter. It had moreover, become common to refer to the Ba'ath in this way since the massacres of Communists in Iraq. The Ba'ath's reign in Iraq was brief, however. The National Guard which it had set up and which had all the characteristics of a military organization had begun to make itself intolerable, especially to the army. The party governed under the cover of a non-Ba'athist President, General Abdul Salem

Aref. This individual was a religious traditionalist and a fervent admirer of Nasser, with little taste for socialism and even less for the secularism of the Ba'athist ideology. In a coup carried out on 18 November 1963, he rid himself of the Ba'ath and established closer links with Cairo.

By the end of 1963 the Arab world had never been more divided. Syria was engaged in a cold war with Egypt and Iraq; her relations with the capitalist Lebanon were far from cordial, and she was hostile to Jordan and Morocco. Egypt and Saudi Arabia were in military conflict in the Yemen, each giving more or less open aid to the opposing sides in the civil war. Outside the Near East itself, Algeria was embroiled in frontier disputes with Morocco (with whom there had been actual military clashes) and Tunisia; these two were themselves at loggerheads over Mauretania. But Israel stirred, and all quarrels were forgotten.

5 ISRAEL SOFTENS

In the course of the general outline just given of Arab political developments from the Suez expedition to the end of 1963, the name of Israel has hardly been mentioned. Certainly no Arab forgot the presence of this outpost of the Western World implanted in the Near East, none forgot the common aim of all Arabs to avenge the humiliating defeats suffered in 1948 and 1956, none was resigned to the loss of forcibly stolen Arab territory nor to the running sore of the refugee problem. Action, however, was always put off until later, to some unspecified time in the future. Some hoped that this time would not be far off, while others wished it as far in the future as possible, even hoping that some unforeseen development might some day solve the problem painlessly. The Arab rulers' principal preoccupations for the moment were in some quarters the creation of a more modern, more independent and more just society, in others to make the maximum profit with the minimum effort out of a society deliberately left archaic, unjust and very largely dependent – albeit profitably dependent – on the outside world. All were also intent on protecting a chosen system, maintaining or conquering power for a given group, or extracting the benefits of power for the class supporting that group. In practice, Israel was a long way down the list of priorities. But no ruler would or could allow Arab rights to go by default – rights which had been violated through sheer brute force. The Arab claims were kept up in verbal proclamations delivered in a more or less impassioned style, coloured by every metaphor in the repertoire of Arab rhetoric and animated by all the fire of total ideological commitment. Various propaganda outlets were made available to the Palestinians, the most violent and most interested group in the Arab world. But a barrier of 'Blue Berets' conveniently prevented any incidents with Egypt, while a garrison of these same U.N. forces enabled shipping to and from Israel to pass the Egyptian Strait of Tiran without difficulty, thus symbolically absolving the U.A.R. from the responsibility of authorizing such traffic. Incidents remained possible and frequently occurred on Israel's frontiers with Jordan, Syria (where the question of demilitarized zones was a continual source of conflict) and even the Lebanon, whose military weakness and mercantile pacifism naturally inclined her towards appeasement. But the incidents were limited and less serious than in the preceding period.

At the same time, Israel felt more secure. Her rulers were able to consider their long-term foreign policy. As in any country benefiting from a relatively peaceful situation, the masses were able to pay more attention to internal problems. A specific pattern in Israeli politics began to emerge.

Ben Gurion was still in power. As ever, his policy was conceived on the global scale. His object was to consolidate Israel's position despite Arab hostility, and force was the only means in which he had any faith. He therefore had to seek the support of the strong. As ever, his main hope lay in the United States; but he also made advances to Great Britain and Federal Germany, and kept up the alliance with France. In the course of a triumphal tour in March 1960, he visited Eisenhower in Washington to extract a vague promise of rockets. He shook Adenauer by the hand in front of press photographers. At the same time he won some substantial advantages, including a loan of 500 million dollars, and a free and secret supply of arms. Also secretly, Israeli troops and officers were trained in the use of the new arms on German territory. These arrangements were best kept secret in view of the sensitivity of Jewish public opinion to reports of dealings with Germans; the deals were nonetheless extremely useful. Also secretly, France helped Israel to build a nuclear reactor, allegedly for 'peaceful purposes'.

Ben Gurion was full of concern for his allies' welfare, and generous with his advice. This advice was obviously as much to Israel's advantage as to her allies'. In 1957, as we have seen, taking advantage of American anti-Communist hysteria, he had offered his services against the supposed threat of a Soviet take-over of

Syria. Nonetheless, his efforts to win a N.A.T.O. guarantee of Israel's frontiers had failed. In 1960 he instructed de Gaulle as to how he, Ben Gurion, would solve the Algerian problem: partition Algeria and keep the most useful areas (the coast and the oil-rich Sahara), leaving the rest to the Arabs; then settle one million Frenchmen from the metropolis in the French zone. De Gaulle replied, appropriately enough but rather obviously, 'What, you want to create a new Israel in Algeria!'*

The support of the great powers remained of paramount importance, but it was always conditional and not entirely reliable. Following the age-old precepts of international diplomacy, it was necessary to have other allies outside the hostile Arab belt. Successful moves followed to achieve an unsigned but firm agreement with Turkey – pro-American, anti-Soviet and estranged from Syria and Iraq by continual disputes; with Iran, likewise in constant difficulties with Iraq; and with Ethiopia, concerned about the possible effects of Nasserite propaganda on the Muslims of Eritrea and Somalia. Further off, Asia and above all Africa offered diplomatic opportunities for making friends and influencing people. It was not advisable for Israel to have all the Third World's votes at the U.N. against her. Israel was able to provide very useful technical advice, notably with regard to agricultural community development. Ben Gurion tried to get the Americans to finance these projects by extolling their usefulness in warding off Communism.

Ben Gurion was getting old. In 1960 he would be seventy-four. There were things that he failed to grasp with his old clarity of vision. For instance, he railed against overseas Zionists. He was particularly exasperated by the predilection exhibited by some of their representatives – notably Nahum Goldmann, president of the World Jewish Congress – to meddle in Israel's internal affairs. He failed, for once, to appreciate that this was the other side of a coin otherwise very valuable to Israel. The support of foreign Zionists was of the most crucial importance. For one thing, it enabled Israel to win the support of the Western powers without having to submit to all their demands. In December 1960 American reconnaisance aircraft discovered the secret

* Michel Bar-Zohar, *Ben Gourion*, op. cit., p. 357.

nuclear reactor built with the aid of France. The Americans were furious at this breach of their own policy of non-dissemination of nuclear secrets. They demanded proof that the device was really only for peaceful purposes. They stormed and threatened, but Ben Gurion would not give way and refused to allow any inspection. The American super-state finally had to give in to the tiny state of Israel, and content itself with the reports from its intelligence agents. Once again, the more responsible Arab statesmen had to face the fact that Israel was strong, very strong indeed. In July 1961 the first Israeli rocket was launched.

From time to time the Americans were also forced to face the fact that Israeli-Arab tension had its disadvantages; it was impossible for them not to support Israel, and this support could not but discredit them in Arab eyes. They decided to work out a plan for the final solution of the problem, and exerted pressure to get it accepted. In 1961-2 Kennedy put forward two successive proposals for a settlement. Both began with a demand for the readmission to Israel of some of the refugees which the U.N. resolution had ordered Israel to take back. But the two parties were too mistrustful of one another, and both plans fell through. Significantly, Kennedy attempted to exert pressure on Ben Gurion through the Hawk missiles he had promised. The missiles would only be delivered if Israel accepted a plan for a settlement. Ben Gurion rejected the plans, and got the missiles all the same.

It should not be thought that he did not want peace. But he wanted it on Israel's terms, and his only strategy was to win it from a position of strength. From the end of the pre-war period, he had been convinced that demonstrations of force were the only way to wring recognition from the Arabs for the state which had been imposed on them. The failure of the 1948 war, the 1956 war and the large number of small frontier engagements to achieve this end could not persuade him of the ineffectiveness of the method. On each occasion, he felt that external circumstances had intervened to spoil the effect. A day would come when the international situation was favourable, and the major powers, behind Israel, would force this stubborn people, so unwilling to accept defeat, to bend the knee. He was not one of those dreamers who spoke of a Jewish Empire extending from the Nile to the

Euphrates according to the promise made to Abraham by Yahweh (although Abraham was also supposed to be the father of the Arabs), a dream which had earlier inspired Herzl; nor had he any sympathy with Right-wing extremists like Menachem Begin and his Heruth party, successor to the old Irgun, who wanted all of Israel's ancient territory on both banks of the Jordan. He was ready to concede what he did not hold and content himself with the territory won in 1948. This was at any rate Ben Gurion's policy for the moment; he would leave to future generations of Israelis the task of constructing their policy on the basis of what he had given them. But he would not give up a single square yard of the land already won, nor allow a single man of those expelled to return. The Arabs, for their part, could not accept less than the announcement of some concession, even in principle, in the direction of the U.N. resolutions, which provided the only legal basis to which reference could be made, even though the Arabs themselves had at first rejected them. In the circumstances it is hardly surprising that Ben Gurion's proposals for a meeting with Nasser should have failed. These attempts were made through various intermediaries, including Tito, in 1962 and the beginning of 1963. Nasser had been wooed with fair words; but the difficulties facing him in the Arab world itself were too great. He could not hope to overcome them if he was handicapped by any gesture made to Israel, which would immediately have been denounced as a surrender. He knew that Ben Gurion was little inclined to make major concessions, and nothing less would enable him to emerge from the negotiations with his reputation more or less intact. In any case, he did not consider the matter urgent.

It all seemed rather a distant problem to the Israelis, too. They were growing used to the makeshift *modus vivendi* with the Arabs. Most Israelis were primarily concerned with their day-to-day difficulties, the economic situation, and with internal policy. Internal tensions were now free to emerge. Ben Gurion's authoritarian rule became increasingly irksome to many Israelis. The Old Man looked to the army, and to his younger colleagues who shared his militant approach: Moshe Dayan, onetime Commander in Chief of the Army, turned politician and subsequently Minister of Agriculture; and Shimon Peres, Director General of the Defence Ministry and then, in 1959, Minister of Defence. The opposition parties, naturally enough, became increasingly censorious of procedures which seemed to them undemocratic. But more seriously, increasingly bitter criticisms began to be heard in the heart of his own party, the Mapai. Sharett had never forgiven Ben Gurion for having forced him out of the government, and no doubt also saw quite clearly where the activists' policy would lead. The faithful Golda Myerson herself (now Golda Meir), Minister of Foreign Affairs, was deeply offended at the major foreign policy initiatives taken behind her back by Ben Gurion and Peres. In March 1963, following the arrest of two Israeli secret agents in Zurich for threatening a German girl whose father, an engineer, worked in Egypt, a loud barrage of propaganda orchestrated by the Israeli secret service was let loose, condemning the collusion of German scientists with Egypt. A tremendously exaggerated picture was painted of the advances being made by Egyptian military technology with the aid of these Germans, all described as former Nazis. Some no doubt were, as no doubt were some of the Germans who make up the body of technicians in military establishments in the German Democratic Republic, and for that matter so were some of those West Germans currently giving aid to Israel and training her soldiers. Before long, every Israeli believed in his country's imminent annihilation under a hail of Arab-Nazi missiles. The Israelis' very understandable anti-German feeling was exacerbated, and Ben Gurion's friendly policy towards Germany was violently attacked. Ben Gurion was greatly embarrassed by the effects of his Intelligence Service's excess of zeal. He found himself opposed by Golda Meir, who was emotionally irreconcilable to a policy of friendship with the Germans. The head of the secret services was obliged to resign.

Ben Gurion then made the fatal mistake of providing the critics of his autocratic tendencies with a focal point of attack. This focal point was the sombre Lavon affair. Lavon, a former Minister of Defence and the sworn enemy of Dayan and Peres, and an influential member of the Mapai, had been convicted by his peers in 1954 of being responsible for an adventurist operation conducted by Israeli secret agents in Egypt, the objects and result of which have been described in an earlier chapter. He felt himself to be the victim of army machinations to place on his shoulders a responsibility which ought properly to have been assigned to certain highly placed officers in the Intelligence Service, perhaps to Peres himself. He felt that the oath of secrecy with regard to military operations had been used to prevent him from vindicating himself. He had since become General Secretary of the Histadruth, but still chafed at the bit, impatient for the day of his revenge. In October 1960 he demanded to be rehabilitated, and made allegations concerning the Army Intelligence services before several parliamentary commissions. Despite Ben Gurion's opposition, the government appointed a special commission of seven members to look into the secret dossiers of the affair. The commission exculpated Lavon. Ben Gurion was furious. He declared war on Lavon, and applied blackmail by threatening to resign. In February 1961 the Central Committee of the Mapai, rather than lose its leader, dismissed Lavon from the General Secretaryship of the Histadruth. But Lavon had attracted great popularity as the victim of the Prime Minister's authoritarianism; Ben Gurion was abandoned by his closest friends; the secret machinations of military cliques, the close extra-parliamentary connexions between the Prime Minister and his favourites, who were quite beyond democratic control, were publicly denounced.

Ben Gurion's stiff-necked behaviour over the Lavon affair did him a profound disservice. It was everywhere seen as a sign of senility, super-imposed on the old man's well recognized authoritarianism. In the spring of 1963 his panic at the still-born pact between Egypt, Syria and Iraq and his appeal for help to the big powers, who were justifiably sceptical of the imminence of any newfound Arab unity, caused his international stock to fall as well.

He was aware of the general hostility surrounding him, knew that he was considered 'past it', that many thought him incapable. On 16 June 1963 he resigned and retired to the *kibbutz* of Sde Boker. He probably hoped that his revenge would soon come. Israel would realize he was indispensable and recall him.

He was succeeded by Levi Eshkol. Eshkol was a man of much less brilliance, hesitant, a poor talker, but a good organizer, realistic, affable and easy-going. Of course he was a convinced Zionist, a member of the Mapai party machine. However, he was by temperament little inclined to military adventure, and he sensed the nation's weariness with the military burden and its small enthusiasm for periodic mobilization. It was in all conscience a strange nation which he represented. Hardly yet formed into a coherent whole, it was profoundly divided, chauvinistic and racialist from the Zionist ideology drummed into it in schools, in the army, in the party organizations, encouraged by reading the bellicose texts of the Old Testament and greatly heightened by the constant hostility of Israel's neighbours. But as soon as a relative relaxation of tension permitted, it was immediately ready to plunge into its internal quarrels, to clamour for reforms, to demobilize. It was largely composed of great numbers of Jews from the Arab countries, who had come to Israel not in the pursuit of any ideological dream, but quite simply because there did not seem to be anywhere else for them to go. How many even of the European Jews had made a practical rather than a spiritual choice, and had simply taken the path mapped out for them by the Zionists. A story told about Golda Meir by one of her friends, an American Zionist, is revealing. The story concerns an incident which occurred during a tour of inspection when she was Minister of Labour.

Once on an inspection trip to a recently completed housing development, Golda was surrounded by disgruntled immigrants from Eastern Europe, who, disdaining preliminary courtesies, besieged her with angry complaints about the houses, the climate, the scarcity of work for professionals and the neighbours. They had expected an easier life. The small four-room cottages assigned each family were unfurnished except for essentials; the plot of land around each house was bare; a hot sun beat down on the treeless, sandy road; and appropriate employment was hard to find. Golda, proud of the well-designed houses with running water, electricity and good plumbing given to destitute immigrants for a few dollars a month, and aware of what it had cost to transport and settle these newcomers, reminded one of the impatient women that flowers and vegetables had to be planted. Why had she come to Israel? 'Because I was afraid to stay in Poland. I don't care about Zionism,' the woman answered unblinkingly. The husband nodded in agreement.

'Not one word of gratitude,' said Golda bitterly to a companion as she left.*

Thus the nation's Zionist consciousness tended to abate the moment there was a let-up in tension. This filled the militant clique with fury, as they saw in it a slide towards the abyss. But Eshkol, without abandoning the fundamental principles of the movement, responded to the pacific urge to demobilize and explored the possibility of an alternative to the activist sabre-rattling foreign policy of his predecessor. He thus inclined towards Sharett's old policy, and going further back still, to the policy of those who had hoped for a conciliatory attitude towards the Arabs. He was led therefore to seek ways of avoiding an arms race, to have recourse to the U.N. instead of despising it, to move towards non-alignment by disengaging himself from exclusive American support and making tentative advances to the Soviet bloc. At all events, he announced his intention of subordinating the military to the civil power and of placing restrictions on military reprisal actions against Israel's neighbours. He caused a stir by the changes he made in his cabinet, refusing to take Dayan and Peres back into the Ministry of Defence.

The awkward problem which threatened to become a major cause of conflict was the question of the diversion of the waters of the River Jordan. As is well known, a large area of Palestine is near-desert. For a long time, a number of schemes had existed to use the water from the River Jordan for irrigation. A large part of this water originated from tributaries of the Jordan flowing through Syria and Lebanon. The main benefits of the proposed irrigation would accrue to Israel and Jordan. Ideally, an agreement between all four countries would have been necessary to arrive at an effective and equitable scheme. The political situation excluded such an agreement. As we have seen, the American Main-Johnston plan failed in 1955 because of Dulles. Fresh approaches in 1957 to get the plan put back on to the agenda proved futile. Jordan then obtained United States aid for a limited irrigation scheme using mainly water from the Yarmuk, a tributary of the

* Marie Syrkin, *Golda Meir: Woman with a Cause,* New York, G. P. Putnam's Sons, 1963, p. 264.

Jordan. Israel then also decided to carry out a national irrigation
plan, which would divert water from the Upper Jordan to the
Negev Desert, which, said the Israelis, could then accommodate a
further four million immigrants. This aroused great consternation
among the Arabs. Jordan immediately feared a diminution in the
river's volume and a proportionate rise in the saline content,
which could have catastrophic effects on Jordan's arable land.
Syria had similar fears for Lake Tiberias. The plan was announced
at the end of 1959. The Arab countries then began a series of
conferences to find a way of hindering its application or decide
on effective retaliation. There was talk of diverting the headwaters
of the Jordan flowing through Syrian and Lebanese territory.
This proved difficult to implement and might not even be very
effective. Israel replied with counter-threats in the time-honoured
aggressive militant style. Officiously one paper stated: 'An attempt
to divert the sources of the Jordan in Syria and the Lebanon will
not be playing merely with water, but also with fire.'*

The first phase of the Israeli project was due for completion in
1964. For many years the Arab countries had made violent threats
in their habitual style against the Israeli project, each outbidding
the other in an attempt to put their neighbours in a difficult
position. The impossibility of doing anything positive at once
often led to conditional threats: 'Just wait and see what will
happen when Israel acts.' The day of reckoning was now near.

In December 1959 Kassem had hit upon the idea of setting up
a Palestine government, on the pattern of the Algerian G.P.R.A.
His intention was to embarrass Egypt and Jordan, both of whom
occupied portions of Mandate Palestine, rather than to attack
Israel. The two Arab states were very well aware of this, and had
reacted violently, accusing Kassem, naturally, of providing grist
for Israel's mill. Nasser called him a criminal and a madman,
alleging that this 'base manoeuvre' had been carried out 'on
the orders of his Zionist, imperialist and Communist masters'.
But the idea nevertheless gained ground, because it met a real
need felt by the Palestinians, both those who had fled from the
territory now occupied by the State of Israel and those remaining

* *Israel Digest*, 6 January 1960, quoted by the *New York Times*, 16
January 1960, p. 7.

on the West Bank of the Jordan, since annexed by the Hashemite Kingdom of Jordan. The Palestinians were very mixed in their social structure, level of culture and political attitudes. Those who had remained on the West Bank or emigrated into Transjordan formed the most dynamic and progressive element in the Hashemite Kingdom of Jordan. The majority of them were opposed to Hussein's pro-Western policy, and could easily have enforced their own point of view – since they outnumbered the indigenous Jordanian population – were it not for the Bedouin tribes supporting the king. The refugees concentrated in the U.N.R.W.A. camps continued to chew over their nation's wrongs in bitterness and vengefulness. The most enterprising of them, or those most favoured by fortune, had succeeded in integrating in the various Arab countries, or at least in finding work. In many places they had settled in groups which behaved like a minority elite. Some had made fantastic fortunes. The intellectuals and militant trade unionists, full of ardour for the political and social struggle, were drawn from among them. But the old semi-tribal structure persisted – especially in the camps – dominated by village notables. All these groups felt themselves united by a common destiny which distinguished them from the Arabs of other countries. Together with their Arab brothers and cousins inside Israel, they formed a torn and scattered national community. Their songs and poems made constant reference to 'the return' in tones which strikingly recalled the nostalgic songs of the Promised Land sung by the exiled Jews of old.

Kassem gradually developed the idea of the so-called Palestinian entity. He launched a Palestinian army, formed of a few volunteers who paraded in Baghdad, and created Palestinian passports. The other Arab countries were not to be outdone. Hussein, who was directly threatened by this manoeuvre, hastily convened a Congress, in May 1960, at which the Palestinians of Jordan reaffirmed their loyalty to his kingdom. Nasser created a radio station, the Voice of Palestine, in Cairo (October 1960). He then consolidated Egyptian rule in the Gaza Strip, giving it a Constitution and a governor general nominated by Egypt (March 1962). Hussein announced a chimerical plan for a solution. Syria called for an Arab military conference (December 1962) and Iraq

demanded separate Palestinian representation at the Arab League
(September 1963). All these moves were primarily directed
towards the final elimination of the ghostly Palestinian Government in Exile, formed in 1948 by the Council of the League and
consisting largely of followers of the former Mufti of Jerusalem,
Haj Amin al Husseini, since widely discredited. Ahmad Shukairy,
a Palestinian who had supporters among the Palestinian notables
and had won friends in several Arab countries (especially Saudi
Arabia), now came to the fore. He had previously been Deputy
General Secretary of the Arab League. He had also been the
Saudi Arabian Minister of State for Palestinian Affairs. In
September 1963 he was appointed to sit on the Political Committee
of the Arab League as official Palestinian delegate, despite
Hussein's protests. At the same time the League, pressed to 'do
something', called for a conference of Arab Chiefs of Staff to study
what riposte to make to Israel's diversion of the waters of the River
Jordan.

One man felt especially endangered by all this activity, which
arose from the necessity to appear to respond to Arab expectations
with regard to Palestine, thus threatening to detonate the whole
explosive situation. This man was Nasser. He had for a long time
advocated patience, bringing forward a convincing historical
argument, the example of the Crusades. The Crusader Kingdoms
had also, in their time, been a bridgehead of the Western World
on Oriental territory. They had finally been eliminated after two
hundred years. Israel would finish up the same way. There was
no call for haste. Nasser was well aware of the weakness of the
Arab armies, and their lack of coordination. His own army was
fully occupied in the Yemen, bogged down in difficult terrain.
He had his work cut out to keep the Egyptian economy from complete collapse, let alone achieve progress.

He was continually accused by his Arab rivals of being perfectly
content with the cordon of U.N. troops which insulated him
from Israel, while they were in daily confrontation with the
Jewish state through numerous border incidents. He was afraid
of the stigma of passivity, which would greatly harm Egyptian
prestige and influence, but even more afraid of being dragged by
irresponsible elements into an unequal contest with the powerful

Israeli army under extremely unfavourable conditions. In June 1962 Akram Hourani, the dissident Ba'athist leader, let loose a broadside aimed at the Egyptian ruler, among others: all the Arab governments, with the exception of Syria, had accepted the Johnston plan for the irrigation of the Jordan valley in concert with Israel in 1955, and in 1959 Nasser had rejected a Syrian proposal for military intervention to prevent diversion of the Jordan waters.

Faced with this threat to his position, Nasser put out a clear warning. On 17 December 1963 an Egyptian journalist with official connexions accused the Jordanians, Syrians and Saudi Arabians of trying to push Egypt into a hornets' nest, and of wanting to stab her in the back by making her attack Israel at an inopportune moment while standing back themselves. 'The U.A.R.', he declared, 'is not going to embark on any adventures. The U.A.R. will not let itself be pushed into a battle with Israel before the attainment of unity among all the Arab countries.'[*] This article provoked violent reactions in the countries concerned. Meanwhile Nasser brought off a great political stroke. In the course of a speech made at Port Said on 23 December he proposed that all the Arab states, so disunited and suspicious of one another, should come together in a summit conference to discuss what measures they should take on the question of the diversion of the waters of the Jordan. From 13 to 17 January 1964 all the Arab sovereigns and heads of state met in Cairo. General reconciliation was the order of the day. Differences were ironed out, or more frequently shelved. A united military command was created, under a high-ranking Egyptian officer. The 'Palestinian entity was to express the wishes of the Palestinians but would not take the form of a government and would have no constitutional authority over the Palestinians'.

The euphoria was great. Everyone went away contented. The danger felt by each of being driven too far by the game of chicken forced on him by his neighbours was removed. Nasser was able to control and canalize Syrian turbulence. Hussein was able to limit the infringement of Jordanian authority represented by all

[*] Malcolm Kerr, *The Arab Cold War 1958–64*, Oxford University Press 1965, p. 131.

the autonomous activities of the Palestinians. More generally, on the level of inter-Arab relations, each realized how futile their internecine struggles were. Verbal broadsides could shake a regime, but they could not overthrow it.

All the back-slapping and embracing in Cairo seemed to herald the opening of a new era. Nasser especially hoped that the peace which he desperately needed was now assured for some considerable time at any rate. Hussein likewise hoped for a long period of peace, and the Syrians were resigned to it. In Israel itself, Eshkol showed signs of adopting a less aggressive policy than his predecessor. Nonetheless, a chain of events, aided by the partisans of confrontation in both camps, was to bring this wise decision to naught, and ultimately, less than three and a half years later, to lead to war.

6 THE ARAB CIRCLE
AND THE WORLD AT LARGE

In his *Philosophy of the Revolution*, Nasser expresses with a great deal of passion and sincerity some of the ideas, doubtless not very original, which had come to guide his political conscience. Egypt was bound by the restrictions of time and space; her policy could not be determined as though she were still in the tenth century (this would appear to be a critical reference to the programme of the Muslim Brotherhood). Moreover, isolationism was futile. Every country is affected by what goes on beyond its frontiers and must inevitably take account of it,

to find the source of the currents which influence it, how it can live with others, how . . . , and how . . . And no state can escape trying to determine its status within its living space, and trying to see what it can do in that space, and what is its field of activities and its positive role in this troubled world.

Sometimes I sit in my study reflecting on the subject, asking myself: What is our positive role in this troubled world, and where is the place in which we should fulfill that role?*

And he discovers three circles, three zones to which Egypt must necessarily devote all her energies. Egypt cannot ignore the existence of an Arab zone surrounding it, the history and interests of which are closely bound up with her own. Nor can she ignore Africa, in which destiny has located her, nor the Muslim world, to which she is bound not only by religion but by a common history.

This clear view of Egypt's geopolitical situation (inspired, moreover, by the Churchillian idea of the three circles within which British policy was conducted) had been deliberately

* Gamal Abdul Nasser, *Egypt's Liberation; The Philosophy of Revolution*, op. cit., pp. 84–5.

distorted by Anglo-French propaganda on the eve of the Suez expedition in order to justify that venture. The analysis supposedly revealed a desire to dominate the three zones in question, a desire which gave credibility to the famous equation Nasser= Hitler. Of course Nasser sought to make Egyptian influence as strong as possible in the zones in which his country was situated. But this is the programme of every political leader, and it had nothing in common with a programme of military conquest. Nasser was enough of a realist not to harbour any grandiose and ridiculous plan of conquering the Muslim world as far as Indonesia, and Africa into the bargain! Even within the Arab world, he had had reservations over the union with Syria. In the Yemen his troops were supporting a friendly regime against the reinforcement and extension of Saudi domination (and of the American influence behind Saudi Arabia) over the entire Arabian Peninsula. It is of course true that once these regions fell into its hands the ruling Egyptian military caste exercised an unbridled authoritarianism there. It need not be supposed either that Egypt's political and military services, both public and secret, did not try to exert the maximum influence in every field of operations, sometimes using highly unsavoury methods. But this is some way from Hitler's project to enslave, in the strongest possible sense of that word, an entire continent.

At all events the Arab zone existed and Egypt could not avoid being interested in it. I have so far been referring only to Egypt and that part of the Arab countries of Asia known as the Fertile Crescent: Iraq, Syria, Lebanon, Palestine, Jordan. These are indeed the only countries directly concerned with the challenge of Israel. But the other Arab countries, especially those recently independent and hence able for the first time to decide their own policy, could not disregard the problem. The differences between the Arab states were great and their peoples had evolved in different ways; they each had their own special problems and could regard the other Arab peoples as to some extent and in a certain sense foreigners. They despised some, joked about others, while others they feared. Nevertheless, over and above Tunisians, Egyptians, Iraqis, they were all Arabs. They were all bound together by the strands of a common history and culture, and any injury done to one people from outside was sharply resented by the others.

Governments may sometimes have been contemptuous of this sentiment. But beyond a certain limit, they could not ignore it without endangering the basis of consent, however passive, on which even the most tyrannical state must in the last resort rely.

It will be enough to cast a brief glance at those Arab states on the periphery of the circle which nonetheless frequently had an important part to play in Arab affairs, and to see what had happened to them since their last mention in these pages.

Of these peripheral states, Saudi Arabia is the nearest to the central stage of the drama. This country, the birthplace of Arabism, had been transformed by the oil-extraction industry which began its operations in 1938. The patriarchal monarchs who ruled over this vast territory, peopled by nomadic tribesmen and their camels, suddenly found themselves the owners of immense fortunes. The exploitation of the oil deposits which brought them their wealth depended on the Aramco company, a giant American trust. In 1965 Aramco paid the Saudi government 618.4 million dollars in taxes and royalties. It has been estimated that in recent years these have accounted for ninety per cent of the national budget. This has made it possible to keep up a relatively powerful army, to subsidize tribal chiefs, and to maintain the hundreds of aristocrats spawned by this polygamous society in unheard-of luxury. Oil revenues have had the usual effect of creating a closed economy, sealed off from the general economic development of the country. The archaic social structure persists. Of course a merchant class has begun to emerge, hoping for some degree of progress, which would like to make its voice heard in the counsels of state. It is also attracted to Arab nationalism. King Saud who ruled from 1953 to 1964, and his brother Feisal have been engaged in a long tussle for power, each playing a complicated game of internal and external alliances made and broken. The constant factors in Saudi politics are a vigilant conservatism more or less aware of the necessity for a minimum of reforms, the American alliance, and hostility to the revolutionary movements gaining ground elsewhere in the Arab world, with interludes of reconciliation. Israel is only of secondary interest to the Saudi monarchs. They recognize a duty to support the Arab cause, firstly because of the sympathies of their people plus some small national feeling of their own, and secondly because of Islam – they are both Guardians of the Holy Cities and leaders of a puritanical and extremist Muslim sect, the Wahhabi. But their contributions to the Arab cause are circumspect, and always made with an eye to their other interests. They prefer to give money rather than send troops, which they might have need of to maintain order at home and which, more importantly, might become contaminated by dangerous ideas. Their heart is Arab, no doubt; but their purse is American.

In the Persian Gulf and in a series of little emirates protected by Great Britain, oil resources have poured sudden immense fortunes into the pockets of a few Bedouin sheikhs. The unrest of the nascent middle class and of the population at large has led them to espouse Arab nationalist principles and follow with enthusiasm the tune called by Cairo and Baghdad. Kuwait has drawn particular benefit from the treasure trove of oil – the sovereign has reserve deposits of more than 200 million pounds sterling in British banks. The other Arab countries have suggested that this wealth might be used for other purposes than ensuring unheard-of prosperity for a tiny desert sheikhdom (6,000 square miles, 330,000 inhabitants; in 1963 the national income was 3,000 dollars per head). Kassem's clumsy and unsuccessful attempt to annexe it has already been mentioned. As a contribution, Kuwait created a Development Fund for the Arab countries which has issued some considerable loans. But many Arab rulers coveted this monopoly of wealth, dreaming of the great things they might accomplish with its help.

In the south, the Yemen has for centuries been the most archaic state in the Peninsula, perhaps in the world. The revolution of 26 September 1962 was a great surprise to the Arab world, and provoked foreign intervention, as we have seen. Since that time, royalist tribesmen supported by Saudi Arabia, Britain, the Americans and a number of neo-fascist European mercenaries have held out against the Republic, supported for its part by the Egyptians. Egyptian aid has since turned into military occupation, partly through force of circumstances and partly because of the authoritarian bent of the Egyptian military caste, and is borne very grudgingly by the Republicans themselves. Developments in the Yemen recall the history of the 'sister republics' created by the armies of the First French Republic. From being a straight fight, the struggle has developed into a three-cornered contest, the Egyptians having fallen foul of their Republican protégés. The Egyptian troops have become bogged down in this mountainous and difficult country, with its tribal social structure of extreme primitiveness, which is only now beginning to show some signs of detribalization and the development of an urban society, including merchants and nationalist intellectuals. Nasser attempted to effect an honourable withdrawal from this hornets' nest, but his negotiations with Saudi Arabia stumbled on all kinds of obstacles. The stalemate still persisted in May 1967, and the only significant result appeared to be a worsening of relations between Nasser and the United States.

South of the Yemen, on the southern coast of the Arabian Peninsula, lie the enclave of Aden (eighty square miles), which had been in British hands since 1839, and the British protectorates of South Arabia (75,000 square miles). Historically and culturally, these territories are part of the Yemen, which has never ceased to lay claim to them. Aden, a large commercial centre, possesses ardently nationalist middle and working classes. The rest of the territory has a thoroughly primitive tribal structure dominated by twenty-six sultans, emirs and sheikhs. In the face of the rising nationalism of the region, manifested in a wave of terrorist outrages, the British created a Federation of the South Arabian emirates in February 1959 in order to appease the nationalists while at the same time retaining control of the area. The union effected between Aden and the Federation in June 1963 was designed to harness the progressive and turbulent forces in Aden to conservative structures which Britain could easily control. The protests were massive and violent, especially in the Adeni trade union movement, which was intensely politically conscious. Guerilla warfare broke out in the sultanates themselves. Great Britain announced that independence would be granted to the Federation from 1968.* No-one believed in her altruism. At all

* In fact she evacuated South Arabia in November 1967.

events, the Egyptians were encouraged to remain in the Yemen, if only to supervise the liquidation of the British legacy in the area. The violence of the events in South Arabia kept alive the flame of the struggle against Western imperialism throughout the Arab world.

To the south of Egypt the Sudan, which had nominally been an Anglo-Egyptian condominium but in practice a British colony, became independent on 1 January 1956. The country suffers from the very severe problem presented by the coexistence of the Arabized, Muslim north (with about seven million inhabitants) and the south, inhabited by about six million Nilotic Negroes, either animists or converts to Christianity. The Negroes of the south have for many years been oppressed by the Arabs of the north, for whom they provided the principal source of slaves. The southerners feared that independence would bring northern domination, and there has certainly been a considerable tendency towards Arabization and Islamization. From the beginning, bloody mutinies broke out in the south, denounced by the north as provoked by British imperialists with the aid of the European Christian missions. Their suppression by the north was no less bloody. Left-wing elements tried to disarm the opposition between north and south by demanding an autonomous regime for the south, and this was even accepted in principle. Civil war continues to this day and is frequently conducted with frightful cruelty. Sudanese governments, whether progressive or reactionary, have been too overwhelmed by these problems to be able to devote much attention to the far-off conflict over Palestine. They have generally assumed the role of mediators, preaching unity among the Arab ranks. Their policy towards the Western powers has oscillated considerably, according to the vagaries of internal politics.

To the west of Egypt lies Libya, a largely desert country, which has lived on Anglo-American aid (plus royalties on recently discovered oil) since the departure of the Italians. Both powers possess strategic bases there, including the American base of Wheelus Field which dominates the whole of the Eastern Mediterranean. The patriarchal and conservative governments of King Idris, head of the religious brotherhood of the Senoussi, has made efforts to limit the influence of the nationalist movement. The movement, which looks to Egypt for sympathy and guidance, has of course suffered oppression, but the King has also tried to disarm it by making minor concessions.

The Arab region which has undergone the most striking transformation in recent years is the Maghreb. This was divided into three countries, one (Algeria) under the direct rule of France, the other two administered under the thinly disguised form of colonialism known as the protectorate (Morocco and Tunisia). The force of the nationalist movement constrained France to grant true independence to Tunisia in 1955 and to Morocco in 1956. The long Algerian war, begun on 1 November 1954, ended in July 1962 with the granting of independence to the Republic of Algeria. Solidarity in the struggle against French colonialism could not disguise the differences and tensions between the three countries. In Morocco and Tunisia the fight for national independence was led by the middle class. But in Morocco the leadership of the movement was partly taken over by the large semi-feudal landed proprietors, who rallied to it late in the day. The movement was broadly based on small traders, craftsmen, clerks and civil servants, with a few manual workers. In Algeria, the existence of an urban proletariat in close contact with the French working class through the large numbers of immigrant workers in France created a different situation. This factor, together with the brutal break with traditional values which colonization had imposed throughout large sectors of the social structure, plus the duration and bitterness of the war and the sacrifices which it entailed, produced in the victors a more revolutionary and social-istic attitude. Ahmed Ben Bella made strenuous though not always well-directed efforts to direct Algeria's political development into radical and socialist channels. However, these efforts were largely thwarted by the resistance of a conservative middle class, traditionalist and suspicious of rapid social and cultural change. Colonel Hwari Boumedienne's military coup (19 June 1965) relied to a large extent on these classes for support. None-theless, Algerian politics have remained more radical in general tone than those of the two neighbouring states. The close eco-nomic links between independent Algeria and Gaullist France have favoured the development of a policy of non-commitment on the part of Algeria towards American hegemony.

The three countries of the Maghreb are a long way from Israel. Their ruling elites have frequently attempted to take up a less intransigent position towards the problem than the Middle-Eastern Arabs. They have been the bridge-builders, they have been the ones to make advances to Israel in the hopes of encountering a more flexible attitude, they have tried to establish contacts with more liberal or Left-wing Israelis. This did not mean that they renounced the cause of Arab solidarity. In Morocco, the increasingly direct pro-American bias has produced a generally passive attitude to Palestinian affairs, despite some concessions, more verbal than concrete, made to the Islamic Right. The Tunisian leader Bourguiba, the most outspokenly pro-Western and secularist Arab ruler, has boldly proposed an Arab strategy which would imply as a starting point some recognition of the Israeli *fait accompli*. As a result, he aroused terrible fury in the East. By contrast, Algerian revolutionarism has been all the more intransigent on the Israeli question for the very reason that the problem was a distant one and presented no danger to the Algerian middle class. Added to this, a complex of 'Western' superiority over the incompetence of the Middle-Eastern Arabs has arisen.

Just for the record, some mention should be made of the largely Arab and very archaic country of Mauretania at the far Western end of the Arab world. Her role in the Israeli-Arab conflict has been limited to providing a point of discord which exacerbated the rivalries between the three states of the Maghreb and made unity of action even less likely.

We may now attempt to summarize the major tendencies emerging from this brief outline. Throughout the Arab world there exists, either suppressed, tolerated or triumphant, a radical nationalist movement, which favours socialistic forms of economic organization in internal policy, and alliance with the group of socialist countries in foreign affairs. This movement has come to hold these positions through the general desire of the masses for independence, through unhappy memories of the colonial period, and through the common desire for a rise in the standard of living, which, like true independence, only seems possible through the medium of autonomous industrialization. Experience seems to show that autonomous industrialization is imperilled by the operation of free enterprise, which tends to result in American hegemony. The same factors which induce the Arab masses to support a radical nationalist ideology have produced intransigence towards Israel, a colony imposed on them by the industrially advanced West. Even the most pro-Western Arab rulers have been unable to do more than remain passive in the face of this prevailing attitude. They have not been able to repudiate it. Moreover, concessions to popular feeling on the Palestine question are easier to make and more agreeable – being mainly verbal and symbolic – than decisions to institute economic change, to revise internal policy, or review their fundamental alignments with the major powers. Thus Arab hostility to Israel is not an artificial phenomenon, a cheap cement for plastering over deep cracks. It is a necessity arising from the nature of the choices open to the Arabs in the modern world, at least as long as Israel appears as a bridgehead of the West in the midst of a profoundly committed area of the under-developed world.

Beyond the Arab world and containing it lies the world of Islam. By this is meant all the countries in which Islam is or was the dominant religion. Basically, these include Turkey, Iran, Afghanistan, Pakistan, Malaysia, Indonesia and part of Black Africa. We may exclude from consideration the Mohammedan Republics of Soviet Central Asia, whose destinies are in general inseparable from those of the Soviet Union, and whose politics are controlled by Moscow; and Albania, where the Communist regime has instituted a thorough-going programme of de-Islamization, and where in any case any feeling of solidarity there might be with other Islamic countries finds no political expression whatsoever.

It is often thought in Europe that the Muslim world is blessed with a strong sense of unity inspired by community of religious faith. Nothing could be further from the truth than this conception, compounded of romanticism, historical idealism and ignorance. In fact the Muslim world is hardly any more united than Christendom. Each country is faced with its own special problems, which arise from its geopolitical situation, and each tries to find its own solution in accordance with a number of special factors principally conditioned by the internal economic and social level of development. Moreover, even from the Islamic standpoint positions are different. The state religion of Iran is Shiism, which the other sectors of Islam regard as a heresy. Turkey, despite the reaction brought about by the rule of the Democratic Party from 1950 to 1960, has remained largely faithful to the 'anti-clerical' (but not anti-religious) secularism of Kemal Ataturk. In contrast, Pakistan deliberately sets out to be a Muslim state, a theocracy obedient to the Religious Law, although the reality is very far removed from this ideal.

Of course feelings of solidarity do exist between Muslims the world over. It is not the content of the Muslim faith which produces this feeling, for real faith in the religious message of Muhammad is everywhere in decline, both quantitatively and qualitatively. It is rather the feeling of belonging to a community extending over a vast area of the earth, held in contempt by the European-American world and the victim of discrimination and persecution. On the other side, there is a feeling of superiority towards infidels and 'barbarians'. This by no means excludes political and emotional attachments to Afro-Asian and Latin American countries which are, to some extent at least, in the same situation.

The Arab countries' political opposition to Israel grasped at every weapon that lay to hand. It proved especially useful to exploit the old religious antagonism between Islam and Judaism, and to quote Mohammed's military engagements with the Jews of Medina celebrated in many verses of the Koran. This kind of appeal was bound to strike a chord in the Arab countries. The Arabs then used it to try to gain the support of other Muslim countries for their anti-Israel policy. Pakistan felt obliged to support them, in conformity with her Muslim ideology, but Iran and Turkey have been much more reluctant, and on the whole maintain good relations with Israel.

The appeal to Mohammedan brotherhood is a political stratagem which has been used on frequent occasions to obtain specific political ends. As we have seen, Nasser did not hesitate to use it to attack his hated competitors, the secularist Ba'ath in Syria, and Kassem, allied to the infidel Communists. The stratagem has its dangers, however, since it appeals to emotions which can be most effectively exploited against Nasser by the religious fanatics of the Muslim Brotherhood. The device has most commonly been used by the reactionary regimes to over-trump revolutionary pan-Arabism, by an appeal to conservative loyalty to Islam. This Islamic loyalty is a feature of the member-countries of C.E.N.T.O., the pro-Atlantic alliance between Turkey, Iran and Pakistan. Such attempts have not, however, met with very wide success. The Arab masses, especially outside the towns, are certainly faithful to Islam, which to them means primarily traditional morality and loyalty towards a threatened identity. But they are well able to make the distinction between their faith and an allegiance to political and social objectives which have nothing to offer them and consequently do not tempt them. It should be added that the version of Islam which is offered to them is generally highly suspect. As an instance of this, we can quote the Islamic alliance established between the Shah of Persia, a Shiite monarch and hence a heretic from the point of view of the majority of Muslims; the King of Saudi Arabia, who also belongs to a sect which, although orthodox Muslim, is not representative of the main body of Islam; Hassan II, King of Morocco, whose assiduous respect for the ritual ceremonies has not erased the memory of his somewhat irreligious youth; and Habib Bourguiba, the very spokesman of secularism, contemptuous of ancient rites, whose Muslim faith can hardly be considered as his guiding inspiration.

Interested in the struggle against European and American domination in all its forms, Arab countries in Africa have joined the Organization for African Unity and have participated in all its efforts to coordinate the African countries' struggle to achieve autonomy. Common stands have been taken by some Arab countries with some of the countries of Black Africa when faced with similar situations. However, a hidden cleavage, never expressed, lies beneath the surface of Afro-Arab relations, which may help to explain some attitudes. The peoples of Black Africa have unhappy memories of the Arabs. Arab traders were long the main organizers of the slave traffic, delivering slaves both to the Islamic world and to white slave-masters. Not so very long ago Arabs living in Negro territories felt more community with the Europeans there than with these 'savages'. This was before Europe began to treat them as 'savages' as well. These unpleasant memories are attenuated but not altogether erased among the numerous Negroes converted to Islam. The civil war in the southern Sudan keeps them alive. Distrust of the Arabs is compensated, to a greater or lesser degree depending on circumstances, by community of interest and attitude towards the European-American peoples. At the same time, the Arabs do not command the respect which is always due to the powerful. They are not the real masters.

The Arabs, for their part, still tend to regard themselves as superior to the black man. Revolutionary intellectuals are usually able to overcome these feelings, and statesmen to dissimulate them. There are still many who make their attitude felt, or even express it openly. These imprecise feelings and emotional responses do not, on the whole, play any significant part in the political decisions taken by members of one or other of the two ethnic groups. Nonetheless, one cannot be certain that they do not from time to time influence political attitudes.

Israel's attempts to exert influence on Black Africa have already been mentioned. These attempts have been successful to a certain extent. The African states have on the whole welcomed Israeli technical aid, especially agricultural aid, where Israeli experience has proved very useful to black communities. Students of agriculture have been sent to Israel on special courses. Israeli officials have been well received in African countries, as was Golda Meir on her various good-will missions. The form of micro-socialism represented by the Israeli *kibbutzim* was especially attractive to those states which could not or would not take a resolutely pro-socialist stand in the world line-up of the powers, but still needed a fashionable socialist label in order to attract sympathy and support. In 1960 Ben Gurion rather cunningly asked for United States credits to finance aid to the Africans, arguing that Israel would thus be contributing to the prevention of Communism in

Africa. He also asked for a free hand in the administration of these funds.

The Third World as a whole shares the embarrassment of the Africans with regard to the Israeli-Arab conflict. The Arabs' struggle against the imperialism of Europe has all their sympathy. Few can bring themselves to regard Israel as *only* an outpost of imperialism, as the Arabs claim. In contrast to the Europeans, the people of the Third World are not encumbered by the age-old vision of the Jews as an oppressed race by nature, which could never be anything but the victim of oppression. It is rather Israel's small size, her social structure and her inoffensiveness beyond the boundaries of the Middle East which make other countries hesitate to copy Arab intransigence. The fact that she is recognized by the U.N. and by the vast majority of the non-Arab states makes the Arab refusal to recognize her appear unreasonable. To those countries and political movements most committed to the socialist or anti-imperialist road, the Arab states' anti-Israel campaigns look like a diversion designed to distract their peoples from an intensification of the internal revolutionary struggle. Israeli disengagement from her imperialist connexions still seems possible. In brief, the conflict is seen rather as a territorial dispute between states whose existence is not called in question like the Indo-Pakistan conflict over Kashmir, than as a struggle to eliminate an illegitimate colonial base, which is how the Arabs see it.

However, in a world dominated by force, it is the powerful who deserve the most attention, and this means those states who dispose of considerable material force with which to impose their will. This does not mean that the power latent in the masses of other countries is quite without importance; merely that this form of power does not make itself felt on the world scale except in so far as it affects the decisions of the real powers, either by its support or by its resistance.

The world is dominated by the formidable power of the United States of America. Economically they far outstrip every rival, and are able to intervene anywhere with the enormous weight which wealth confers. Militarily, they possess armaments capable of annihilating the whole world in a matter of seconds. How do they use this power in their relations with the rest of the world and how does it affect the problem under consideration?

A spectre is haunting the Americans: the spectre of Communism. Communism, that demonic, protean, sophistic, elusive force, seems to them to be the very essence of evil. Such is the strange, malignant power of this monster that if it is given an inch of territory, the smallest part of a population, or even the tiniest concession in the soul of man, it quickly swallows all the rest. Unflagging vigilance is needed against such an enemy, readiness to act, to repel, to track down. Men and nations must be constantly prepared to resist the unaccountable temptations which this repellent phantom holds out. Communism is in truth the modern face of Satan.

In 1917 Satan acquired, through his foul machinations, a terrestrial base, the Soviet Union. He then subjugated and tortured the Russian people and the other races subject to the Russians. An American, Franklin Delano Roosevelt, attracted profound suspicion when he attempted to strike a bargain with this evil power – an attempt which was taken as a sure sign of derangement. He had thought it necessary to make this pact with the Devil in order to combat the monstrosity of Hitlerism which he wrongly thought the greater evil. He had granted to Satan the power to oppress yet more peoples in Eastern Europe and had allowed him to acquire a dangerous influence in world affairs. Fortunately, Roosevelt died, having outlived his time. A true American, Harry S. Truman, then did his best to retrieve the sadly deteriorated situation, and to contain the monster until the time came to destroy it in its lair.

Of course this view of things was pure ideological myth. Behind it lay deeper, sub-conscious motives. Regrettably, however, the world is shaped by the delusions of the powerful.

From the beginning of the Cold War, the United States have been committed to the containment of revolutionary movements, always allegedly inspired by the U.S.S.R. and its diabolic nerve-centre, the Kremlin. A military barrier had to be constructed around the U.S.S.R. and its satellites, ready to stifle any Soviet attempt to break out of its provisional limits. As has been remarked, the United States' efforts to enrol the Arabs in the coalition encircling the Communist world had in fact driven the Arab peoples, profoundly disinterested in the struggle for world mastery, into a sympathetic attitude towards the hated power.

The Americans found it difficult to distinguish between the movements and states in the Third World which for one reason or another entertained relations with the Enemy. They found it hard to determine which of a number of more or less revolutionary states, more or less rejecting capitalist hegemony both in the world and in their own country, could be saved and which could not. One certain sign of the unredeemable was any attack on major American interests; this damned the Latin American states of Cuba and Guatemala. Another criterion was quite simply membership of the international brotherhood of Communist Parties; this meant China was out. The two criteria were to some extent combined in the Philippines and in Vietnam, where an anti-imperialist movement under predominantly Communist leadership attacked a state which was practically an American colony.

Beyond these clear-cut cases, diagnosis was more difficult. It could even happen, as in the case of Titoist Yugoslavia, that a Communist state was encouraged to detach itself from the bloc, at that time still monolithic, and still keep its internal structure. Ideology, strategy and material interest combined in complex ways to formulate the judgement. Any measure of socialization was always suspect as undermining religion and free enterprise, and, more materially, as presenting an obstacle to the penetration of American capital. However, if all the other criteria were favourable, the Americans were always willing to understand that situations very different from those obtaining in the classical capitalist countries might demand different sorts of solutions. There was great understanding for the feelings of movements directed primarily against the interests of non-American imperialism – despite the fact that these were perforce the allies of the United States. The old American anti-colonialist ideology of the distant past would then be resurrected specially for the occasion.

This helps to explain the American attitude at the time of Suez. Ben Gurion had every reason to suppose, as did everybody else, that in the Eastern Mediterranean the Americans would leave the field clear for the free play of English and French policy. His agreement with the British and French ought therefore to have been sufficient protection from the reactions of the rest of the world. But the Americans were already heavily committed in the area – both in Greece and Turkey. Above all, they considered it their duty to safeguard the general interests of the anti-Communist struggle, even if this led them into conflict with their allies, blinded by their selfish imperialist interests into hasty and harmful policies. The Americans could be very perceptive of the blindness and folly of others. The British, French and Israelis threw themselves on Nasser's Egypt, hoping to overthrow Nasser by force. Nasser seemed to the Americans eminently recoverable for the Western cause. Of course the purchase of Czech arms and the nationalization of the Suez Canal had been regrettable gestures. It was recognized, however, that he had been forced into them by the attitude of the Western powers. He had been taught a serious lesson by the refusal to finance the Aswan High Dam. But he ought to have been left to digest the lesson, not pushed into a final break with the West. Above all, such behaviour was a self-condemnation before the whole Third World, proof that the imperialist bloc was unregenerate and still liable to resort to acts of brutal provocation on the nineteenth-century pattern. The French, British and Israelis had, by their action, compromised the chances of mobilizing the Arabs against the Communist menace, which the Americans still hoped to make clear to them. Despite his flirtation with the East, Nasser had never burnt his bridges to the Capitalist West, had not as yet resorted to socialist measures, and was by no means committed body and soul to the Eastern bloc. His sympathies lay with the neutralists, with Nehru, with Tito, and with Sukarno. The immorality of wishing to remain neutral between Good and Evil was deplored; but these were sensible people, and it was possible, the Americans hoped, to bring them to reason and attract them to the right side.

This train of events pushed the Nasser regime towards greater socialization and into closer relations with the Soviet Union. Nevertheless, Nasser made sure of keeping his independence of this bloc, and he kept up his relations with the Western capitalist world. Under the pressure of events, the American attitude began imperceptibly to change.

The socialist or socialistic countries slowly began to segregate, and the monolithic bloc of earlier days increasingly came to resemble a constellation of fairly independent units, each with its own interests, its own aspirations and its own policy. The U.S.S.R. began to exercise less and less control over their decisions. At the same time she made considerable strides in nuclear technology, and it became apparent that it would be impossible to attack her directly and inflict a decisive defeat without risking apocalyptic reprisals, tens of millions of American dead, even, possibly, total but mutual annihilation. The result might be an armistice in the Cold War. This is what happened, eventually, when the nuclear test-ban treaty was signed on 5 August 1963. But it was now known that the U.S.S.R. had her difficulties, in differing degrees, with socialist and even Communist states, principally China and Albania, to a lesser degree with Rumania, and still, of course, with Yugoslavia. She could not automatically protect them, and such protection as she gave would not always be effective, as was demonstrated by the trial of strength over Cuba in October 1962, and by her attitude to Vietnam.

From that time on, American policy towards the more or less socialistic nations of the Third World was given more room for manoeuvre, and at the same time became more determined. These countries' attitude towards the U.S.S.R. ceased to be a determining factor. Every movement which was in any way revolutionary might by its own dynamism represent a danger to American hegemony, and it now became possible to dispose of these movements without imperilling the world balance between the two super-powers. In October 1965 Indonesian army officers, supported as many believed by the C.I.A., overthrew Sukarno's regime, which was too prone to take socialistic attitudes and under which the Communists were acquiring too much weight. In April 1967 a similar alliance established a military dictatorship in Greece, to prevent the country from sliding towards the Left.

Nasser (not to speak of the Syrians) thus came to be classified among the irredeemables, or at any rate among those who were leading their country down a potentially dangerous road.

Notwithstanding his preference for conciliation, his dislike of fanatical radicalism, and the presence in his government of notoriously pro-Western elements, he represented a danger despite himself. He had opted decisively for socialist solutions to internal problems, and had shown his hostility to Western interference in Arab affairs. In the Yemen he was in conflict with the royalists, supported for their part by Saudi Arabia and, behind her, by the United States. Despite their mutual antagonism, not to say hatred, he supported Syrian policy in so far as it was anti-imperialist. In the Lebanon the Nasserites represented an alternative to the generally pro-Western attitudes of the commercial middle class and militant anti-Muslim elements in the Christian community. Nasser also supported Algeria's resistance to American economic hegemony, and maintained his hostility to the reactionary states throughout the Arab world, which were at the same time pro-American. He had to be got rid of, whatever his motivations. Israel did not fail to appreciate this hardening of the United States' attitude towards Nasser. This was an extremely important factor in the events of June 1967.

Of the United States' own allies, Great Britain and France had taken opposite directions. The Suez disaster put paid to all British pretensions to conduct a general independent Middle Eastern policy out of step with the policy of the United States. Great Britain now directed all her attentions to her oil interests in the Persian Gulf and to maintaining her political influence in East and South Arabia. In the Yemen her interests coincided with those of the United States, and here again Nasser was the common enemy. Obviously none of this gave her any cause to diverge from American policy, and other factors pressed her to pursue the same course in the broader field of world policy.

Israel's original attitude towards the British had been chilly. The memory of the Balfour Declaration, without which Israel could never have come into being, had long been effaced by the memory of the ill-will of British officials at the time of the mandate, of the White Paper, of the brutality of the British army in the face of Jewish terrorism, and of Bevin's policy. This could be explained either by a deep-seated anti-Semitism, or by an infatuation for the Arabs brought on by the needs of Empire, or by both factors at once. At all events, most Israelis still thought of England as perfidious Albion. From 1958 on, Ben Gurion had followed a policy of *rapprochement* with Great Britain, making great play of the danger to British interests represented by 'revolutionary' Arab policies. This unfroze Anglo-Israeli relations, but not Israeli public opinion, which remained mistrustful. On the British side, it helped to create a pro-Israeli orientation, although still hesitant, and dependent on the attitude provoked by the various Arab policies towards the West. This attitude towards the Arabs was complex, discriminatory and fluctuating. In general it may be noted that no really major interest prevented Britain from following, in the main, the lead of her senior partner, the United States.

France pursued quite a different path. The Algerian war had provoked a wave of anti-Arab feeling among many Frenchmen. The presence of numerous Algerians and other North Africans in France forming a kind of sub-proletarian layer employed mainly in dirty, dangerous and unpleasant occupations had the kind of consequences one might expect. It is a not uncommon sociological phenomenon for a sector of the population which is placed in despicable conditions to be widely despised. Although the degree of Algerian assimilation in the French population was relatively advanced, backwardness in catching up with French modes of living persisted and made them feel strangers. Competition from outsiders asking for little and being paid little aroused irritation in the French working class. The ill-defined but pervasive political temper and ideology of French society, strongly anti-racist in France itself at any rate, and frequently so even in the colonies, tended to succumb to a situation highly favourable to the development of racialism. It was resisted only by the liberal intellectuals, especially the Left-wing Christians and the members of the non-Communist Left, including some who left the Party because of its passive attitude on the question. They embraced the Algerian cause with all the more enthusiasm in that their revolutionary ardour found little outlet in French politics themselves. They were gradually joined – though certainly without any great militancy - by elements of the Right and Centre, who were beginning to understand, as the Algerian campaign became more hopeless, the folly of wishing to maintain French domination for ever over an increasingly rebellious population. In contrast, the Socialist Party leadership did not dare to make peace and face a revolt by the French settlers in Algeria and other conservative elements; they used every conceivable Left-wing argument to justify the continuation of the struggle against the Algerian National Liberation Front. They even allied themselves with the nationalist Right in denouncing what they regarded as the root-causes of the whole problem, in the vain hope of gaining some easy victory outside Algeria. The origins of the Suez expedition lay in this attitude, which expressed itself in a general condemnation of Arab nationalism and of its figurehead, Nasser, as reactionary and even Fascist. The natural tendency of the Arab peoples to strive for a certain degree of political unity corresponding to the relative unity which existed on the social and cultural plane, was denounced as 'pan-Arabism', which had unpleasant overtones evoking the pan-Germanism and pan-Slavism of the nineteenth century (pan-Italianism was not mentioned) and had a reactionary ring. Clearly these attitudes only reinforced the anti-Arab feeling in France. From then on the alliance with Israel had a dual function: to provide military support in the East, and a justification to the liberal and Left-wing conscience. Support for a state widely accepted as socialist, support for the Jews whom Hitlerite persecution had turned into the living symbol of the minority oppressed by Fascism, all this lent the anti-Algerian faction a spurious but effective aura of militant anti-Fascism.

As usually happens, the capitulation to Algerian nationalism, so wounding to the national pride and so harmful to the interests of a large number of Frenchmen, could only be made acceptable by a Right-wing government, or at least one which could not be accused of sacrificing the nation to some universalist ideology. This was the historic role of Charles de Gaulle, who had already in a rather similar fashion made the anti-Hitler alliance with Stalin and the French Communists respectable in the eyes of the French bourgeoisie. Of course his personal ambition also played its part. But once peace had been made in 1962, the causes of conflict with Arab interests in general faded into insignificance. For a man as detached from ideological and sentimental enthusiasms as France's new master, the obvious policy was one of strict neutrality in the Arab–Israel conflict, or rather of coming down firmly on both sides. When the factors guiding his general policy led de Gaulle in the direction of disengagement from the American bloc, and towards a policy of support for the aspirations of the Third World, he naturally became more favourably inclined to the Arab cause, without ever breaking with Israel. His followers, however, conservative and nationalist and deeply imbued with the anti-Arab feeling of the preceding period, did not relish their new role.

As for Federal Germany, her national interests and the violent anti-Communist conservatism of her political leaders bound her to the American band-wagon. Wishing to prove that she had broken radically with Hitler Germany's brutal expansionism and bestial doctrines of national purity, she was induced to make spectacular gestures of reparation to the persecuted Jews, whoever and wherever they might be. This was the easiest, and in the long run the cheapest way of breaking with the past. Moreover this method helped to disarm the ill-will of the American Jewish community, a pressure-group with powerful influence on the policies of the world's dominant power. It was nonetheless necessary to maintain good relations with the Arabs, and this sometimes led to difficulties. All these more or less contradictory needs were classified in order of importance by reference to a compass-needle which always pointed to Washington.

The preoccupations of the Communist states were not, in fact, at all those attributed to them by the Americans and many others. Their strategy was for many years wholly determined by the Russians of the Soviet Union and by the Georgian who had paradoxically come to lead them and incarnate them. Certainly the World Revolution was the ultimate end prescribed by Communist ideology, and in his own way Stalin believed in it. But very early on, while Lenin was still alive, Stalin's solid, brutal realism led him to relegate the accomplishment of Marx's prophecies to a distant and uncertain future. For the moment, Russia was weak and backward. Within the country itself, an elite – itself not entirely trustworthy – imposed for the future good of the nation a programme of austerity unattractive to the tens of millions of benighted muzhiks and to the hardly more enlightened sons and daughters of muzhiks, who now hoped to enjoy the fruits of the revolution but found such hopes premature. The first priority was to strengthen Russia. Severe internal and external shocks had to be avoided as far as possible. Allies had to be found – any allies, no matter who. Only after these priorities had been fulfilled would it be possible to develop, slowly, Russia's internal resources, and raise the cultural level and the standard of living. Any opportunity of recovering the territories lost to the infant Soviet Republics in the civil war and through foreign intervention had to be seized. Any opportunity of acquiring new territory would be jumped at. The new state needed room to enable it to keep any attack from outside at arm's length; it needed a sphere of influence which would act as an insulating layer. Nothing and nobody could be trusted. The Soviets would, of course, have to withdraw into their shell at the first sign of danger from the reaction to these movements. Finally the State ideology provided, in the various national Communist Parties, groups of dedicated men ready for any sacrifice on Russia's behalf, supported in their turn by a constellation of 'honest innocents', as Stalin called them. They would have to be used; but used for the benefit of the Soviet Union, and consequently in the final analysis for the good of humanity. They could not be allowed to think up and follow objectives of their own. Failing to appreciate the delicacy of Russia's situation, they might in their haste compromise the safety of the bastion of socialism for the sake of illusory gain and hence endanger the distant Millennium which they claimed to cherish.

Stalin believed in force. The powers which had to be taken into account were those which really had force at their command: the United States, Great Britain, Hitler Germany, Japan, and, until 1940, France. The rest were a mere helpless litter of small states subject, either by right or in fact, to the decisions made by these, the great and powerful. In what was later to be called the Third World, the starving masses, possessed of only the most embryonic forms of political organization, attached themselves either to political frauds or dreamers. At times they could be exploited to inflict insect bites on the big powers. No available weapon is ever entirely useless. But it was dangerous to over-estimate the strength of this ridiculous rabble, or the chances of success of their Communist Parties in particular.

The Arab countries and Israel were mere specks amidst the cloud of minor states. Stalin did at one time play with the idea of exploiting Israel against Great Britain, which might have caused the British Lion some embarrassment. This would have meant a complete break with all the previous theories pronounced by his movement, and amounted to sacrificing the Arab Communist Parties. These were not obstacles likely to cause Stalin any loss of sleep, as he demonstrated at the time of his pact with Hitler. But he shortly realized the pointlessness of such a move and how little he could expect to gain from Israel. The Arab states and the Arabist movements seemed just as unpromising. Apart from the Communists, the groups active in these countries were mere bands of conspirators in the pay of one power or the other, exploiting the emotions of backward masses. Thus the Free Egyptian officers were denounced, in 1952, as nothing more nor less than American agents. Even chance identity of interest with some other group and the occasional current of sympathy for the U.S.S.R. were to be exploited if possible, but too much hope could not be placed in them.

The development of the situation resulted in a corresponding change in Soviet political thinking. This change already began to show itself in the terrible Josef Vissarionovitch at the end of his life. The American attitude showed that in the face of the advance in Soviet military power, the United States would resist the temptation, however strong, to attack the Soviet Union. In 1952, in his last ideological statement, a paper on the *Economic Problems of Socialism*, Stalin considered wars between capitalist countries more likely than between the 'imperialist camp' and the 'anti-imperialist camp'. It follows from this that the latter would be able to make a free choice of allies among the rival groups of states confronting one another within the capitalist world. So far as the Third World was concerned, Soviet strategists were mostly strongly impressed by the growing force of national movements, and by the fact that countries achieving their independence under middle-class leadership did not, for all that, necessarily endorse American policy. The Bandung Conference and the policy moves made by Nasser (among others) in 1955 were proof of this. Khruschevian empiricism could not ignore potential allies of such importance. Moreover, the Twentieth Congress of the Communist Party of the Soviet Union, held in February 1956, foresaw a lengthy period of peaceful coexistence with the capitalist world, and also admitted the possibility of different roads to socialism, including parliamentary and non-violent evolution. The colonial bourgeoisie itself – subjected to intemperate abuse in the preceding period – could therefore be led painlessly on to the road to socialism. Much more important, this class could be won over as an ally, on many points at least, in the Cold War, because of its sincere desire of independence of Western, and especially American, hegemony.

Seen in this light, it became obvious that the Arab countries would be much more useful clients than Israel. Israel, armed to the teeth behind the walls of her tiny besieged fortress, was driven by factors which have already been discussed into alliance with the Western powers. The Zionist ideology could not fail to have an undesirable influence on the Jews of the Soviet Union. The Arab countries, constantly threatened by the superiority of the West in their struggle for self-determination and moderniz-ation, were peopled by masses who would long remain faithful to these objectives against Western hostility, whatever particular government they might have at any given time. The general aspirations of the people usually won in the end, or at least created powerful opposition movements if pro-American rulers remained in power. The choice was clear-cut, since the concili-ation hoped for in 1947–8 had proved impossible. Respect for the U.N. Charter (which was greatly to the Soviet Union's advantage) and for U.N. decisions, fear of Jewish and pro-Jewish opinion throughout the world, and the support in Israel for the Communist Party and even the Mapam prevented the Soviet Union from refusing to recognize Israel's existence, as did the Arabs. But the Soviet Union affected to recognize Israel only within the limits of the frontiers granted by the U.N. in the partition plan of November 1947. The conquests made in the war of 1948 were regarded as quite without validity. Soviet schoolchildren still have to learn Israel's 'legal' area as well as her actual area (2,587,000 square miles greater) and their atlases are coloured to show the situation as it ought to have been, although some charitable cross-hatching informs them of the true situation.

For many years, the countries of the Communist bloc followed the strategic directives issued to them from the Kremlin. In Stalin's day, they were rationed to a very few decisions deviating from the strict Soviet road, and they were told what these should be. For instance, at the birth of the State of Israel, it was the Czechs who supplied her with arms, while Rumania, Poland and Bulgaria opened their gates to Jewish emigrants to the Promised Land. The Soviet Union was able to harvest some of the fruits of these policies, to observe their implementation and effects, without having to bear any of the responsibility. Only much later did Rumania embark on a distinctly independent policy.

As everyone knows, Yugoslavia broke with the bloc in 1948. The difficulties which faced Tito and his lieutenants in safeguarding themselves from possible Soviet attack while maintaining an essentially Communist system internally led them to seek alliances with the neutralist states of the Third World. More than this, Yugoslavia's leaders had to try to achieve a fairly lasting coalition, able to exert international influence as a 'third force'. Hence Tito's great personal friendship with Nehru and Nasser. For Nasser, Tito was a respected counsellor, a man of greater maturity, with long experience and a consequent thorough understanding of European affairs. This friendship was even worth the Communist hostility which it sometimes called down on Nasser. Khaled Begdash frequently denounced him to the Communist International as an accomplice in the Titoist heresy. But the same factors which drove the U.S.S.R. to support the Arabs pushed Tito in that direction too, despite his eagerness to stay on the right side of the United States. Support for the Arabs was directly in line with the political currents in the Third World. By contrast, support for Israel, closely bound up with Western policy, could have done nothing but harm without bringing any concomitant advantage.

One power remains to be discussed: China. When the new Communist power began to be able to formulate independent political attitudes, there was nothing to attract it towards Israel. Her position with regard to the Arab states was somewhat equivocal: her Communist fundamentalism made her hostile to reactionary regimes, whereas a realist recognition of her interests as a great power often pulled her in the opposite direction. A clear example of this is provided by the coup d'état in Iraq on 8 February 1963, when the new regime celebrated its accession to power by a wholesale massacre of Communists. Relations between Iraq and the U.S.S.R. cooled markedly; but China leapt into the breach and made advances to the new regime. The Arab Communists are not likely to forget this episode very quickly.

The feelings of the Arab Left towards Communist China were fluctuating and ambivalent. The liberalism of the period of the Hundred Flowers attracted those irked by Soviet dogmatism. Development on the Chinese pattern seemed more appropriate to the Middle East's problems than the solution represented by the U.S.S.R. – too European in many eyes, and also too advanced. When the schism with the Russian leadership occurred, many at first shifted their sympathies towards Peking. But the militant extremism of the Chinese, their call to armed struggle, their mistrust, whether implicit or explicit, of bourgeoisie politicians were to arouse powerful antipathies. The Arab Communists themselves had been conditioned to loyalty to the Soviet Union, and had received their political education in the Popular front era of parliamentary alliances with the nationalist middle class. They could not see themselves acting the role of subversives against their anti-imperialist allies. With regard to Israel, the Chinese counselled a war on the Vietnam pattern, without explaining precisely how this recipe was to be applied to the Middle East. They did however give warning of the terrible dangers, the great suffering and massive destruction liable to follow from such a strategy. The Middle Eastern peoples had not known a war of this nature since the Mongol invasions of the thirteenth century. The apocalyptic prophecies of the Chinese were enough to make the stoutest heart quail. The Cultural Revolution was a shock to the extreme Left, which a long period of militant nationalism had taught to respect the heritage of an ancient culture, even though they were but poorly acquainted with it. Naturally some extreme

Left-wing elements were attracted, as were dissidents of every colour, including, apparently at least, the most extreme partisans of the struggle against Israel, even if they were middle class. For the moment however they were a tiny minority. Nonetheless, the intensification of the conflict and disillusionment with present ruling cliques and their Soviet ally might, in the future, attract many of the more dynamic elements to the Chinese approach.

True enough, a third alternative did exist – that of 'open', liberal Communism on the Castro model, which might seem especially appropriate in view of its special concern with the problems of the Third World. Ben Bella, for example, had been particularly drawn by the attractions of Castroism. However, the radicalism of the Cuban system, its unbuttoned style, and the rupture it entailed with all ancient traditions frightened off the Arab middle class, whose nationalist past, however radically anti-imperialist, had given them a profound respect for traditional values, and made them very conscious of their power. The campaign against these values, if undertaken at all, is conducted with exemplary prudence and expediency, by means of an infinite number of tiny transitional reforms. The Cubans, for their part, do not understand the Arab intransigence towards the Israelis. They are mistrustful of the bourgeoisie character of the Arab ruling parties, and tend to see the Israel question as a decoy, a diversion from the radical revolutionary struggle to throw off all the values of the past, which they consider just as necessary in the Arab world as elsewhere. They refuse to accept that the political elimination of Israel is a self-validating revolutionary objective, even though they accept the Arab critique of Israel.

This, in broad outline, is how the nations of the world and their political movements are divided up. It helps to explain many attitudes and many factors influencing the struggle over the last few years and the events of 1967. But beyond these fundamental standpoints, there are further factors at work which experience has shown to be very powerful. There is the public opinion of the two world camps to be considered.

Public opinion generally moves along simple lines in problems relating to distant events which do not touch it directly. Once the public ceases to be indifferent, it tends to relate these distant problems not to the real facts, of which it is ignorant, but to facts with which it is familiar – in fact to its own problems, in so far as such identification is possible. Moreover it uses as its reference a few stereotyped images which basic education, current popular literature and the mass media have succeeded in establishing. This is obviously the cause of the gross discrepancies between the reality and its distant image. During the period we are discussing, Western public opinion knew nothing of the real Palestine. Only believers knew anything at all, and then but little: Palestine was the Holy Land. This might have had the effect of convincing some that the Christian Church had rights over some Christian sanctuaries. Others with some little knowledge of religious history (usually Protestants) knew that it was the land given by God to the Hebrews. Beyond this nothing much was known, except that the whole question had something to do with two peoples with which the public was reasonably familiar: the Jews and the Arabs.

As for the Jews, the West had good grounds for thinking it knew them well. Many people still had some notion of an old rival and accursed religion, to which belonged the murderers of Christ. The distressing notion that it was also the religion to which the founders and most highly venerated figures of Christianity – Jesus, the Virgin Mary and the Apostles – themselves belonged, and in which they firmly believed, was pushed as far back from the conscious mind as possible, like most disturbing ideas. Some innovating pioneers within the Church were forcing attention back to this unwelcome fact, and were beginning to gain a hearing among Catholic churchmen. Without realizing it, they were in tune with a widespread trend.

During the decade from 1930 to 1939, the Jews began to be violently persecuted in Germany and were the victims of more or less vexatious discrimination in Eastern Europe and the Balkans. Those who found refuge in Western Europe or America often arrived after the loss of all their possessions, wretched, supplicant and spreading uneasiness. German propaganda represented them as the children of the Devil, evil by nature, revolutionary by instinct, strangers wherever they went, ready to drain any nation of its substance, to pollute its essential nature and despoil it of its traditions. This they did from above, through the banks which they controlled, and from below, through revolutionary movements which they allegedly inspired. This fantastic picture was widely accepted, because there were a number of apparent facts which seemed to confirm it. In any case, it did not need much in the way of facts to win support, for Western opinion had a terrible grievance against the Jews. This grievance, difficult to express openly, glimmered weakly through a smokescreen of false arguments: the Jews troubled the West's self-satisfied tranquillity, and this was the best reason for mistrusting and hating them. The Germans never ceased to proclaim that they asked nothing more than to live in peace with all their Aryan brothers, that only the Jews sowed discord between them. Obsessed by the memory of millions of dead and disabled and of the enormous sufferings of the 1914–18 war, Westerners wondered if they were to be dragged once more into the same terrible cataclysm, attended by the same frightful slaughter, and all because of the Jews. Many repeated under their breath an adaptation of the terrible phrase pronounced nineteen centuries earlier by a Jewish High Priest in Jerusalem: it is better that one man should die for the people than that the whole nation should perish. Was it not better to sacrifice this group of people to the vindictiveness of a menacing neighbour in order to avoid consequences which would be disastrous for everybody? Of course a great number of justifications were adduced to show that the Jews were suspect, even guilty. They must in some way be responsible for the hatred which they aroused. Any vigorous policy towards Germany henceforth became suspect of having been inspired by this accursed group, ready to allow millions of good Frenchmen, Englishmen, Americans, Russians, etc. to die for its own interests. Governments animated by any spirit of resistance to Hitler had to forestall criticism from their own public opinion by demonstrating that their attitude was in no way dictated by any desire to placate the Jews. They had to dissociate themselves as far as possible from pro-Jewish feeling.

The war came, and persecution gave way to wholesale massacre such as had not been seen in the West for centuries. The Germans were directly responsible, but all the peoples of the West, except for a few pockets of resistance, were accomplices in the deed. The Poles, whom a hardly better fate awaited, watched the destruction of the Warsaw Ghetto as though it were a circus; French militia and police arrested Jews to deliver them up to their executioners; many moral authorities were silent; a number of bishops blessed the persecutors and mass-murderers. Even outside occupied Europe, the British and American governments resisted any energetic and effective measures against the great massacre.

When peace came and it was no longer possible to close one's eyes to the extent of the crime, when books, newspapers, films, the radio gave detailed accounts of the abominations practised on the Jews, the Western world was seized by a terrible feeling of guilt for its complicity, if only by abstention. The feeling was no more than a vague disquiet, and any straw blowing in the opposite direction would have transformed it at once into a clamour of self-justification. But everything, or nearly everything, pointed in a different direction. Western Jews were no longer pariah refugees, but, increasingly integrated into general society, they had become pillars of respectability. There was no reason to sacrifice them in any cause. Widespread prosperity gave no grounds, as poverty and fear had done, to look for scapegoats. The new Germany won a place in the community of the rich and powerful by spectacular gestures of contrition. The sum of complex forces which were driving the Catholic Church to renew its ideas and its internal structure helped it to discover, all of a sudden, the errors and misdeeds it had committed over fifteen centuries, and to seek common ground with rival denominations. Everywhere, anathema became dialogue. The Catholic Church suddenly became aware of the part it played in the development of anti-Semitism, and set out, in its habitual stately and unhurried fashion to retrace its steps in an effort to make amends.

To the peoples of the West, the Israelis were first and foremost Jews. Unable to rid their minds of the Jewish tragedy of 1939–45, in Palestine they saw only the survivors of the massacre. This persecuted people had fled and recongregated in the land which historically was theirs, as the Bible shows; they had worked that land, and proved that they possessed the qualitites which the West prizes above all: technical efficiency and military prowess.

Settled in this distant country, they lost all the disagreeable characteristics (chiefly that of being different) which had blighted their life in Europe. Purified by distance and national regeneration, they now represented the quintessence of Europe amidst the dirty and backward masses of the languid and verminous Orient.

Israeli and Zionist propaganda reinforced, as it was bound to do, these images. Israel, it was said, *was* the Jewish people. The fund of good will towards the Jews was mobilized in the service of Israel. The identification of Israel with the Jews, with all the Jews, was total. The West felt bound to make good the wrongs historically perpetrated on the Jews, whether as members of the Jewish religious community or of the Jewish race, by supporting Israel, their historical representative. The history of the Jews and the history of Israel have everywhere been written from this point of view, in learned works just as much as in popularizations and vulgarizations at every level, including that of the novel (vide *Exodus* by Leon Uris, translated into every language and sold in millions of copies, in which the historical reality is carefully inflected to suit the Zionist view of things), the cinema, right down to music-hall songs. Israeli propaganda also stressed Israel's undeniable achievements, the dedication of the communities working in the *kibbutzim*, the flowering of the desert, the romance of the watch on the frontier. The Western urbanite could have his dreams of a free and healthy life fulfilled by proxy. The sympathy of the self-satisfied classes of Western society was won by developing Israel without renouncing free enterprise; the sympathy of the revolutionary or vaguely socialistic by the vision of the *kibbutzim*, representing a socialism without dictatorship, without deportations, without purges, without firing squads. Above all, none of this represented the remotest danger, the slightest threat to the masses of the West. All the disadvantages were on the other side – the Arab side.

If these pictures enchanted the non-Jewish masses, it is then hardly surprising that they should have won over all those who might in any way be termed 'Jew'. The authorities of religious Judaism had always been violently hostile to Zionism, a secular nationalist movement which wished to achieve by human strength that which belonged to God alone. Neither the Jewish community in mandate Palestine nor the State of Israel seemed to them to resemble the messianic image of the mythic Israel which was to return to Palestine at the end of time. But the rabbis, with a few exceptions, were not long able to resist the enthusiasm of their flocks, all the more shrill and vibrant the further away they were and stayed from the new state; nor the peace-offerings held out to them by the new state itself. Non-practising Jews, for their part, did not resist assimilation with the society around them, with the culture of the country where they had found a home, of which they felt themselves to be citizens and even fully integrated members in many respects. But they attempted to combine this with loyalty to Israel, without realizing the contradiction or inconsistency this might involve. The general admiration for that country reflected on to them, and it would not have been human to reject such flattery altogether, despite the unease which many felt at their dual loyalty, and the disgust they must sometimes have experienced to hear such fulsome praise from erstwhile anti-Semites. In France, the synagogues which had been deserted by the assimilated Jews, who wanted above all to be Frenchmen with no trace of a specific Jewish culture, were refilled by a wave of Algerian Jews of French nationality. These came from close-knit communities with their own traditions, their own way of life, their own customs and culture. Full of bitterness against the Arabs and against Islam, they were first and foremost Jews, the Jewish cause was their cause on whatever battleground it was defended. This battleground was now Israel.

As for the Arabs, the West's ideas about them were less clear-cut and had less basis in experience. But at all events, they were strangers to the European world. Popular culture, compounded of half-digested history and geography lessons in childhood and adolescence, romances, and tales handed down through the ages, presented an image of half-starved and wild-eyed nomadic Bedouin on the one hand, and of harems, concubines, and lubricious and cruel despots on the other. Added to this, tales were told of the oil potentates with their immense fortunes – hardly modernized versions of the legendary Haroun al Rashid. Colonial enterprise added its own touches to these pictures, to suit the predilections of the nations engaged in it. For the conservative and traditionally patriotic English, Lawrence of Arabia aroused sympathy towards the Arab dynasts, chivalrous allies of the Empire. Their rivals therefore tended towards greater sympathy with Israel. The French thought more in terms of the destructive Bedouin, and of the Maghreb villager buried in his archaic and barbaric traditions. The French Right and the patriotic lobby were outraged at Algerian terrorism, and found it hard to swallow France's capitulation to this backward people. Since independence, to their mind ill-gotten, these barbarians had seemingly exhibited nothing but disorder and ineptitude. The revolutionary Left, by contrast, had been fired with enthusiasm by the Algerian cause. The disappointment was all the greater when the new Arab states proved to be very far removed from the Left's vision of a socialist society where liberty would reign at every level, and archaic values, the suffocating grip of out-dated traditions, would be thrown off. The Arab world, seen in this way, had little weight to place in the balance of sympathies, against a virile, modern and forward-looking Israel, embodiment of the Jewry to which such a heavy debt was owed.

As for public opinion in the Communist countries, it tended to take the same side, despite the pro-Arab attitude of their governments, and partly because of it. Government propaganda methods had succeeded in arousing automatic distrust towards everything the government said. In the U.S.S.R. this propaganda had made strenuous efforts to represent Israel as an ordinary country, as against the Jewish religious and Zionist idealization. This was perfectly correct in principle. But it was delivered in the violent, rabble-rousing manner habitual to the Soviets. Israel was presented as a vale of blood and tears, where poverty-stricken proletarians languished under the whip of hardship and oppression. Not many believed in this grotesque image, which therefore had the effect of encouraging a boundless idealization. An ironic comment on this is furnished by the story of the reaction of Soviet Orthodox Jews when Elie Wiesel, a Western religious Zionist, showed them a Hebrew newspaper from Tel Aviv. Seeing the usual collection of daily news items, including thefts, crimes, strikes, political and social crises, etc., they immediately suspected him of being a secret government agent showing them a forgery fabricated in the headquarters of the political police. Anti-religious propaganda pamphlets directed against Judaism – similar to those attacking the other religions – were not very successful in making the radical distinction between anti-Judaism and anti-Semitism. The liberal intelligentsia spoke out against this official anti-Israeli and anti-Judaic propaganda. It seemed to them a continuation of the traditional anti-Semitism of the old reactionary governments and of Stalin's anti-Semitic machinations after 1949. They also judged the problems of distant Palestine by reference to their own problems, as is only natural, and identified Israel with the Jewish cause. They were afraid that government propaganda would reinforce the traditional anti-Semitism of the masses. It would seem, however, that this popular anti-Semitism, while it did not perhaps abate at all, was counterbalanced to some extent by an even stronger sentiment: implacable hostility to everything which emanated from the government. In addition to this, the Arabs reminded all the Balkan peoples of the Muslim Turks who had been their overlords for many centuries and for whom they had little love.

Such is the world in which the latest phases of the Israeli–Arab conflict have taken place. It is clear that the factors favouring Israel were by far the stronger. This was to have its effect on the attitudes and political decisions of both sides.

7 FROM DISENGAGEMENT TO ARMED VIGIL

At the beginning of 1964 the general tendency in the Arab world seemed to be towards some degree of disengagement. Nasser was visibly most interested in consolidating his rule and in promoting economic progress at home. His foreign policy was conditioned by these primary considerations, except in the Yemen where the weight of earlier decisions, the need to avoid loss of face, and the interests of the Egyptian military caste were dragging the army deeper into the quagmire of a hopeless, costly and generally damaging conflict. However, this was a distant and secondary field of action – one might almost say colonial. Broadly speaking, Egypt was anxious for peace – and Egypt was the determining factor in the Arab world.

In March 1964 a constitutional proclamation abrogated the provisional constitution of 1958, and gave the National Assembly the power to dismiss the government. But the President retained the power to dissolve the National Assembly if it came into conflict with him. Nevertheless, the newly elected Assembly preserved some trace of the effort made to enlarge the regime's popular base. 188 out of 350 deputies were workers or peasants. But the formation of a new cadre among the lower ranks of the population desired by Nasser and the small ruling group which shared his preoccupations was continually being thwarted by the contradictions inherent in the regime. The cabinet was led by Ali Sabri, a strict Nasserite, and consisted of Vice-Presidents, almost all representing the military interest, to whom the civilian ministers were responsible. The true centre of power in the regime kept the newly-emerging cadres in leading strings, while it was supposed to be encouraging them, at a time when they were needed at the controls to effect vital economic developments.

In March the last Communist internees were freed. This was a further sign of the attempt to build up popular cadres. In May Khruschev was invited to attend and participate in the solemn inauguration of the Aswan High Dam. Nasser was proclaimed a 'Hero of the Soviet Union' and decorated with the Order of Lenin. In the course of the banquets and other festivities, the host and his guest found themselves opposed in courteous controversy. Khruschev said that he was disturbed by the nationalist tone of the movement for Arab unity, which implied conciliation towards reactionary regimes and classes. Nasser replied somewhat evasively. He was constricted by the class support to which he owed his position, and his inter-Arab policy effectively undermined the programme of radicalization implied by his ideology.

His desire to withdraw from the competitive propaganda-escalation practised by the Arab governments and to pacify the Arab front drove him to make concessions which contrasted with his ambition to lead the neutralist trend and the movements of liberation in the Third World. He bargained with the governments associated with the American bloc, while at the same time denouncing that bloc. In October 1964 a conference of the non-aligned nations was held in Cairo. At this conference, even those countries which had become more or less compromised by association with the United States were forced into a strenuously anti-imperialist pose. With the support of the Africans, Nasser affronted Tshombe by holding him prisoner in a Cairo hotel before sending him back to the Congo.

But the economic situation was grave. The government's investment effort, the massive purchases of capital equipment abroad, and the military costs piling up as a result of the war in the Yemen were draining the country's foreign reserves. The balance of payments deficit was enormous. It was becoming impossible to purchase foodstuffs, and the Nile valley was only able to produce quantities quite inadequate to feed a population which was increasing at a terrifying rate. The increase in the area under cultivation, even with the High Dam, was insufficient. Birth control was officially encouraged, but met with every kind of obstacle in such an untutored population, and in any case it would be very slow to take effect. Unemployment was endemic, and the immense mass of the destitute sub-proletariat only diminished very slowly. Egypt was reduced to awaiting anxiously the arrival of American grain consignments. The United States drove a hard bargain, supplying the precious grain only in return for arms control, economic measures and, implicitly, acceptable political attitudes. The consignments became smaller, were suspended, then started again. This was to show the Egyptians that it was in their interest to behave themselves and stop their pranks.

Although this attitude helped to weld the patriotic ruling group around Nasser, its consequences provoked growing and ever more dangerous popular discontent. While the clandestine Egyptian Communist Party, which had long since been won over to Nasser's policies, made the solemn gesture in April 1965 of formally disbanding itself, Right-wing opposition became more and more virulent. The despair and nostalgia of the dispossessed bourgeoisie found expression at the funeral of the old leader of the Wafd, Mustapha Nahas, in September 1965. The Muslim Brotherhood, a clerical and Fascist organization with a popular following, was more dangerous. In August police who tried to arrest a Muslim Brother conspirator in a village ten miles from Cairo were attacked by the local population. Four people were killed, three of them policemen, and martial law was declared in the region. A large-scale police swoop covering an entire quarter of the city of Cairo resulted in hundreds of arrests.

In October Nasser entrusted the leadership of the government to Zakaria Mohieddin, one of the leading officers. Zakaria Mohieddin is known both for his pro-Western tendencies and economic liberalism, and for the firmness of his hand. He was just the man to carry out the repression of the Right. Hundreds of Muslim Brothers were dragged before the tribunals. Many were accused of having conspired against the life of Nasser, among other things. Seven were condemned to death and three of them were executed. One of these was the ideological theoretician Sayeed Kotb, a highly regarded intellectual. Telegrams flooded in from all parts of the Muslim world pleading for clemency, but in vain; demonstrations against the execution took place in Khartoum, Amman and other places. To counterbalance these effects, some twenty pro-Chinese Communists were condemned to terms of hard labour. The goods and chattels of 169 families were seized, numerous 'feudalists' in the towns were placed under house arrest, and local government offices were purged, following two outrages against members of the Socialist Union committed in two villages at the instigation of wealthy landed proprietors.

In foreign policy the pendulum now swung towards the West. American grain consignments immediately began to arrive more regularly. Relations with France became very cordial; those with the Soviet Union remained good.

In September 1966 the 'strong-man' was replaced by a techno-crat, Sidki Suleiman, erstwhile Minister for the Aswan High Dam. The significance of this change appears to be that the time for repression was past, the regime was again securely in the saddle and constructive tasks were once again given priority. The eco-nomic plan was revised, and the anti-feudal purge continued. Policy towards the great powers was conducted apparently much as before, but in January 1967 a crisis arose in relations with the United States. This crisis seems once again to have been connected with grain deliveries and the Americans' demands to exercise control over Egypt's armaments and foreign policy. It seems that after the brief honeymoon of Zakaria Mohieddin's rule, the Americans had returned to their attitude of mistrust, even out-right hostility, to Nasser and Nasserism.

In any case, from 1964 to the beginning of 1967 Egypt did not waver from her habitual policy with regard to Israel: verbal intransigence, and passivity in practice. Nothing seemed to be pushing Nasser to seek armed conflict; quite the reverse.

In Syria, events took a different turn. Relations with Egypt had improved somewhat, it seemed. But in April 1964 the Ba'athist government had to undergo a trial of strength. The urban trades-people and small manufacturers on whom the Ba'ath had long relied for some of its support objected to the party's socialistic policies. Seen in terms of Hethnic/religious communities, most of the members of this group were Sunnite Muslims, while the Ba'athists had many supporters – especially in the services – from minority groups, notably the Alawi. Of the thirteen members of the Central Committee of the Syrian Ba'ath Party, only five were Sunnites. An alarm-call of Alawi domination went up. Ideologi-cally, the opposition was divided into the Muslim Brotherhood, rampart of Sunnite fundamentalism and Nasserism, which seemed from the outside to be a guarantee of pugnacious Arab nationalism. At the same time both ideologies, however opposed to one another they might be in Egypt, seemed to offer safeguards against a too radical revolutionary policy. The respectful religiosity of Nasserism still seemed a safeguard against Ba'athist secularism. Very violent demonstrations against the regime broke out in the towns, supported by sermons in the mosques and accompanied by a strike of tradesmen and shop closures. The minority groups, the workers and the peasantry, who had benefited from the Ba'athist regime's reforms, combined in its defence and the army did the rest, i.e. the main work of restoring order. A mosque in which some members of the Muslim Brotherhood had taken refuge and which they used as a snipers' post was demolished by artillery fire. With bold but dangerous opportunism, the Nasserite press condemned the impiety of the Ba'athists, despite the fact that the Muslim Brotherhood was Nasser's most dreaded foe. Damascus made violent accusations against Cairo and Baghdad to the effect that they had supported, if not instigated, the revolt. Syria stood alone.

In order to escape from this isolation, the Ba'athist leaders were obliged to swallow their fundamental antipathy for Nasser and work for a *rapprochement* with him—a move already attempted on several previous occasions. Periods of reconciliation and renewed hostility followed one another, marked by distrust on both sides. In order to explain these changes of attitude to his followers, General Amin al Hafez, for the moment the strong-man of the Syrian regime, drew a distinction between Nasser, whom he exalted as an 'Arab hero', and his entourage which 'often misled him into error'. In 1965 the party veered sharply to the left and undertook an impressive series of nationalization measures. These measures were considered in many circles to have little economic justification, and to be unnecessarily provocative. They met with great resistance. The trial of strength against the urban shopkeepers, still supported by the Ulema, was won thanks to the energy of the measures taken and to the support of the groups mentioned above. An extraordinary military tribunal was set up. Fairly radical agrarian reform was undertaken, with some success it appears. Friendship with the U.S.S.R. and the other Soviet bloc countries was strengthened.

But the Ba'ath was torn with internal dissensions. A number of groups confronted one another behind the scenes, each backed in differing degrees by sections of the army. This factional struggle arose partly out of a conflict of ideologies. The old leaders of the party had based their attitude on unitary Arab nationalism, with some provision for socialist aspirations – but with the latter relegated to a definitely subordinate position. As long as the principal aim was still to overthrow the old bourgeois ruling groups and to mobilize the masses in support of traditional Arab claims and of a consistent anti-imperialist line, this ideology had been adequate. But now that the party was itself in power and confronted with the ineluctable decisions that power involved, the Arab nationalist ideology as presented in the rather nebulous theories of Michel Aflaq seemed a less certain guide. A new generation of young militants appeared, just as little attracted to institutional Communism as their elders. Many of the members of this younger generation had in the course of their studies (often in Paris) met with a form of Marxism liberated from the shackles of Communist Party dogma and the organizational bonds which this necessarily entailed. Some had lent their support to the Algerian Revolution, and had found the same ideas in some of the ruling circles of the F.L.N. Marxism, or Scientific Socialism as these young men called it, represented for them the need to integrate their own struggle in the context of the world struggle against imperialism, and to face the tasks of economic construction freed from the burden of capitalist privilege. It also entailed a refusal to abandon any universally valid principle on the pretext of an appeal to specific national or religious interests. They were just as strongly attached to national values as their adversaries; but they appreciated that although the problems facing them had an undeniable Arab or Muslim cast, this was not fundamental, and that basically these problems were the same as those faced by the peoples of other nations. This did not mean that the national question was without importance, and the Ba'ath had been right in principle to combine nationalism with socialism. However, its traditional leaders seemed to them to have sacrificed socialism to a narrow nationalism, which would in the long run prove fatal to national objectives themselves.

The active arm of this young generation of Ba'athists was a clandestine organization of army officers, the most noted of which was to be General Salah Jedid. At the Sixth Congress of the party, held in October 1963, the 'Marxist' Left gained the upper hand. The Right and Centre resorted to underhand manoeuvres to maintain their hegemony, alliances formed and re-formed in the shadows, playing off the party's various bodies against one another. Finally, on 23 February 1966, a military putsch prepared by the Jedid group overthrew the Right-wing Ba'athist government. A new government was formed under Youssef Zuain in which two Communists figured. The Ba'athist leaders of the Right and Centre were imprisoned.

The new ruling team lost no time in making its presence felt. Nationalization was continued. An iron hand descended on those opponents who denounced the 'atheistic power hostile to Arabism and to Islam'. A military conspiracy provided the opportunity for setting up a popular militia, to which arms were distributed. Khaled Begdash was permitted to return to Damascus, and the Communist Party newspaper made its reappearance in public. But the Party was still banned, and mutual distrust persisted. The Communist ministers had been appointed on their individual merits only, and Begdash's appeal for the formation of a national Progressive Front in which his party would play an open role fell on deaf ears. He denounced, in measured terms, the inadequacies of the government's social programme and pronounced his disdainful verdict on this group of young upstarts who might, at best, be credited with a few good intentions, but could not claim to hold the key to 'true' Marxism since they were not Communists.

This by no means excluded the establishment of strikingly cordial relations between the ruling group and the Soviet Union. This group had no illusions about the sentiments harboured by the C.I.A. towards it nor about American designs in general, which could only be aimed at its destruction. One of the first signs of this was, as usual, tension with Turkey. Foreign policy on several fronts was dictated by the situation. The friendship of Gaullist France was guaranteed to these French-trained anti-

Americans. Among the Arabs, the choice was easy. Good relations were only possible with states which had given proof of sufficiently sincere and radical anti-imperialist intentions to alarm the Americans. This was true of Egypt, Algeria and the Yemen Republic. Consequently, a very close relationship was established with Nasser, even though the Egyptian leader may have viewed the turbulence and pugnacity of his youthful allies with some disquiet. He was at pains to exercise a moderating influence in their dispute with the mighty Iraq Petroleum Company (I.P.C.), which had given the Syrians offence. On 4 November 1966 a joint defence agreement was signed between the U.A.R. and Syria, in circumstances which will be analyzed later. Naturally enough, it was intended mainly for the benefit of Israel. The Syrians felt themselves to be the special target of American hatred. They wondered from which direction the threatened blow would come. They took stock of all the pro-American regimes in the area: Jordan; Turkey; but above all the great military power represented by Israel. Besides, the defence agreement was in accordance with the intransigent attitude to Israel which their general philosophy dictated, as we shall see later. Also, Nasser was in a position to render effective support in case of attack. On the other side, the Egyptian leader hoped to be able to moderate and control any dangerous initiatives by his allies.

The two Middle Eastern Arab countries which took socialist anti-imperialism most seriously were thus brought together as allies by force of circumstances. Outside their immediate area they were, as has already been mentioned, decidedly sympathetic towards Algeria and the Yemeni Republicans. The latter, for their part, were somewhat torn between their anti-imperialist feeling and the difficulties they were having with the Egyptian troops, who while providing reinforcements to the Republicans, acted at the same time like an army of occupation. The other Arab governments found themselves in a delicate situation. Many were violently hostile to Syria and Egypt, whose political programme represented a grave threat to their privileges. But, with an eye to public opinion, they could not openly disapprove of all the anti-imperialist measures taken by these states, nor avoid showing some solidarity with them when such measures aroused reactions from the capitalist powers. This should be enough to demonstrate the political importance of Arab public opinion, which Western authors have often been tempted to dismiss as a myth. Within the Arab League, an unwieldy official body, conservative through sheer inertia, these rulers were in spite of everything forced at least to pretend to support the general interests of Arab nationalism. In the eyes of the masses, these interests seemed to coincide at least to a large extent with Syrian and Egyptian policies.

One means of escaping the dilemma had always been open. This entailed taking advantage of feelings of identification with the Muslim community. The remedy was well known, and, significantly, American circles interested in the Near East had long since developed a strategy for it, projecting a bloc uniting the forces of religion against atheistic materialism. I myself wrote an article as early as 1955 entitled 'Is Allah American?',[*] based on the ideological moves being taken in this direction. Early in 1966 King Feisal of Saudi Arabia cautiously advanced the idea of an 'Islamic summit'. The advantages were obvious. A general alliance of Muslim powers would make it possible to drown Egypt, Syria and Algeria in a gathering in which the non-Arab, conservative Muslim states, principally Turkey and Iran, would carry great weight. An appeal to Islamic solidarity would be an effective counterblast to the call of revolutionary Arab nationalism. Too radical measures of socialization could be criticized as contrary to the principles of Islam, and opposition to the capitalist West reduced to its proper proportions of a bargaining position in which the lion's share would go to the powerful Western interests. The support of the socialist countries sought by the revolutionary Arab regimes could be denounced in the name of the protest against the anti-religious attitude exhibited by the U.S.S.R. and by China in the Mohammedan areas of Central Asia. The struggle against the shackles which the West continued to impose on the self-determination and freedom of decision of the Arab world could be countered by a denunciation of Russian and Chinese oppression of the Uzbeks, Tadzhiks, Uighurs and other Muslims of that region. Among other demagogic devices used by Feisal

[*] *Democratie nouvelle*, May 1955, pp. 28–37.

to render his project acceptable to the Arabs, prominence was of course given to the support that the whole of Islam would give to Arab claims regarding Israel. The aim was a radical transformation of the political struggle for Palestine into a religious claim brought by Islam against Judaism. The implications of such a transformation were by no means all welcome to all the participants in the proposed bloc, notably Turkey and Iran; but things had not yet reached this stage, and initially the scheme would bring considerable advantages.

The revolutionary regimes at once understood the aims of the Saudi manoeuvre, and nobody in the Arab world was naïve enough to see in it an outburst of religious faith. The reactions of the socialistic states were violent in the extreme, despite Feisal's oratorical precautions. The Lebanon was understandably hostile, in view of its position on the duality of Islam and Christianity in the framework of Arab nationalism. Hussein of Jordan was the first and most enthusiastic convert. Ironically, and significantly, one of the Arab rulers most interested by the plan was Habib Bourguiba, who had shown the most determination (and courage) in his efforts to make Tunisia a truly secular state, in the French-revolutionary sense. Nothing could more clearly demonstrate the political nature of the project. In view of the mixed response to the plan, many even of the more reactionary Arab rulers thought it wise to reserve their opinion.

The project of an Islamic pact only accentuated the rift between socialistic and pro-Western states in the Arab world. The principal bone of contention was the Yemen. Nasser, enmeshed in the impenetrable jungle of the Yemeni conflict, had on several occasions tried to rid himself of the problem by a compromise with Saudi Arabia, which as we have seen supported the Yemeni Royalists, backed by the Americans and British. The difficulty was that since neither party had any decisive advantage, each was ready to compromise only up to a certain point. The affair was complicated by the private interests of the Egyptian military, by those of their Yemeni protégés, by the revolt of the Republicans against Egyptian authoritarianism, and by a thousand and one tribal squabbles. The Saudi Arabians could only be induced to withdraw their support for the Imam Badr in the framework of a general settlement guaranteeing them advantages elsewhere. But in fact, like their American and British protectors, they had throughout this period every reason to add to Nasser's difficulties. The latter, by contrast, appears to have genuinely desired disengagement for some time. But he would have had to obtain conditions enabling him to save face and not seem to be abandoning his protégés to the gibbet of triumphant reaction. He was subjected to powerful pressures by his own troops. Finally, the announcement by the British of their forthcoming withdrawal from South Arabia – which Yemeni nationalists call 'occupied Yemen' – made up his mind not to abandon a position which could shortly prove to be of paramount importance.

Many factors tended to push Israel into the background of the real conflicts in which the Arab countries were currently engaged. None could remove the elimination of this colonial enclave from their future programme. But whatever the solution was to be, it could be put off till a later date. This was what Nasser had wisely decided to do, as we have seen. His mouthpiece Haykal and he himself eventually came to spell it out more and more explicitly. The Arabs ought not to embark rashly on an adventurist war. The diversion of the waters of the Jordan was not a threat to the Arab world, and it was pointless to waste time and money on civil engineering works to divert the Jordan's headwaters in reprisal. In order to get the Arabs to swallow this counsel of restraint, Nasser declared that coexistence was not possible in the long term, and reminded his audience that the Muslims in the Middle Ages had waited seventy years for their first major victory over the Latin colony established by the Crusaders. The idol of Arabism was also anxious to prove his devotion to the Arab cause, but without running any immediate risks; he therefore delivered conditional warnings, threatening a preventive war if Israel began to arm herself with atomic weapons, and pledging military support to any Arab country attacked by the Jewish State.

However, two important factors – to stay for the moment in the Arab world – were working in the opposite direction. Two pressure-groups with telling motives for maintaining a state of warlike tension with Israel happened to find themselves in a position to do so. Both were very well aware that such a policy threatened to provoke a sharp response from the besieged Israeli fortress. They also knew that on their own they could never hope to defeat Israel if she decided, as she generally did, to resort to arms. But they counted on the force of Arab nationalist feeling in the masses to push the more lukewarm Arab states into supporting them. In any case, they had little to lose. These two groups were the Palestinian Arab organizations and the Syrian revolutionary Left.

The first Arab 'summit' in January 1964 has already been mentioned. This was organized by Nasser in an attempt to draw the sting of the Palestine question; the Arab governments were to be forced to face up to the responsibilities entailed by their brave words and gestures, and abandon the tiresome and dangerous game of one-upmanship so embarrassing to their neighbours. It was decided that those who were especially preoccupied by the problem should be given a bone to gnaw to keep them quiet. A united military command was to be set up, which would work, in a leisurely fashion, towards the establishment of a common military front against Israel. A 'Palestinian entity' was to be created to give expression to the desires of the Palestinians, who were the most interested party, without taking a form which might embarrass the constituted Arab states. This was with particular consideration for Jordan, whose King, Hussein, ruled over more than one million Palestinians.

The organization of this 'entity' – which was specifically excluded from taking the form of a government – had been entrusted to Ahmed Shukairy. This individual's rise to prominence has already been traced in an earlier chapter. He was apparently Nasser's choice for the job, possibly because of the small moral influence which he wielded, which would prevent him, it was thought, from setting himself up as an independent force and taking personal initiatives which might prove dangerous. His new appointment was greeted with suspicion by Hussein and with violent protest on the part of the previous leader of the Palestinians, Haj Amin al Husseini, ex-Mufti of Jerusalem and Chairman of the moribund Palestine Arab Higher Committee. These protests were ignored. Shukairy set about creating institutions on which he could base real power. In May 1964 a Palestine National Congress consisting of delegates nominated by Shukairy met at Jerusalem and founded a Palestine Liberation Organization, electing him as President. This enabled the Arab League to rid itself of the tiresome Mufti and to confer on Palestine some international significance. In September 1964 the League appointed Shukairy Palestinian delegate at the United Nations, and from that time on the Organization had its own seat at the League. The P.L.O. decided to create a Palestine Liberation Army (P.L.A.) from conscripts recruited among the Palestinians scattered through the various Arab countries. The Organization's budget was financed by contributions from the Arab countries and by a tax levied on the Palestinians. But since it was not a government and had no territory of its own, it depended on the good will of the various Arab countries in which the Palestinians now lived.

Ahmed Shukairy could have regarded himself as the obedient instrument of the League, or rather, since the League was by no means united either in sentiment or policy, as holding the balance between the different tendencies at work within it. This would no doubt have led him to align himself with the less militant and to stir things up as little as possible. But he was a politician schooled in factional strife, rather muddle-headed, inclined to be carried away by his own words, with a taste for the grand gesture, and capable of making two equally shattering and totally contradictory pronouncements in the same breath. He had succeeded in creating a network of clients among the Palestinians and he was anxious to keep them happy in order to retain their support. Surprising as it seems, circumstances had elevated him to a position in which he was the apparent equal of monarchs and heads of state. Ambition and interest drove him to play an independent role. However, some degree of sincere patriotism cannot be excluded from the motivations acting on this Palestinian.

He therefore took his role seriously. This implied setting a course which of necessity came into fatal conflict with the desires of some of the members of the Arab League. Hussein's reservations shortly turned into implacable hostility, not unexpectedly in view of the threat which an independent Palestinian initiative represented for the Kingdom of Jordan, swollen by the annexation of non-Israeli Palestine. Saudi Arabia, Shukairy's erstwhile patron, also became violently hostile. The Lebanon, a small country already concerned to avoid an internal explosion, was not prepared to face the powerful Israeli army with its own 12,000 poorly equipped and inexperienced troops, and she refused to harbour on her territory troops answerable to a unified Arab command. Jordan followed suit. Each feared that they might be compromised by supposedly friendly troops which might take action in the interests of their neighbours.

Shukairy and the P.L.O. found their main support in the socialistic states, Egypt and Syria, although these were never prepared to give him a blank cheque. He vilified other states which expressed their reservations. Following certain declarations by Bourguiba, to be discussed later, he demanded Tunisia's expulsion from the Arab League. In September 1965 all the demands which he presented to the Arab Summit Conference at Casablanca were rejected. The League became disturbed about the running of the P.L.O.'s budget; the Organization was reproached for wasteful and purposeless extravagance. Shukairy, thwarted by the majority of the Arab states, then sought support elsewhere. He paid a visit to Kosygin; warm relations were established between this wealthy bourgeois and the Chinese, who were by definition in favour of any armed revolutionary struggle. Mao benevolently counselled him not to attach too much importance to the number of casualties to be expected from the liberation struggle.

All this drove Shukairy to take up a position of aggression, which was to remain largely verbal. The justification for the existence of the P.L.O. was the struggle against Israel, and the Palestinians were impatient for the struggle to take on some real substance. The example of Algeria was in everyone's thoughts – a country which had just won its independence through guerilla warfare and terrorism, defeating a great nation and an extremely powerful army. Diplomacy had extracted no gains whatever from Israel. All directly concerned with the problem considered that the only effective recourse was to armed revolutionary struggle. Shukairy followed the current – or pretended to. Threats of large-scale armed raids on Israel abounded, but very little action followed. One of the major obstacles to the P.L.O. seemed to be Hussein, who refused to allow the Organization to conduct raids from his territory, since he would have to suffer the consequences. The P.L.O. made one unsuccessful attempt to overthrow him. Shukairy declared that he saw no difference between Hussein and Eshkol.

This somewhat fruitless agitation necessarily ended in splitting the Organization itself. Rivals to Shukairy appeared. Conspiracies became rife. Shukairy several times offered to resign. His 'unconstitutional methods' were attacked. Insinuations were made to the effect that his hangers-on had embezzled funds. In February 1967, his principal rival was made the object of an assassination attempt in Beirut and was taken to hospital with a bullet in his leg.

The Organization had been created to enable the Arab states, acting in concert, to canalize the claims and aspirations of the Palestinians, to keep a close watch over them and render them harmless, except when the common interest of all dictated otherwise. But the new organ had taken on a life of its own. Amongst states torn by dissension, it was able to take sides. At all events, it had brought into the foreground the Palestinian demand for energetic and immediate action, to take the form of armed intervention against Israel.

Naturally enough, those Palestinians who took this programme seriously grew impatient with Shukairy's prevarications and compromises, and with his preoccupation with the complex play of forces between the various Arab states. A clandestine 'Movement for Palestinian Liberation' had been set up some time before. This movement was determined to move into action regardless of political calculations. It took the name *al Fath*, combining the initials of its title in the Arab word meaning 'conquest' or 'victory', which evokes for all Muslims a passage in the Koran which speaks of a 'coming victory'. It set up a commando organization called *al Asifa*, 'the storm'. In January 1965 al Asifa published a communiqué boasting of a raid on Israel in which 12 Israelis were killed and 18 injured. From then on, similar communiqués appeared at fairly short intervals.

The free-lancing activities of these terrorists caused official Arab bodies considerable embarrassment. In January 1966 the heads of the Arab delegations to the Arab-Israel Armistice Commission condemned them as ineffective. Shukairy announced talks to coordinate activities. Nothing further was heard of this plan. Instead, the creation of new organizations of a similar type was announced. Their relations with those already existing were obscure. In contrast to the previous situation, a full-blown movement of armed struggle against Israel was being built up, which most if not all the Arab states were completely impotent to control.

All of these movements did, nevertheless, find an ally among the Arab states: Syria. Such support was essential to make their activities possible at all. Palestinian commandos could not very well launch their attacks from Egyptian territory, which was cut off from Israel by the Blue Berets of the U.N. and the Egyptian authorities were hardly cooperative. Jordan and Lebanon, fearing Israeli reprisals, forbade the use of their territory as a base and also tried, in varying degrees and at different times, to suppress this activity. Only one Israeli frontier was left: the Syrian frontier. Instead of hostility, the Palestinians met with the warmest cooperation.

How the Syrian Left came to power and how the most radical elements, the younger Marxist or neo-Marxist generation, came to lead it has already been described. The logic of their situation drove them inexorably into an aggressive attitude towards Israel. Ba'athist governments, after a long period of wordy inaction, had finally embarked on the social transformation of their country. Whether or not such action was praiseworthy in every respect or whether it was inadequate is not the point at issue here. The author is not in possession of sufficient documentation to enable him to give a sound judgement on this point. It is nevertheless indisputable that such a programme was undertaken. But in an under-developed country like Syria, dependent in many respects on the powerful economies of the capitalist world, every programme of social reform must come up against international interests. Furthermore, such a policy met with very strong opposition from inside the country, not only from the privileged classes but also from the lower-middle class – tradesmen and shopkeepers. Consequently the masses had to be mobilized if this programme of reform was to have any chance of success. The Ba'ath's vaunted secularism, its desire to transcend communal divisions which hindered all progressive action in these countries, the strong following it enjoyed (for various sociological reasons) among the non-Sunnite minorities, all dictated an attitude of pugnacious intransigence on the national level. The argument best calculated to appeal to the masses, which had for decades been committed to the struggle for national liberation, consisted in making the social struggle appear as the logical extension of the national struggle. No national struggle was possible without taking account of Israel. It should not be forgotten that in the 1920s Palestine was still thought of as a southern province of Syria, that the ties between the populations of the two areas were numerous and close, that Syria had 135,000 registered Palestinian refugees on her territory. Also, Syria intended to uphold what she considered to be her rights over the demilitarized zones – those very areas over which Israel claimed inalienable sovereignty, and emphasized it by cultivating them from time to time. It was extremely difficult to make an appeal for mobilization against Western imperialism while at the same time adopting a soft, conciliatory attitude towards what everybody regarded as the colonization of Arab, and more specifically Syrian, territory. This colonization was itself a manifestation of Western imperialism that directly touched Syria; it had been carried out by Western elements, and was supported by the West. Conciliation would have been difficult for any Syrian government; it would have been fatal to a leadership open to charges of cosmopolitanism, one which had claimed to want to break with the purely verbal nationalism of its predecessors, and which counted among its most ardent followers many members of those minority groups which had, in the past, often been used as instruments by foreign oppressors.

All this made it impossible for any Left-wing government to obstruct the action of the Palestinian commandos; indeed it pressed it to give its active support. However, no-one could afford to turn a blind eye to Israel's strength and the danger of the reprisals which this action might unleash. Everyone knew that Damascus, less than fifty miles from the Israeli frontier at its nearest point, could be bombed by Israeli aeroplanes minutes after take-off from their bases. All harboured doubts (rightly) as to the Syrian army's capacity to defend the Damascus road against Israeli tanks. The Syrian government's actions therefore showed the courage of despair, and could properly be regarded as irrational. Any counsel of moderation on the Palestinian question seemed a betrayal of the revolution. On 16 September 1965 the secretary of the Ba'ath for the region (i.e. Syria), Munif al Razzaz, said to the correspondent of *Le Monde* that his government did not consider that an armed conflict between the Arab countries and Israel was either possible or desirable in the short term. 'We do not know what the future holds in store for us', he said, 'and whether the Palestinian question will be decided by force or not, in view of the changes which will take place in the meantime in the world situation and within Israel itself.' He showed scepticism on the usefulness of diverting the headwaters of the Jordan. Despite his insistence on the need to prepare for the worst and set up a powerful and unified Arab military apparatus, his pronouncement aroused a storm of indignation. It undoubtedly contributed to the defeat of the Ba'athist Centre and its replacement by an extremist group. In October a delegation from a 'fraternal party', the French P.S.U. (United Socialist Party), visited Damascus. An attempt was made to work out a joint declaration with the Ba'ath containing a paragraph on the Israel question which would be acceptable to both sides. The P.S.U., of course, had no intention of endorsing the Ba'ath's warlike enthusiasm. The first draft, drawn up jointly, was rejected by the Ba'athist delegates after a few hours' reflection; it could have brought about the party's fall from power. The final text, still very moderate by Syrian standards, nonetheless provoked a wave of protests from the rank and file of the French party.

From this it may be understood why the Syrian press, official publications and radio were marked by an extreme bellicosity. The Palestinian commandos of al-Fath, the P.L.O. and other organizations were at the very least encouraged by this propaganda. The strict measures taken against them by Jordan and the Lebanon were not applied by Syria. They probably even received a certain amount of aid. However that may be, it did not prevent the Syrians from protesting vehemently, albeit illogically, against Israel's retaliatory measures. The Syrian government assumed a posture which was warlike in every respect. But it recoiled from the consequences of its own attitude. World opinion could, with some difficulty, have come to appreciate the merits of Syria's arguments against Israel as such. What it could not understand was how one could conduct an underground war and then protest at the military measures taken to counter it.

The Ba'athist leadership's despair went even deeper than this, at times. The total revolution which it desired was faced with obstacles which must have seemed insurmountable: the revolution had to be conducted on a restricted territory, unable to support itself, and without any realistic hope of unification to form a larger unit; Syria had no allies in the Arab world that were not at the same time rivals and competitors; and the Syrian Ba'ath popular following was backward and intractable. Furthermore, there was the ever-present threat of action by Syria's terrible neighbour, armed to the teeth and backed by the most powerful nation on earth. At times, the governing group was tempted to embark on a cataclysmic trial of strength, in which Syria would be annihilated, but would inflict terrible wounds on her enemy; it would be a flamboyant example of life sacrificed but dearly sold, a legacy to the Arab world similar to that once given to European socialism by the Paris Commune.

Two incidents clearly illuminated for the whole world to see the absurdity of the position in which the Arabs were placed by the installation of Israel on their territory. To recognize Israel, i.e. to establish normal diplomatic relations with her, would have meant accepting the defeat inflicted by the European-American world as final, it would have meant unconditional surrender, when in fact resources for a future come-back seemed virtually inexhaustible. Just as the United States and Federal Germany cannot resign themselves to accepting the *fait accompli* of a Communist regime in China and in East Germany, thereby declaring that the battle is over and won by their enemies, the Arab states could not resign themselves to announcing to their incensed peoples that there was nothing more to be done and that the struggle was being abandoned. This kind of situation might have been bearable as long as mutual hostility, institutionalized by the witholding of recognition, did not break out into actual military action. This had been well understood by Nasser, Hussein and the Lebanese – all of them directly involved. But a revolutionary regime like that in Syria, preaching the active engagement of the masses in a revolution at once social and national, would have condemned itself irredeemably if it had tried to halt the engagement on the front most sensitive to the mass consciousness. The contradiction was insurmountable.

In February and March 1965 the Tunisian President Habib Bourguiba went on a good-will tour through the countries of the Arab East. He visited every country in turn except Syria. He was everywhere warmly greeted by the crowds and by the rulers, who were willing to forget their old differences with him. In Jordan he was taken round the camps of Palestinian refugees. But on 6 March, at Amman, he made a declaration, and repeated it in substance on the 11th at Beirut, amounting to a proposal that Israel be recognized. He had been shocked by the wholly unrealistic conjunction of warlike phrases with obvious incapacity to conduct a real war. Faced with the violent reaction to his statements, he specified that recognition should be placed in the context of a negotiated settlement on the refugees and the frontiers, the frontiers proposed in the U.N. partition plan of November 1947 to be taken as a point of reference. This immediately aroused a point-blank refusal from the Israelis, who had at first been favourably impressed. Nonetheless, he had proposed at least partial recognition of the Israeli *fait accompli*, holding out at the end for the benefit of the dissatisfied the possibility of going back on this if the occasion, as yet unforeseen, should arise.

Bourguiba left for home pursued by the insults of the mob, by declarations of inalterable hostility on the part of the more committed leaders, and the rejection of all, with the exception of some Arab Christian politicians in the Lebanon. His realism was the realism of a man not involved in the problem. No pressures drove him to commit himself to the struggle against Israel – neither Muslim fundamentalism, nor a profound sense of Arab solidarity, nor anti-imperialist revolutionary ardour. He was a man of the Arab West, and was quite unaware of the depths of passion which the problem stirred up in the East. He would have been far more careful with his words if a similar situation had arisen in Algeria, for example. The purpose of his speech was, one might think, a perfectly rational one. But diplomatically speaking, he was compromising the value of the Arab trump-card of non-recognition by announcing from the start that he was prepared to give it up; more than this, in the eyes of the masses he was proposing capitulation without compensation of any kind. Only Israel's acceptance in principle of a discussion on the basis of the 1947 partition plan and on the return of the refugees would have saved his position. The prospects of this were extremely thin. It should be added that Bourguiba's close relations with the American camp were hardly calculated to win him sympathizers or to enhance his proposals in the eyes of the Eastern Arabs, who were likely to regard them as inspired by the Western imperialism they so hated.

The international situation could not have been less favourable at this time. Rumours abounded concerning secret negotiations on the supply of American arms to Israel, compensated it is true by similar deliveries to Saudi Arabia, Iraq, Jordan and the Lebanon. In February and at the beginning of March it was learned that Federal Germany was to supply arms and economic aid to Israel, and that she was about to accord formal recognition to the Israeli state. Such recognition was a pure formality, since close relations already existed between the two states, as intimated earlier; German reparation payments constituted one of the main sources of revenue enabling the Israeli government to balance their payments. There had been massive supplies of arms and equipment to Israel from the Bundeswehr since 1960, but it seems that a threshold had been reached beyond which the Federal German government simply redirected, with United States permission, consignments of American arms. This was an expedient to camouflage American arms supplies to Israel in order to avoid Arab reactions. But word got around. The Arabs were furious and tried to exert pressure on Federal Germany. Nasser threatened to recognize East Germany, whose President, Walter Ulbricht, happened to be visiting Egypt at the time. West Germany gave way, or seemed to, on the arms question, but stuck to her decision to establish diplomatic relations with Israel. In May 1965 this decision was put into effect. At once most of the Arab states broke off diplomatic relations with Bonn. The exceptions were Morocco, Tunisia and Libya (the German Federal Republic is the largest purchaser of Libyan oil).

Chancellor Erhard pointed out in a message to Nasser, quite logically, that seventy-eight other states maintained diplomatic relations with Israel. These included countries from the Western bloc as well as from the socialist bloc and from among the non-aligned nations. The Arab states had not broken off their relations with these states, and indeed were on extremely good terms with some. The German Chancellor might have added that the Arab states maintained good relations with states which supplied arms to Israel. Why, therefore, this sudden reaction against West Germany alone? Nasser's reply was rather laboured. He saw in the German gesture one move in a sinister large-scale operation which constituted a provocation against the Arab nations. Bourguiba, on the other hand, supported the German Chancellor's argument, showing the inconsistency of the Arab reaction.

This inconsistency was indubitable and, moreover, perfectly obvious. But the Arab gesture followed naturally from equally obvious political imperatives. Israel and the Arab states stood in a state of war, which hung fire militarily speaking except for minor incidents on the Syrian frontier. In these circumstances, the masses and the mass parties seized every opportunity for demonstrations of anger against the enemy. The news of the arms deliveries and the German recognition of Israel provided one such opportunity, among many others. The states less committed than Syria had to demonstrate from time to time that they understood and supported the aspirations of their peoples. This was an opportunity which did not cost them very much. A similar reaction against the United States, for example, would have been much more difficult and costly. Rather pathetically, the Arab governments resigned themselves to making this spectacular gesture. It meant that they lost some of the advantages of relations with Western Germany, but it was not an irreparable loss. And in any case they took good care not to press their demonstration too far, to burn all their bridges by recognizing East Germany, for instance. At least this concrete gesture added a credit to the balance of their contribution to the Arab national struggle. It may also be observed in passing that West Germany's application of the Hallstein Doctrine conforms no better with strict logic than the Arab attitude.

What of Israel? What was going on inside the besieged fortress while its enemies were dancing their war-dance around its walls? What was her reaction to the bellicose proclamations, spectacular diplomatic gestures, to Arab arms purchases, and last but not least to the small-scale military actions of the Palestinian commandos and the Syrians?

Levi Eshkol had been in power since June 1963. This old Mapai militant, previously accustomed to the ungrateful task of treasurer, had inaugurated a policy of reaction against the frenzied activism of his predecessor. Eshkol was an Israeli patriot and convinced Zionist. But he sensed the transformation taking place within the country, its ardent desire for peace, and he was determined to explore all possibilities of fulfilling the aspirations of his people in some other way than by a permanent state of mobilization, punctuated by punitive expeditions to terrorize the enemy.

The relative security which Israel enjoyed at this time helped his plans, as well as the profound transformation which Israeli society was undergoing. Israel was becoming comfortable and bourgeois. The year 1965 saw a veritable boom in industry and commerce. The standard of living rose. The per capita income reached the level of the more prosperous European countries. Of course this meant that differences between the various sections of the population became more marked. The mass of Jews which had come from the Arab countries since 1948 provided a relatively cheap source of labour, although still better paid than in the under-developed countries, especially the neighbouring Arab states. A minor economic crisis occurred in 1966; but it was characterized by an inflationary level of activity, partly caused by the pressure for a rise in the standard of living, and only reinforced the tendency to move away from the mode of living and the ideals of the Jewish pioneers.

Israel became increasingly 'normal' as a nation. The social model inherited from the time of the colonization of Palestine before independence, with its idealization of the *kibbutz* and its soldier-monks, was gradually disappearing. The life of the upper classes, mostly 'veteran' pre-1948 immigrants, was becoming luxurious. The newcomers showed little interest in the ideologies which had animated the founders of the state. The Oriental Jews, the least ideologically inspired of all, increased in numbers, and the day seemed not far off when they would be in the majority. The Israeli people was little interested in the objectives of Zionism as such. They wanted to live in peace and live well within the limits acquired by the founding fathers. Everyone was aware of the Arab menace. But a state of mind was gaining ground which favoured concessions to buy peace from these turbulent neighbours, without worrying about maintaining or extending a base to accommodate a trickle of immigrants from the European countries or elsewhere. Nowhere, moreover, was any real wave of anti-semitism apparent. Jews in every part of the world felt reasonably secure, and very few decided to emigrate to Israel. Those who retained any fervour in the Zionist ideal were content to express it symbolically through monetary donations, their militancy reduced to occasional evening meetings. Even this activity was gradually declining. It was easy to be a Zionist in New York, London or Paris. In Israel, those able to make the comparison were inclined to prefer a 'normal state' to a 'normal' state, and to recognize that the European-American world had many advantages over the Promised Land. Members of the upper echelons were fleeing Israel and accepting attractive posts offered to them in the United States and Europe. Immigration fell to an all-time low. The forecast for 1966 had predicted 50 to 60,000 immigrants. The actual number was some 15,000.

The Israeli people had become amenable to the prospect of peace initiatives by means other than those traditionally resorted to. An incident took place which clearly demonstrated this, by a kind of *reductio ad absurdum*. In February 1966 a one-time Israeli airman, who had become the owner of a fashionable restaurant in Tel Aviv frequented by a snobbish Bohemian intellectual clique, left for Egypt in a monoplane to see President Nasser. He was forced to land at Port Said, where he was received by the Governor after spending the night in the aliens' prison. After an exchange of friendly words, gifts and other courtesies, the bold pilot was given a tank full of fuel, his machine was repaired and he was despatched back home to Israel. Some Israelis demanded that he be locked up for treason; but he was greeted on his return by a delirious crowd. This mad expedition on the part of a man who might reasonably be suspected of hankering after publicity and of being slightly unbalanced ended in a massive demonstration for peace.

There were other signs, more serious, which pointed in the same direction. Eshkol had made a great show of 'energetic' gestures, declaring that his policy was in no way different from that of his predecessor. But Ben Gurion and his clique accused him of treason for being less inclined than they to a policy of punitive, or even preventive, military raids. Dayan and Peres had been obliged to resign from their posts at the Ministry of Defence. The Old Man was not reconciled to finding himself put in the wrong over the Lavon affair. He was still campaigning for electoral reform to introduce a two-party system on the British model, which would place the reins of power in the hands of a strong government. He resigned from the Central Committee of the Mapai in November 1964, setting up his own parliamentary group and founding a new party, the Rafi.

The elections of November 1965 were significant. The Rafi, associated with the names of Ben Gurion, Dayan and Peres, who stood for the maintenance of Israel's security by means of 'energetic' and dazzling strokes, suffered a catastrophic defeat. It won only 10 out of 120 seats. Eshkol received his mandate; the Mapai and its ally the Achduth Havodah (Union of Labour) returned 49 Deputies (including 4 Arabs). The Right lost ground slightly. One small event, without any real parliamentary importance, was nonetheless significant. One Deputy of a phantom party, created specially for the occasion, was elected. This was Uri Avneri, publisher of the most widely read magazine in Israel, *Ha-olam Ha-zeh* ('This low world'). Avneri, who had an excellent service record in the fighting which had ended in the creation of Israel, had long been preoccupied with the Arab problem. He had tried various ways of establishing peaceful relations, rejecting the Ben Gurion approach. He had tried to found a movement for 'Semitic' federation of the Middle East, in which Israel would be represented side by side with the Arab states. He preached the transformation of Israel into an ordinary Middle Eastern state, freed from Zionist ideology and from international Zionism. The Semitic Movement met with little success, and he then hit on the idea of broadcasting his views through the medium of a periodical attracting its readership by means of photographs of female nudes – condemned as pornographic by Israeli puritans and by his enemies. He also let fly against the restrictions imposed on the Israeli population by the Jewish clericalists, thanks to their privileged position as a decisive electoral pressure-group. He presented himself at the polls and, against all expectation, was elected. Indubitably, the majority of the votes cast for him were in support of his struggle against clerical tyranny and of his protest against a Libel Bill, which if passed would effectively gag all journalists not covered by parliamentary privilege. Yet everybody was well acquainted with his views on the problem of relations with the Arabs and he was still elected despite this.

The elections encouraged Eshkol to press his policies further. He replaced Golda Meir by Abba Even (or Eban, according to the usual mode of transcription). Eban, a Cambridge graduate, had violently attacked Ben Gurion's foreign policy, which he called 'adventurist' and 'bitter-endist'. He was disposed to explore new paths. From the beginning, he spoke of the need for the two peoples to modify their image of each other. This was to admit that the Israelis' image of the Arabs had as little validity as the Arabs' image of the Israelis, a sacrilegious assumption to traditional Zionism. Yet he was unable to offer the Arabs any more than his predecessors. His pet scheme seems to have been to induce the Soviet Union to intervene as guarantor of the status quo. It should not be forgotten that the U.S.S.R. had been one of the founders of the State of Israel and had never withdrawn recognition, although this was limited, it is true, to the frontiers of the U.N. partition plan of November 1947. Eban was encouraged in this no doubt by certain discreet signs of Soviet support for the position of the old-guard Israeli Communist Party. This Party was committed to the existence of the state, and had furthermore recently lost its Arab elements through an internal split.

Eban's policy broke with the pro-Western exclusivism of Israeli foreign policy by appealing to the spirit of Tashkent, where the U.S.S.R. had helped to soften the Indo-Pakistani conflict. He visited Warsaw – the first time an Israeli minister had set foot in any socialist country. Close relations were established with Rumania; Israel recognized the Oder-Neisse Line.

Eshkol also made some moves in the same direction. He suspended the raids on the sites at which the Syrians were carrying out the diversion of the headwaters of the Jordan. The name of the Histadruth ('Federation of Jewish Workers') was changed to 'Israel Federation of Labour', in recognition of the recent admission of Arab members. Arabs were finally accepted as fully fledged trade unionists. It was announced that the military administration still governing the major part of Arab territory in Israel would shortly be abolished.

These gestures certainly fell far short of satisfying Arab claims. But they were the first steps towards the establishment of a new climate in Israel. This new climate might some day promote a new understanding between the two camps. Before this could happen, two essential conditions had to be fulfilled: Israeli parties' policy of outbidding each other would have to cease; all apparent or real threats on the part of the Arab states would have to disappear. Neither of these opportunities for peaceful development was granted.

The new foreign policy and its approval by the majority of the Israeli people aroused the anger and indignation of the activist clique. This was the road to the precipice. The demobilization of the Israeli masses and the downward trend of immigration had to be halted. Dayan warned of the danger of 'levantinization'. The numerical preponderance of the Oriental Jews, the expected result of their greater fecundity, would have a detrimental effect on the culture of the state and on its politics. The end result threatened to be an ordinary Middle Eastern state having no use for Zionist dreams. The cultural alignment with the Middle East which these activists saw as the likely result of Eshkol's and Eban's pacifism was liable to end up as a political alignment. Ben Gurion declared: 'We do not want the Israelis to turn into Arabs. We must fight against the levantine spirit, which corrupts men and societies, and preserve the authentically Jewish values which have been developed in the Diaspora.'*

Added to these general fears aroused by the direction in which Israeli society was evolving, the old chief, full of personal rancour, suffered from a profound mistrust for the policies of his successors. At the beginning of 1966 he loudly accused Eshkol of 'irresponsible decisions' in the realm of national defence, 'acts seriously compromising the security of the nation, which could bring disaster in the four or five years which lie ahead'.† These mysterious accusations plunged the nation into perplexity. Ben Gurion sought allies to help him shake the Eshkol-Eban policy, and drew closer to his onetime hated rival, Menachem Begin, old chief of the Irgun and now leader of the Right-wing expansionist party, the Heruth. The bloody disputes of the period of struggle against the British were forgotten before the imperative need to halt Israel's current disastrous course. The Right-wing opposition joined forces and won an electoral victory, the mayoralty of Jerusalem.

It cannot be supposed that the activist clan of Ben Gurionist 'Young Turks', Dayan and Peres, remained passive. They had certainly retained close relations with circles inside the Ministry of Defence, from which they had themselves been expelled. It is thought that a 'shadow General Staff' was set up under their leadership, controlled by the Rafi. The Lavon affair (among others) had thrown light on the independent policy which various branches of the army followed when need arose – especially the Intelligence Corps. Be that as it may, pressure was certainly brought to bear on Eshkol to pursue an 'energetic' policy. He could not allow himself to be accused of softness with regard to Israel's security. It seems at least highly probable that the Army was one of the groups through which this pressure was exerted.

The actions of the Palestinian commandos of al-Fath and the P.L.O., more or less supported by the Syrians, were admirably calculated to further the ends of Israeli extremism. At the beginning of 1965 hydraulic engineers pointed out that even if the

* Reported by Eric Rouleau, *Le Monde*, 9 March 1966, p. 4.

† See Centre d'information du Proche-Orient et de l'Afrique, *Bulletin hebdomadaire*, no. 564, 10 February 1966, p. 10.

Arabs succeeded in diverting all the waters of the Jordan's principal tributaries, they still would fall well below the quantity which
had been allocated to them by the Johnston plan. An Israeli
expert further declared that the Arab project would not reach the
'operational stage' in less than twelve to fifteen years. The similarly sceptical view held by the head of the Syrian government of
the time has already been mentioned. Nevertheless, Israel resumed her attacks on the sites at which the diversion work was
being carried out in the spring of 1966, and the Israeli Chief of
Staff, General Rabin, threatened the Syrians with full-scale military intervention. Acts of sabotage on the frontier, accompanied
by inflammatory Syrian propaganda, were cited in justification
of a reprisal raid on Syrian territory conducted by the Israeli Air
Force on 15 July. At the same time Israel complained to Washington that she was getting fewer Western arms than the Arab
countries, which already benefited from Soviet arms aid. In May
a large delivery of American tactical aircraft was announced, to
be supplied at very favourable prices. In June 1966 Eshkol
replied to the violent attacks of the Rafi's First Congress that he
had won a promise from the United States to ensure that a balance
of power was maintained in the Middle East, and that this was a
revolution in American thinking with regard to the problems of
the area.

On 11 September 1966, in an interview given to the Israeli
army newspaper, General Rabin declared:

> The Syrians are the spiritual fathers of the al-Fath group. . . . The
> military engagements which Israel has to conduct in Syria in reprisal
> for the sabotage raids she suffers are therefore directed against the
> Syrian regime. . . . Our aim is to make the Syrian government change
> its mind, and to eliminate the cause of the raids.*

On the 18th, the hesitant Eshkol piped the tune called by his
Chief of Staff, as he has often done. He declared that from now on
Syria would be held responsible for all acts of sabotage committed
by terrorist infiltrators from any adjacent Arab country. This
seemed a direct threat against the Syrians, and they then sought
to protect themselves. Talks with Nasser were begun, and on 4

* See *Cahiers de l'Orient contemporain*, no. 63, December 1966, p. 43.

November a joint defence agreement between Syria and Egypt was signed. Despite the cautious declaration made on 18 November by Nasser's mouthpiece, Haykal, to the effect that the agreement did not mean 'that the Egyptian Army would immediately intervene against any Israeli attack on Syrian positions',* nevertheless a train of events had been set in motion which was to force Egypt to take direct part in the Israeli-Syrian confrontation.

On 13 November a mine exploded on an Israeli road running along the Jordanian frontier, near Hebron, killing three Israeli soldiers and wounding a further six. Eshkol refused to apply the doctrine of reprisals against Syria, officially held unconditionally responsible for all acts of sabotage. Despite undoubted pressure from activist civil and military circles, he refused to provoke Nasser into acting on the Egyptian-Syrian pact, perhaps even the U.S.S.R. into intervention on Syria's behalf. He gave way on the principle of a reprisal operation, but it was to be aimed at an apparently less dangerous point. The operation authorized was directed against the Jordanian village closest to the place at which the act of sabotage had been committed. 125 houses in the village of Samu' (including the dispensary and the school) were destroyed after being evacuated by the inhabitants. Jordanian troops appeared on the scene, and a fight started which lasted more than three hours, until U.N. observers intervened. 18 Jordanians were killed in the operation, and 134 injured. 80 tanks and a dozen French Mirage aircraft had taken part. It seems likely that the army exceeded the government's instructions, pleading the intervention of the Jordanian troops in justification. Eshkol made efforts to minimize the casualty figures, and declared that he hoped the operation would be the last and that reprisals 'were not an integral part of Israeli policy'. Eban stated on the French radio: 'Our action was originally intended to be more limited in its scope and effects than it proved in practice.'

The blow was a terrible one for Jordan, and had far-reaching repercussions. The Palestinians of the West Bank held violent demonstrations, complaining that they were being abandoned, demanding arms, accusing Hussein of weakness towards Israel and of betrayal. He was reproached for his refusal to allow troops

* *al- Ahrâm*, 18 November 1966.

of the P.L.O. and of the Unified Arab command on to Jordanian territory. The regime came close to being overthrown. Order was restored with great difficulty by the Arab Legion, at the cost of a number of casualties, both dead and wounded, among the demonstrators in Palestinian towns. No-one has ever been able to find out the exact number. To deflect the blame, Hussein accused Nasser of having remained passive. Those who spoke of Arab nationalism might at least have been principled enough not to leave him to face Israeli reprisals alone. The great Nasser could talk as much as he liked of intransigence towards Israel. The Blue Berets gave him an easy excuse for not moving on the southern frontier and for allowing Israeli military supplies to pass the Strait of Tiran unmolested.

Early in 1967 the 'energetic' measures forced through by the Israeli activist clique, thanks to the aid given them by the miniature military operations of the Palestinian commandos, supported by revolutionary Syria, had succeeded in placing the proponents of the peaceful solution – Nasser, Hussein, Eshkol and Eban – in a very difficult position. The two latter could not afford to appear to condemn action which allegedly ensured the everyday security of Israeli citizens. The parliamentary opposition was impotent; the Rafi had even split, counterbalancing Ben Gurion's move towards Begin and his 'gang of fascists', as Ben Gurion had so recently called them. Yet the Israeli rulers were subjected to a campaign of denigration which was all the more dangerous for the fact it emanated partly from activist groups with powerful support in the army. Every cause of discontent in Israel was seized upon and attributed to Eshkol and his supposed softness. Demobilization had reached its limit, educated Jews were leaving Israel, and the economic situation was worsening. A highly popular anecdote circulating at the time ran: A notice has been put up on Lod aerodrome, saying 'Will the last to leave kindly turn out the light.' Eshkol could not allow himself the slightest 'weakness.' Similarly, the Arab leaders could not allow themselves to show too much passivity, nor too much hostility towards the militant elements which expressed in their actions the general claims nurtured by all Arabs, claims which none could afford to repudiate.

Moreover the Arabs, nervous of Israel's military strength and increasingly aware that they could not forever avoid becoming caught up in the deadly merry-go-round of frontier incidents and reprisals, were led to look for outside support, in particular suppliers of arms. Syria was driven to depend more and more on the Soviet Union, who began to find this friendly base in the region really useful. Again possibly through the influence of the military, the attitude of the Soviet Union towards Syria became increasingly protective, despite the mild anti-Communism of the Syrian ruling party.

At the same time there were rumours in Europe towards the end of 1966 that the close relations established between the U.S.S.R., Egypt and Syria had led to a 'rude awakening' in Washington. The Americans were supposed to be in the process of working out a new strategy for the 'defence of the Near East' based on the two pillars of Turkey and Israel. The Arabs also caught wind of some such development.

In January 1967 the familiar sporadic firing broke out in the region of the demilitarized zones ('seasonal' U Thant called it). But it was augmented this time by firing on the Lake of Tiberias, by acts of sabotage and various other operations carried out by the al-Fath commandos which grew in strength, efficiency and organization. News of troop concentrations on both sides of the armistice line filtered out. Israeli activists demanded a reprisal raid. For instance Peres, in an interview with the French Zionist newspaper *La Terre retrouvée*, observed that the Syrians were the only ones 'never to have felt any real blow from the Israelis'. 'Perhaps the time has now come', he added, 'to teach the Syrians a good lesson.' He mocked at the 'spirit of Tashkent' to which Eban had appealed. Eshkol and Eban fought back, and made 'energetic' statements to clear themselves of the charge of softness. On 25 January the Syrian-Israeli Armistice Commission met on the bridge of the Daughters of Jacob, at the instigation of U Thant; yet Eban had in December made the startling announcement that Israel was withdrawing from this body. The two parties pledged themselves to avoid all acts of aggression and hostility. But the Syrians wanted to discuss the status of the demilitarized zones, whereas the Israelis refused to talk about anything but the cessation of frontier incidents. Israeli statements proclaimed that sovereignty over these zones was not negotiable; the Syrians tried to disarm their own internal opposition by declaring that the struggle for the liberation of Palestine would continue. A mine was discovered on Israeli territory. The discussions broke down.

Once again Eshkol was accused of weakness. The Syrian government was accused of having suspended the raids of the *fedayeen* under Egyptian and Soviet pressure. The usual pattern of events recurred in April. Eshkol gave or authorized an order that the demilitarized zones were to be cultivated. The Syrians opened fire. Before long both sides were shelling each other's positions, then Israeli aircraft intervened, shooting down at least six Syrian Migs and penetrating as far as the suburbs of Damascus. Eshkol was in practice saying to his critics: 'I am not weak. It is I who, for the first time, have brought aircraft into the reprisal raids.'

Rabin said that he hoped the Syrians would understand 'the lesson which has been administered to them'. He nonetheless considered it 'inadequate'. Israelis who were nervous of Arab retaliation were told that, as in the raid on Samu', the riposte would be a verbal one only.

The Israeli activists had succeeded in forcing Eshkol to adopt their policy, helped by Palestinian sabotage and Syrian frontier incidents. The Israeli cries of victory at the 'good lesson' which had been administered could not but incite the Arabs to revenge and banish all possibility of moves towards a peaceful settlement. Nasser in particular came increasingly under attack for remaining passive under the pretext of the curtain of Blue Berets separating him from Israel, while the Israeli generals were inflicting one 'good lesson' after another, first on the Jordanians and then on the Syrians.

Was a further 'good lesson' being prepared? The Syrians at any rate took the prospect seriously and wondered how extensive it would be this time. A flood of menacing and disquieting declarations issued from Israel. All trace of the Spirit of Tashkent had vanished. At the beginning of April Rabin declared:

Israel, and not Syria, will in future determine the form which military operations resulting from Syrian aggression shall take. On this occasion the Israeli Air Force was brought into action as a result of frontier incidents. It might in future intervene in other circumstances, and it is in the Syrians' own interest to take heed of this warning.*

Eshkol spoke in rather less harsh tones, but his words contained the same threat. An act of sabotage committed by the al-Fath near to the Jordanian frontier moved him to threaten Syria. As well, he brandished the Americans' promised support for Israel, made manifest by the presence of the Sixth Fleet in Mediterranean waters.

More than anything, this last threat sounded the alarm for the Syrians. They had long been convinced – and with good reason – that they were the Americans' pet hate, and that the U.S.A. was planning the downfall of the Syrian regime by one means or another. The danger drew closer. On 21 April the army seized power in Greece and progressive opinion everywhere – even many other sectors of opinion – saw the hand of the C.I.A. behind this coup (perhaps wrongly, but the suspicion was there). The United States, after Guatemala, Ghana and Indonesia, now turned their hand to destroying Left-wing regimes or regimes which might possibly become Left-wing in the Eastern Mediterranean. Their obstinate commitment in Vietnam, to which the U.S.S.R. submitted apparently without reaction, seemed to prove their aggressiveness and their power. The vulgar Marxist image which had taken hold of this vast sector of opinion, the image of a monolithic imperialism extending its tentacles one after the other to seize nations longing for their freedom, was all the more popular now that many facts had emerged to confirm it, its only defect being an excessive schematization. The Syrians and Nasser saw themselves as the next victims of the octopus, possibly following the Makarios regime in Cyprus. What form would the attack take? Would it come from within or from outside? If from outside, then from which direction?

General Rabin seemed to give the answer when he declared, on 12 May, that until the revolutionary regime in Damascus had

* *La Terre retrouvée*, 15 April 1967, p. 2.

been overthrown no government in the Middle East could feel safc. A few days before, the Israeli newspaper *Ha-aretz*, quoting sources in the Ministry of Defence, wrote that 'a head-on collision with Syria would become inevitable if the Syrians did not stop its encouragement of terrorist raids on Israeli territory'. On 11 May, according to the Associated Press, a high Israeli officer had threatened military occupation of Damascus in order to put an end to the acts of sabotage. The Israeli government itself advised that if al-Fath raids continued it would take drastic punitive action against Syria. Press accounts of these statements also seemed so inflammatory to U.S. State Department officials that they expressed concern to Israeli authorities.*

* See Charles W. Yost, 'The Arab–Israeli War, how it began', *Foreign Affairs*, vol. 46, no. 2, January 1968, pp. 304–320.

8 CRISIS

It is now understood that, at around this time, when rumours were circulating in Syrian governmental circles of an Israeli plan to launch an imminent attack on Syria, credence was given to these rumours.

On 8 May 1967 Nasser was apprised of Syrian fears of an Israeli attack. Suspicious, he demanded proof. Reports from the Lebanon, from Syria, from Soviet circles and from his own Intelligence services confirmed that there were Israeli troop-concentrations on the Syrian frontier. Rabin's statements published in the British press on the 13th also seemed to confirm it. It seems that Soviet reports were the decisive factor in convincing the Egyptian leader of the reality of the threat.

Was there any real threat? The Israelis deny it, claiming that their words were very far from becoming deeds (an argument which they reject when used by their adversaries). It has been claimed that an Israeli contingency plan, like those prepared by all General Staffs of whatever nation to cover all possible eventualities, had been stolen by the Soviet secret services and presented to Nasser as a plan for a real and imminent attack. It has also been said that some of the reinforcements sent to the north at the time of the serious April incident with Syria had been left there, giving the false appearance of an aggressive troop-concentration. Eshkol offered the Soviet ambassador the opportunity of verifying for himself that no troop-concentration existed. The offer was refused. Indeed a diplomat might not feel himself entirely qualified to spot military concentrations. U.N. observers reported that no concentration or major troop movements had been noticed. On the other hand, the Israelis are able to mobilize very quickly and invisibly, as they have demonstrated. No conclusive evidence is for the moment available, on one side or the other, as to the reality of the threat. The hypothesis has been advanced that the Israeli General Staff sought to give the Soviet Union and the Arabs the impression that an attack was imminent. To this end they allegedly made use of calculated leaks, perhaps – according to an anonymous French general who appears to have private sources of information – deliberately planting false information by means of radio messages exchanged by a fictitious operational network, and intercepted by Soviet ships patrolling in the Mediterranean and by Syrian and Egyptian listening posts. Of course this supposition cannot be proved, but the statements made by Rabin and by other military spokesmen certainly accord with the theory. Was the desired object merely to frighten the Syrians, as the military men who hold this theory believe? Was it hoped that by this means support for the Palestinian commando raids would be cut short once and for all? Such a hope would have exhibited a profound lack of understanding of the reactions to be expected from Syrian and Arab leaders in general – a mistake fairly common among Israeli politicians but much less likely to be made by the military, and especially not by the Intelligence services. It is difficult not to give some credit to the subsidiary hypothesis: that the situation was stirred up by the Israeli activist clique as part of a manoeuvre to provoke an Arab reaction which would force Israel to assume an 'energetic' policy and bring them back into power.

It is certain at all events that the threat to Syria was not an absurd hypothesis and that Nasser believed in it. Likewise, the Soviets undoubtedly feared an American attack (and probably a combined American-Israeli attack) on Syria sooner or later. They saw in the Israeli threats, which may or may not have been confirmed by secret information, an announcement that such an attack was imminent, and they seem to have encouraged Nasser to make some concrete demonstration of solidarity with Syria. They no doubt hoped that such a display would dampen Israeli inclinations towards possible aggression. Evidently Nasser also thought so. His solidarity had been called in question in recent months by his Arab rivals. They had all condemned his passivity at the time of the Israeli reprisal raids in November (on Samu') and April (the air-raids on Damascus). It was impossible for him to maintain this passivity. An Egyptian general was at the head of the 'unified Arab command'. He had made his headquarters in Cairo, and was in theory, responsible for the defence of all the Arab countries. At the time of the two Israeli raids, he had not lifted a finger. Nasser urgently needed to demonstrate, in some spectacular fashion, his active devotion to the Arab cause. Yet at the same time precautions had to be taken to ensure that he was not dragged into war.

On 15 May Israel organized a military parade in Jerusalem to celebrate the anniversary of the foundation of the state, at the same time demonstrating her rejection of U.N. decisions. The U.N. did not recognize any legal sovereignty on the part of the Hebrew State over the Holy City, still less the right to establish its capital or to mass troops there. Consequently the majority of foreign ambassadors boycotted this display of strength. On the same day troops, armoured cars and lorries from the south ostentatiously crossed Cairo in the direction of Sinai and the Israeli frontier. The Chief of the Egyptian General Staff was at Damascus to assure the Syrians of Egypt's support. Syria laid a complaint before the United Nations and dissociated herself from the activities of the Palestine commandos. If 500,000 American soldiers could not prevent infiltration between the two Vietnams, how was she supposed to control the Israeli-Syrian frontier better than the Israelis themselves?

However, the Syrians, Jordanians and Israelis declared themselves unconvinced by the military movements in Egypt. The old charge was levelled at Nasser once again – that he was only too grateful for the cordon of U.N. troops which prevented any Israeli-Egyptian confrontation. On the 16th Nasser made a further gesture. In the evening, a telegram from the Chief of the Egyptian General Staff, Mohammed Fawzi, was presented to the Indian general Indar Rikhye commanding the U.N. forces. This letter, which U Thant was to call 'cryptic', 'obscure' and 'unacceptable', asked General Rikhye to evacuate observation posts on the frontier. It made no reference to Gaza, let alone Sharm-el-Sheikh which is far from the frontier. The Israelis saw in this a sign that Nasser wished to make a symbolic gesture showing his determination, but no more.

General Rikhye then declared that any decision relating to U.N. troops would have to be taken by the United Nations Secretary General. Steps would have to be taken on the political level, and it was up to the Egyptian President to make direct representations to U Thant. The latter, in New York, asked for further details. He seems to have wanted to prevent Nasser from pursuing his request – itself a bluff, to his mind. He informed him that the Egyptian President had no power to order any movement on the part of U.N. forces. All he had the right to do was to withdraw the authorization accorded in 1956 whereby these troops were permitted to be stationed on Egyptian territory. It was all or nothing. It should be recalled that Israel had always refused any parallel authorization to allow a cordon of U.N. troops to form a protective curtain on Israeli territory. U.N.E.F. had hitherto been able to function effectively only because of an informal U.A.R. agreement that its force would be held 2,000 metres back from the Armistice line in Sinai (Israeli forces patrolled right up to the line).

Nasser, after some hesitation, decided that he could not now draw back. He was still subject to continuous pressure from within and without. Jordan Radio had suddenly recalled the existence of Sharm-el-Sheikh, and derided Nasser's inoffensive moves as mere gratuitous sabre-rattling. The Syrians were also harrassing him. At midday on Thursday the 18th, the Egyptian ambassador in New York presented a formal note to U Thant demanding that U.N. forces be withdrawn from Egyptian territory. The Secretary General acceded at once, for reasons which are not well understood. It is true that the Indians and Yugoslavs had threatened to withdraw their contingents from the U.N. force and that the Egyptian troops had already begun to advance on the Israeli frontier. U Thant probably thought that he would be able to defuse the dangerous train of events later, through diplomatic channels. The Secretary General received the Israeli representative who presented his government's view that the U.N.E.F. withdrawal should not be achieved by a unilateral U.A.R. request alone and asserting Israel's right to a voice in the matter. When, however, the Secretary General raised the possibility of stationing U.N.E.F. on the Israeli side of the line, the representative replied that this would be entirely unacceptable to his government.* Egyptian units immediately took up positions on the Israeli frontier. On Friday the last observation post was evacuated. Some Palestinian units from Gaza took up positions alongside Egyptian contingents. The U.A.R., Syria and Israel placed their forces in a state of alert. The world began to be seriously disturbed. The United Nations Association in Great Britain asked Israel to accept the Blue Berets on her territory. Eshkol refused.

However, the Egyptian troop movements did not yet seem to present a grave threat. The Egyptian 4th Armoured Division had not crossed the Suez Canal. The Israelis remembered a similar military concentration in Sinai in 1960, at the time of an Israeli reprisal action against the Syrians. Nothing had come of it. Now they feared some spectacular coup by the Egyptians, like an air-raid on the Dimona nuclear reactor, perhaps to be presented as an act of reprisal, but feared no real aggression. U Thant announced his departure for Cairo. It was thought that he would try to revive the Egyptian-Israeli Armistice Commission.

As yet, peace was not threatened. The Egyptian Commander for Sinai declared that a simple incident would not be enough to unleash military action. Only an Israeli attack on Syria would produce such a result. Shukairy himself stated that he had placed his troops in Gaza under Egyptian command, and that Hussein would have to be overthrown before there could be any thought of a war of liberation against Israel.

The crucial problem was that of the Strait of Tiran. From the moment that the U.N. forces left Egyptian territory, Nasser found himself without any pretext for not reoccupying Sharm-el-Sheikh, which commands the Strait and hence the outlet from the Gulf of Aqaba to the Red Sea. On Sunday 21 May, Egyptian forces replaced the Blue Berets in Sharm-el-Sheikh.

Nasser then had to make a decision on Israeli navigation through the Strait, the navigable passage of which is so narrow that the smallest firearm can prevent ships from passing. He hesitated, and Field-Marshal Amer told the Egyptian officers in Sinai that the Strait would not be closed. The Russians claimed that they had not been consulted. From 1948 to 1956 the Strait

* Charles W. Yost, *Foreign Affairs*, op. cit.

was controlled by the Egyptians, who in theory thus blockaded the port of Eilat at the head of the Gulf, a port built by Israel on the eight miles of beach which the Israeli army had conquered in March 1949. Israeli ships were not permitted to pass the Strait and foreign vessels had to inform the Commanders of Port Said or of Suez of the time they wished to cross. At the time of the Suez expedition the military post of Sharm-el-Sheikh had been conquered by the Israelis and then evacuated, under American pressure, together with the rest of the conquered territory; but Israeli troops had been replaced by those of the United Nations, and ships had been allowed free passage ever since. In point of fact Israeli ships passing the Strait were very rare, but foreign ships making for or returning from Eilat were fairly frequent. Only five per cent of all Israel's foreign trade was conducted through this route; at the same time the major part of Israel's oil supplies came this way. A pipeline which for the moment only reached as far as Beersheba, but which was to be continued northwards, carried the precious liquid towards Haifa. It was for the most part delivered to Eilat by ships not flying the Israeli flag. A canal had been projected which could one day enable Israel, and perhaps others also, to avoid the passage through the Suez Canal and still pass from the Red Sea to the Mediterranean and vice-versa.

In the night of 22 to 23 May Nasser made up his mind. In the small hours, he announced his intention to bar the Gulf of Aqaba to Israeli shipping. Shortly afterwards he specified that non-Israeli ships carrying strategic materials or oil to Eilat would also be stopped. Here at last was an action which gave the lie to all the accusations of softness and even of complicity with Zionism which had been thrown in Nasser's face or insinuated in the whole of the Arab world, even inside Egypt. The free passage of the Strait of Tiran was the only positive gain from the Suez campaign which the Israelis had been able to keep. In taking it away from them, Nasser saved Syria and at the same time won a victory – the Arabs' first victory for a very long time. He had wiped out the last trace of the Israeli victory of 1956. He had recovered Egypt's full sovereignty over the whole of her territory. None could deny it, nor continue to doubt his devotion or his contributions to the common cause.

Of course this action was fraught with danger. Nasser had weighed the risks and considered himself strong enough to face them. In March 1957 the Ben Gurion government, subject to heavy pressure from the U.N. and especially from the United States, had only agreed to evacuate Gaza and Sharm-el-Sheikh after a dogged resistance, and in exchange for the installation of the U.N. troops on Egyptian territory. Golda Meir had declared before the U.N. that Israel reserved the right to intervene militarily again if snipers recommenced their activities from their base in Gaza or if the freedom of passage to Eilat were to fall into jeopardy. Representatives of fourteen maritime powers (including the United States, France and Great Britain) had 'guaranteed' freedom of passage and proclaimed the Strait an international waterway. This might have become the object of unending and obscure controversy on a point of international law. Egypt had of course rejected this principle; at the same time she accepted the presence of the Blue Berets, so enabling it to be applied in practice. Israel delivered warnings on several occasions, stating that she would not accept that the right of free passage should ever be called in question.

No doubt Nasser thought there was a good chance that Israel would make no move – whatever he was to say a few days later. He knew that he could count on the protection of the Soviet Union and on the understanding at least of many of the nations at the U.N., and that of the Secretary General. He even had powerful friends in the State Department, and knew that Johnson, preoccupied with Vietnam, was not eager to involve himself in the Middle East. He now had all the Arab states ranged willy-nilly behind him, driven by public opinion to support him; he was in a position to drive a hard bargain. He knew that Eshkol and Eban would try to find a peaceful solution. After all, all that had happened was a return to the situation as it was before 1956.

On the 23rd he received U Thant in Cairo and concluded a secret agreement with him. No new move would be taken which might increase tension; a representative of the Secretary General would do the rounds between Cairo and Tel Aviv in an attempt to find some common ground. While waiting for a compromise to be reached, U Thant would ask the maritime powers to refrain from delivering strategic materials to Israel via Eilat. All they needed to do was use Haifa instead. Thus Egypt would be absolved from the responsibility of taking any provocative action by exercising the right of control from Sharm-el-Sheikh.

But Nasser failed to take full account of a number of important factors. He had set a mechanism in motion which was to turn on him and grind all his calculations into dust.

Up to 22 May his moves had been spectacular but innocuous. None was really liable to unleash a serious riposte from Israel. Everyone knew this very well – friends, enemies and neutrals. The situation had reached a state of tension – a commonplace occurrence. At most, all it was likely to do was to make Israel think twice before launching an attack on the Syrian regime. This had been the object of the exercise, and it was, for the moment, successful. The result was that the other Arab states and Arab movements in competition with Nasserism looked on these manoeuvres with undisguised scepticism. In their eyes this was just another Egyptian bluff, designed to polish up Nasser's image. In addition they viewed the Syrian regime with something less than warm affection and would have been delighted if Israel were to rid them of it. If Nasser were dragged down together with the Syrian Ba'athists, so much the better. Hence throughout this period Nasser and the Syrians, instead of denouncing Israel, denounced the American-Israeli conspiracy supported by the reactionary Arab states. They called for revolution against these states – Jordan and Saudi Arabia in particular. Abuse was also directed at the more distant Hassan II and Bourguiba, accusing them of being the accomplices of imperialism. Nasser rejected a suggestion to call a meeting of the Defence Council of the Arab League, declaring that Egypt was not prepared 'to reveal her military secrets to governments in the pay of the C.I.A. and the British Intelligence Service'.* On 20 May the Commander of the Syrian People's Army announced that the forces of his army 'would help to carry the war on to Palestine's usurped territory and to overthrow the reactionary Arab thrones, in particular that

* See *Le Monde*, 23 May 1967, p. 3.

of King Hussein'.* On 21 May a major incident flared up between Jordan and Syria. A Syrian car blew up while being examined by the Jordanian customs. The Jordanians alleged that the vehicle was being used by the Syrian secret service, and had been intended to explode in the centre of Amman. On the 23rd Jordan broke off diplomatic relations with Syria.

All this changed the day after the declaration of the blockade of the Strait of Tiran, 23 May. No Arab government, whatever its true sentiments, could repudiate this joint victory for the Arab people. On the other hand, there was now a serious danger of a riposte from Israel.

Sure enough, the Israeli activists were triumphant and strident in their demands. This was what Eshkol's and Eban's policy of weakness had led to. It would never have happened had 'The Old Man' been in charge, with Dayan and Peres. The press, almost entirely Ben Gurionist, kept up the refrain. Heavy pressure was being exerted on the cabinet. A renewed blockade of the Strait of Tiran had once been defined as a *casus belli*. Israel should strike back before it was too late, attack before the Arabs attacked, as they were bound to do before long. Ben Gurion would never have hesitated for so long.

The military leaders wanted to strike at once. If the Arabs attacked first, they said, the country would be in the gravest peril. Yet, in self-contradiction, they became angry when certain civilians cast doubts on the strength of the army and argued from this that the question ought to be settled via diplomatic channels. To everyone's surprise, one of these civilians was David Ben Gurion himself. The explanation lay in the fact that he felt his successors, especially Eshkol whom he had come to detest, must have been letting this army which he had forged deteriorate.

Eshkol was forced to shift his ground. From 23 May he began to grant some responsibilities to the activist opposition. He convoked the interdepartmental Committee of National Defence, and procured the participation of Dayan, Peres and Begin, among others. The generals gave a survey of the situation. A communi-

* Quoted by *Cahiers de l'Orient contemporain*, no. 67, October 1967, p. 10.

cation was read out from the President of the United States, counselling patience.

Despite opposition from the activists, Eshkol sent Eban on a round tour of all the big powers to sound out their attitudes and ask for their aid. On the 24th, Eban saw de Gaulle in Paris, who urgently advised Israel not to attack. The General-cum-President called for a conference between the four great powers – the United States, the U.S.S.R., Great Britain and France. Eban passed on to London, where Wilson told him that he would associate himself with any American or U.N. action to reopen the Strait of Tiran. On 25 May the Israeli Minister for Foreign Affairs arrived in Washington, where the Pentagon showed itself very well-informed. It had no doubt whatever of Israel's overwhelming superiority, and confidently expected that her army was about to attack. Johnson received Eban; he begged for restraint, promising him that the Strait of Tiran would be reopened by hook or by crook.

In fact the Western powers at once accepted the Israeli thesis on the closure of the Strait. Yet Egypt could bring forward what were at the very least powerful arguments in any legal discussion on this difficult question of international law. In the absence of any specific international convention, was any state obliged to grant passage, through coastal waters extending less than two miles from its shores, to strategic material intended for another state with which it is legally at war? Besides, all that had been effected was a return to the situation operating from 1949 to 1956. What precisely was the definition of an international waterway? Experts did not agree on the matter, and there was at least sufficient material for lengthy discussion before the International Court of Justice in the Hague. Yet on the evening of 23 May, Johnson had asserted that the Strait was an international waterway and that free passage through it ought to be ensured. His ambassador in Cairo proposed to Egypt a plan which would annul the effects of the latest Egyptian move. Cairo rejected the plan. Also on the 23rd Senator Robert Kennedy, speaking at a meeting of the American Jewish Association B'nai B'rith, demanded that a U.N. naval force should be sent to the Strait. On the 24th Harold Wilson, without mentioning the U.N., stated his readiness to participate in international action with the object of reopening the Strait by force.

On the evening of the 27th Eban returned to Tel Aviv satisfied with the promises made by Britain and the United States and convinced that a peaceful settlement was possible. But he found the situation at home greatly changed. The activists had gained ground – and the Arabs had given them very considerable help.

The theatrical gesture of closing the Strait of Tiran had elated the Arabs beyond all measure. This bloodless victory, representing the annulment of Israel's last gain from the Suez campaign, filled them with ardour and confidence, all the more since Israel's reaction was slow in coming and Soviet support seemed an effective counterweight to the Anglo-Saxon aid given to the Jewish State. France was a friendly neutral. Israel seemed to have been driven back into acceptance of defeat. The mob and the propagandists of the press immediately jumped from this diplomatic defeat to the conclusion that the hour had perhaps come for them to inflict the final military defeat to which they had looked forward for so many years. Their exaltation grew, expressing itself in the traditional manner of Arab prose and poetry, inspired by the braggadocio usually displayed by the fighters of the desert. The adversary was promised a thousand deaths, with the most exquisite refinements in the description of his impending annihilation, of the revenge which must surely come, of the cruelties he would be made to suffer. The caricaturists set to with relish; one would have to go back to the war of 1914–18 to find anything to compare with these vengeful drawings, in which the enemy is depicted in the most odious guise, and his forthcoming demise horribly prefigured. None could stay aloof from the general enthusiasm; even the most moderate among the Arabs were carried along by it, down to Bourguiba, so recently the apostle of peace.

Everyone was swept along by the current. The result was a sacred union based on the simplest and most universal of sentiments: the feelings of patriotism and of nationalism. Religion was enlisted in the campaign. Muftis and ulemas, as well as Christian patriarchs, all called down curses upon Israel. The Arab governments could only follow the stream. Distinctions based on political and social attitudes were no longer in fashion. Only the revolutionary leaders in Damascus resisted the flow, and adamantly refused to ally themselves with the reactionary regimes.

Nasser had at first thought military retaliations by Israel unlikely, and his secret dealings had been directed towards achieving an arrangement whereby he would retain the moral benefits of his spectacular gesture, while reducing its practical disadvantages for Israel. However, the flame which he himself had fanned was beginning to scorch him. It seems that especially strong pressure was exerted on him by the officers engaged in the Yemen and by those in Cairo who reflected their attitudes. Just like in any army anywhere in the world, the Egyptian officers, engaged in a distant war against an invisible enemy, felt themselves betrayed and abandoned by the civil power – even though governed by a lieutenant-colonel – which doled out arms and reinforcements in restricted doses and seemed at times to be bargaining with the enemy. They at any rate pressed for an energetic attitude towards Israel, demanding that every advantage should be taken of the situation, in which they thought their country now had the upper hand. Their Syrian allies also urged Nasser to assume a pugnacious attitude.

In the other direction, the Soviets now began to fear a real conflict. They were afraid that a flare-up might lead to a general conflagration and end in world war. They hesitated, urging moderation on Nasser. Very likely, they used the 'hot line' to the White House. Moscow favoured joint action with Johnson, preferring an entente between the two super-powers to the four-power conference proposed by de Gaulle. After a long delay, de Gaulle's plan was rejected (30 May). Meanwhile Gromyko had meetings with George Brown in Moscow on the 24th and 25th, while the Egyptian Minister of War also held talks in Moscow with his Soviet counterpart.

In any case, Nasser sent the 4th Armoured Division into Sinai some time on the 24th or 25th. Unsure of himself, he gave increased expression to the Arab threat, both verbally and by his troop movements. He began to consider the possibility of some military reaction on the part of Israel, perhaps even of a preventive action by the Arabs. On the 26th he declared that *if Israel attacked Syria or Egypt* the war thus unleashed would become total. The objective would then be the destruction of Israel. In reality he seems at one time to have accepted the idea that if the worst came to the worst, the Israelis would attack, gaining some ground in Sinai at first, but subsequently being halted by United Nations' intervention, which would enable a final and comprehensive settlement of the problem. The Israeli service chiefs, for their part, became increasingly insistent on attack, and accused the pacifists of treason for their shillyshallying. The press depicted Israel as threatened by annihilation unless she acted at once. The threats issued by the Arab radio and press reached paroxysms of violence, mobilizing the entire Israeli population, which saw in this propaganda the promise of its approaching doom. World public opinion reached a tremendous emotional pitch. The basic sympathy for Israel, the reasons for which have been enumerated earlier, was inflamed by the prospect that this little people, including a great number of escapees from the Nazi massacre, might be wiped out in blood and flames by hysterical mobs infinitely superior in numbers and, it was thought, in strength.

On Sunday 28 May two events of major importance took place. A meeting of Israeli ministers had been called on the previous evening to receive Eban. His report was considered disappointing. There was scepticism as to the value of the Anglo-American promise to reopen the Strait of Tiran. Must they then give way to the pleas of the military and attack? The meeting was evenly divided on the question: nine ministers were in favour and nine against. This time Eshkol was for attack, together with the majority of the Mapai ministers. Was he really convinced by the military arguments? Or foreseeing that he would be forced to follow the current, did he prefer to retain some control of it? At all events, he did not put the matter to the vote, procrastinating once again. The council dispersed at one in the morning. Shortly afterwards the Soviet and American ambassadors came in turn to deliver messages to Eshkol from Kosygin and Johnson respectively. The messages pleaded for calm. At a second meeting held the same day Eshkol, convinced by these pleas, persuaded all his ministers save one that all diplomatic measures should be exhausted before having recourse to arms. This was the doves' last victory. The generals were enraged. They hurled insults at Eshkol and his ministers, threatened resignation, and spoke of a coup d'état. Rabin declared: 'It is becoming increasingly evident that the only force which can be relied upon in this country is the army.'* Public opinion was disturbed, and found little reassurance in a hesitant speech by Eshkol. Daily threatened on the air by the Arabs, the population was won over in advance to a policy of force which, it was thought, would remove the menace.

More or less similar scenes took place in Cairo. Nasser was subjected, in secret, to increasingly powerful pressures. Field-Marshal Amer and the younger officers were on the attack. They, too, desired a preventive action before Israel moved. On the other side, the emissaries from Johnson and Kosygin again counselled patience. On 28 May Nasser gave a press conference. He appeared nervous and irritable. He, too, hoped to retain control of the current by making verbal concessions. He spoke violently, enumerating Israel's past violations of U.N. resolutions. 'If Israel wants to attack us, our answer is: You are welcome!'† The Palestinians had the right to attack, to recover the rights of which they had been robbed. 'If the war of liberation becomes a total war in the Middle East, we are ready for the struggle.'

He used a phrase which recalled the principle of permanent struggle, the fundamental refusal to accept Israel: 'We shall never accept any kind of coexistence with Israel, for the very creation of this state constitutes an aggression against the Arabs.' However, he immediately followed this statement with an indication that the door to negotiation was still open. He announced that he was ready to serve again on the Joint Israeli-Egyptian Armistice Commission, if Israel would agree to its revival as asked for by U Thant (Israel had put an end to it in 1956). The condition for this was the evacuation of the al-Auja demilitarized zone, occupied by Israel in 1955, and the installation of U.N. troops there instead of the Israelis. This would mean the return of the Blue Berets to the Egypt-Israeli frontier and Israel would in practice be recognized. He also considered the possibility of an all-embracing

* According to Eliahu Ben Elissar and Zeev Schiff, *La guerre israélo-arabe, 5–10 juin 1967*, Paris, Julliard, 1967, p. 97.

† See *Le Monde*, 30 May, 1967, p. 3.

discussion of the Palestine problem; all outstanding questions would be subject to negotiation through the intermediary of disinterested powers. In the course of the next few days, while the Egyptian head of state was delivering himself of a string of pugnacious proclamations, his own higher officials and diplomats gave peaceful assurances behind the scenes. Egypt was ready to negotiate on the right of passage through Tiran, and even through the Suez Canal, if the discussions covered the U.N. resolutions taken between 1947 and 1950 as well – resolutions which Israel had refused to apply. A really major piece of bargaining could be undertaken.

Nasser's words, the most menacing of which were picked out by the world press and by the Israelis, persuaded world opinion that an Arab attack was imminent. People everywhere took the Arabs' sabre-rattling at its face value. Of course the memory of the crushing defeat inflicted on the Egyptians in 1956 was still strong; but surely things were a little different this time? Then Egyptian and Syrian armies had been well-supplied with modern arms by the U.S.S.R. Comparative tables were drawn up showing Israel at a disadvantage. Over the eleven years which had elapsed, Nasser must surely have remedied the shortcomings of his army. Moreover this time the Arabs showed a united front (or almost). Israel no longer enjoyed the advantage of the air cover provided in 1956 by Great Britain and France.

A vital element was missing from the Arab front: Jordan. Hussein was daily covered in vituperation by Cairo and Damascus, and had no desire whatsoever to join forces with his enemies; very likely he hoped they would be defeated. He had been assured that Israel would not attack him if he made no aggressive move. He had announced that he would remain neutral. But he was won over by the general confidence in an Arab victory. If war broke out, his people would never accept neutrality, and his throne would crumble. If the Arabs were victorious, he would be all the more certainly dragged down in Israel's fall. Perhaps he was also inspired by some sincere patriotism. At any rate on the morning of 30 May he took the controls of a civil aircraft and took off for Cairo, accompanied by his Prime Minister and Chief of Staff. At 3 p.m. the text of a joint Egyptian-Jordanian defence pact which had just been signed was read out over the radio. In the afternoon Hussein returned to Amman, this time taking with him an Egyptian general and Ahmed Shukairy. Until that moment, the latter had been banned from Jordan. Now there was a general reconciliation. On the following day Shukairy reopened the P.L.O. office in the Old City of Jerusalem, which Hussein had had closed down. Also on the 31st Iraq decided to send troops as reinforcements to Jordan. Algeria and Morocco also decided to send military units.

'The world will see that in the hour of need, the Arabs will unite', Nasser had declared in his welcoming address to Hussein. It is true that the conflict had passed imperceptibly into a new phase, limited for the moment to verbal demonstrations and troop movements. This new phase was marked by the declaration of the closure of the Strait of Tiran, and was confirmed by the reconciliation with Hussein. The Left-wing Israeli orientalist, Simha Flapan, has tried to show, as against Isaac Deutscher, that the change was from an anti-imperialist phase directed against the United States with the principal object of deflecting the threat (real or imaginary) facing Syria, to a purely nationalist and chauvinist phase in which the object was Israel's destruction. This is not the case. What is true is that Nasser widened the area of dispute. From a threat intended to dissuade Israel from attacking Syria, he hoped to be able to move on to a heavier threat which would oblige Israel to negotiate on all the problems entailed by her creation. He thought that this threat might perhaps force Israel for the first time to make major concessions on the question of the return of the refugees and of the territory conquered in 1948. Here it was no longer a question of defending the Syrian regime, but of returning to the fundamental claims which no Arab could abandon. Any alliance was worth-while if it helped to frighten Israel. Moreover if the Egyptian leader could close the ranks behind him, he would have his hands free in the final grand negotiation But the risks were great. Israel might attack. Nasser thought Israel would feel herself at a disadvantage and would not do so. Was she really too weak? If so, why not attack himself, as his Right-wing critics, especially the military, urged him to do? The populace, unaware of the true balance of forces, also pushed him in this direction. There was, however, every indication that the Egyptian leader had no intention of giving way to the temptation.

The Syrians for their part were thinking chiefly of their internal problems and saw the Israeli-Arab conflict in terms of the struggle of the exploited Third World against American imperialism. They saw no reason to abandon this theory. To do so would have meant reconciliation with their enemies within and without, and the abandonment, at least partially, of their revolutionary programme and possibly in the end of their power as well. They had absolutely no desire for a war of the traditional type, which was the surest way of bringing Israeli tanks rumbling into the streets of Damascus. The Palestinian commandos' call for revolutionary struggle against Israel was far more to their taste. Certainly they threatened Israel. But they had no intention of letting the threat unleash a conventional war, nor obscure the revolutionary ideal underlying the struggle. They therefore bridled at the reconciliation with Hussein.

To make his deterrent more credible and to bring Israel to the negotiating table, Nasser needed American neutrality and the good offices of American diplomacy. The Soviet Union had no objections to such a course. They encouraged Nasser in his deterrent measures at the beginning of the crisis, designed to protect the Syrian regime, and were no doubt not unhappy to embarrass the United States. They wanted to give notice to the Americans that they would not sit idly by for ever and watch their friends and allies be coerced. Their pressure very likely helped to prevent the Americans from intervening and opening the Strait of Tiran by force. But now they were afraid that the Arabs were going too far, and that they themselves would be drawn into a confrontation with the United States for which they had no appetite. They pressed for conciliation. In the night of 26 to 27 May, at 3.30 a.m., a Soviet diplomat woke Nasser to deliver a message from Kosygin urging him not to give way to those who were pressing him to attack.

In his press conference on 28 May Nasser protested his good faith towards the United States. He deplored exhortations to blow up oil installations in the Arab countries, which had been common in the immediately preceding period. The Americans, in return, made a gesture of their own. On the 29th Charles Yost, a State Department adviser on Middle Eastern affairs, arrived in Cairo. He entered into intense private negotiations with the Egyptians.

The Israeli people, however, knew nothing of Nasser's private intentions or of these secret moves. Their attention had not been drawn to the prudent and responsible phrases, pointing to a way out of the impasse, which had followed all the vitriolic rantings. They heard the Arabs' threats, which now reached an unprecedented pitch; they saw themselves surrounded by a monolithic hostile coalition, and fully expected that if war came they would suffer a terrible massacre, which Shukairy was already promising them in lurid detail. The Jordanians were at their gates. The United States showed signs of weakening in their support. France had already abandoned them. The homeland was in danger. Every Israeli Jew was ready to defend it, even those who showed the most understanding for the Arabs' claims: sections of the Mapai, most of the Jewish Communists, Avneri, the Bohemian intelligentsia. Pressure from the service chiefs and activist politicians became irresistible now that Hussein had joined the Arab front. Eshkol was thought too weak and too vaccillating. Pressure was exerted on him to relinquish the Ministry of Defence in favour of Dayan. The Right-wing ministers threatened to withdraw their support, the generals threatened resignation. Eshkol was ready to abandon the Defence Ministry, but did not want to see Dayan take his place, fearing that he would take dangerous initiatives. He offered Dayan a ministry without portfolio, then the Egyptian command. Dayan refused. He wanted the Ministry of Defence. On 31 May the Mapai secretariat, despite Eshkol's and Golda Meir's opposition, decided to replace Eshkol as Minister of Defence by Dayan. On 1 June the government ratified the Mapai's decision. A Ministry of National Unity was formed. Begin, who had four days earlier been spectacularly reconciled with Ben Gurion, was made a minister. Golda Meir departed.

The activist group had won. Whatever the true intentions of either party at the time of the threats directed against Syria before

15 May, two weeks of crisis had sufficed to bring the militants to power, winning a post from which they could directly influence events. Dayan had the great majority of the population behind him. Terrorized by the Arab threat, they had faith in the determination and boldness of the victor of Sinai. They forgot the military leaders who had carefully been preparing the army on behalf of this figurehead. The victory of the moderates at the elections of 1965, the divisions, the party clashes, the disillusionment with Zionism, all was forgotten. Holy unity was the order of the day.

This was the moment, according to Israeli sources, at which the decision to attack was taken. The only point on which there is still dispute is the precise date. Whatever the truth of the matter, by Saturday the 3rd, in the morning, the divisional commanders received their orders to attack on the following Monday. To increase the element of surprise, many troops were granted sabbatical leave. Dayan gave a press conference on the same Saturday, spoke of patience, and said that, together with the rest of the government, he would await the outcome of the diplomatic approaches then being made.

In the Arab camp, the verbal intemperance continued. Shukairy especially distinguished himself, declaring that after the coming war there would be practically no survivors. He announced that it was possible, even probable, that the Jordanian army would fire the first shot. Hussein and Nasser, who stuck to their policy of wait-and-see, were horrified. The Jordanian press censored some of the remarks made by the head of the P.L.O. and Shukairy himself was obliged to swallow some of his words. Disunity was rife, despite the recruitment of Iraq, on the evening of Sunday the 4th, to the Jordanian-Egyptian defence pact. This same pact was still rejected by Damascus, and the Syrian press withheld announcement of it. Instead, news was published of disturbances in the Jordanian army, where revolutionary elements were said to be bridling against Hussein's hostility to Syria. The Algerians too denounced this alliance with a pro-Western monarch, who sullied the purity of the revolutionary Arab movement. Saudi Arabia was also upset by the pact, for opposite reasons, and suspended arms deliveries to the Hashemite king – an unreliable ally, now in league with her enemies. The United States, on whom practically half of the Jordanian exchequer depended, applied similar sanctions against Hussein.

No doubt the pressure on Nasser continued to grow. Amer and some of the army feared that Israel would strike the first blow. Hussein thought, and stated, that he was afraid the Israelis would profit from a moment's inattention. But he did not think the danger immediate, and did not therefore urge attack. The Syrians, too, thought they could make substantial gains through diplomatic action, without giving up the idea of eventual guerrilla war, and it seems that this was the burden of the Syrian Foreign Minister's discussions with Nasser.

Nasser feared an Israeli attack, and must have been tempted to launch a preventive action. He was very well aware of the Israelis' exasperation. However, he had little faith in his Arab allies. He knew that American public opinion, as well as a large part of the Administration, was hostile to him, that they would not forgive a military attack on his part. Both the United States and the Soviet union continually urged him to show patience. Soviet diplomats must have promised that, in return, the Americans would prevent the Israelis from attacking, and it is true that both the Soviets and the Americans made similar representations to Eshkol. Nasser therefore stepped up his diplomatic activity. The crisis was so grave that Israel would surely take fright and make concessions. Nasser kept the bidding very high, but he did leave room for negotiation. In the Security Council his representative put forward a draft resolution which once again proposed to take advantage of the situation to achieve a general settlement. Israel would be enjoined in accordance with U Thant's requirements to revive the Egyptian-Israeli Joint Armistice Commission, which would have its headquarters at al-Auja in the previously demilitarized zone, occupied by Israel since 1955. This was an open invitation to return to the conditions which followed the 1948 war, including what had amounted to *de facto* recognition of Israel. At the same time it would mean ratification of the *fait accompli* at Tiran. The proposal met with Western opposition. Nasser was made to realize that he was asking too much, and that the most he could expect was an agreement which would allow him to retain some of the benefit of his gesture in blockading the Strait – viz. recognition in principle of Egyptian sovereignty.

In Cairo Johnson's envoy, Charles Yost, concluded a secret agreement in principle with the Egyptian Foreign Minister. Diplomatic channels were to remain open. Egypt would not object to the question of the Strait of Tiran's being put before the Court of Justice in the Hague. Nasser's second-in-command, Zakaria Mohieddin, First Vice-President of the Republic, was to visit Washington to negotiate a compromise. Egypt was inclined to allow oil through the Strait of Tiran, limiting her controls to strategic materials. On 3 June Yost left Cairo, having given an assurance that Israel would not attack as long as diplomatic activity was maintained. Both Moscow and Tel Aviv were informed of the attempts to achieve a compromise which were under way. It seems however that Left-wing ministers were not informed, still less was public opinion. The Soviet Union was very alarmed at the prospect of war, and let it be known in the corridors of the United Nations that she might be induced to accept the four-power conference proposed by de Gaulle. They wanted to know if Israel would accept a compromise like that to be negotiated by Yost. Diplomatic circles, notably the British, turned their attention to solving the problem: to safeguard Israel's existence in return for a concession to Nasser enabling him to keep some of the winnings of his gesture and to save face.

Public opinion everywhere feared an Arab attack on Israel, while the diplomats were more afraid of an Israeli move. In London, New York, Paris and elsewhere demonstrations of support for Israel multiplied. Shukairy's threats and the cartoons in Syrian newspapers were enough to show that Israel's annihilation and the general massacre of her inhabitants was imminent.

On 2 June de Gaulle, who had just received the Syrian Foreign Minister, announced that the state which first resorted to arms would have neither the approval nor the support of France. He again put forward the idea of a four-power conference to work out solutions to all the outstanding problems concerning Palestine. He was visibly supported in this by both the Egyptians and the Syrians.

Public excitement both in Israel and in the Arab countries had reached fever-pitch. The propaganda war seemed to show that war was inevitable. Therefore why not get it over with? It was not thought necessary to inform the Israelis of Yost's negotiations nor of the Egyptian concessions then being formulated. The Israelis wanted to react to the menace hanging over them and which they thought very serious. They would win the victory, or die fighting. The Arabs, intoxicated by their own propaganda, believed in their military superiority. Therefore it was time this poisonous problem were done away with. The Arab peoples were moreover completely unaware of the sufferings which such a conflict could entail for themselves. Their armies were powerful and well equipped. They would win without any trouble.

The Egyptian and Syrian governments thought that the war of nerves and Israel's apparent diplomatic isolation would force her to yield, and prevent her attacking. The only remaining problem was the extent of the concession which could be obtained.

The Israeli government was of the same mind. The diplomatists would force them to yield up something of that which they had till then clung to with such tenacity. At most, the return of the refugees and the evacuation of the occupied demilitarized zones, possibly even more. At least, they would have to yield something of their present absolute freedom of passage through the Strait of Tiran. In return it would be possible for them to obtain some sort of *de facto* recognition, a kind of declaration of non-belligerence. But this was not enough.

Did the military chiefs and the activist clique really believe that if the Arabs struck first they had a chance of success? It seems unlikely. The Commander in Chief of the Israeli Air Force is said to have informed Eshkol that he could take his time: whatever happened, the Arabs' air power would be liquidated in the first attack. But these elements did believe that such an attack by the Arabs would at least make their own plans for aggression more difficult to put into practice. The possible gains to be had by diplomacy did not seem to them worth the human and strategic sacrifices it would mean for Israel. Some, at any rate, thought less in terms of defence than of attack. It was an ideal point at which to strike a heavy blow and administer the promised 'good lesson' to

the Arabs. After that the diplomats could have free rein. Infiltration and sabotage would be stopped; at the very least there
would be some readjustment in Israel's favour of the more
strategically disadvantageous sections of the frontier. At most –
the sky was the limit.

Civilian leaders and the more pacific of the politicians were
afraid of a kind of second Munich. They were afraid of the Arabs.
Any peaceful solution without first some demonstration of force
would entail Israeli concessions. The major powers would perhaps
be able to enforce these concessions. Concessions are only possible
between nations which have a certain degree of confidence in one
another. But no Arab dared lay emphasis on the advantages which
Israel could win from these concessions, on the guarantees which
could be granted to her, even if secret negotiations did highlight
these points, and although some reading between the lines of
Arab declarations allowed them to be deduced. From that time on
every concession was considered to be a dismantling of one of
Israel's defences, a stage in the progress to that destruction which
a thousand virulent pronouncements promised them. The Israeli
population felt themselves physically threatened, and it is
undeniable that the Arabs gave them some cause to feel so. Everyone remembered Munich, where the abandonment of the
Sudetenland forced on the Czechs by the great powers and morally
justified in the name of national self-determination led to Czechoslovakia's subjugation the moment her defences had been
breached.

The installation of the Israeli colony had conditioned the Arabs'
reactions. Arab reactions in turn affected Israeli attitudes. The
Arab position of moderation in practice could not carry the day,
given the obligatory verbal intransigence imposed on every Arab
ruler, and the signs of impending guerrilla warfare. The Israelis
did not, in such conditions, have enough reason for confidence in
the safety not only of their state and institutions but of their very
lives. No-one in Israel had arguments strong enough to maintain
against the activism which believed in safeguarding the state by
demonstrations of force, by rebuilding the country in the shape of
a modern Sparta, hard and pure. On Monday 5 June, at 7 in the
morning (Israel time), the Israeli air force left the tarmac. Less

than two hours later, the Arab air force had to all intents and purposes ceased to exist. The war, which was to last another six days, was virtually won.

What then?

9 CONCLUSION

The aim of this book has been to give the reader a picture of the broad outlines of the Israeli-Arab conflict. The study has been historical in essence, with a few fundamental sociological observations included here and there. Some of the assertions made may appear astonishing, since they go against widely held opinions. Nonetheless they have in every case been scrupulously documented, and in other works which, unlike the present study, demand the deployment of an academic armoury I have quoted the arguments and references which support them.* Of course this does not mean to say that the arguments which I have advanced are irrefutable. I am no more infallible than anyone else in the selection and evaluation of facts. I merely wish to point out to those disposed to contradict me that their criticisms will have to be more firmly based than on assertions which they believe to be undeniable simply because they are current in their milieu or country. They will likewise have to bring forward attested facts, supported by serious documentation.

The facts in themselves are of course numberless. Like every historian, I have had to be selective in recounting them. I have chosen those facts which seemed to me to illuminate aspects of the conflict which are fundamental. Here again it is possible that I have made mistakes. But those who would contradict me will have to show that the facts which they adduce – given that they are well-

* See particularly: M. Rodinson, 'Israel, une lutte de libération nationale' (*Partisans*, No. 21, June–August 1965, pp. 34–40); 'Les Arabes et Israel' (*Revue française de science politique*, vol. 16, No.4, August 1966, pp. 785–98); 'Israël, fait colonial' (*Temps Modernes*, No. 253 bis, 1967, pp. 17–88); 'The Israeli-Arab War and the Future of Socialism' (*International Socialist Journal* [Rome], No. 22, August 1967, pp. 503–18).

attested – will throw light on an aspect which I have overlooked and which refutes one of my conclusions.

Such observations may seem self-evident, and so they are. A historical or sociological analysis can usually dispense with them. But the problem with which this book deals has aroused an unusual flood of passion. Rarely has opinion been so one-sidedly informed; the information available to it further reinforced an already strong tendency to make judgements favouring one particular side of the question. It must be admitted moreover that these tendencies partially sprang from highly honourable, even praiseworthy motives. Unusual precautions have therefore been doubly necessary.

The facts which have so far been advanced, with the minimum of argumentation accompanying them or entailed by their selection, are intended to enable the reader to form a well-founded judgement of the nature of the Israeli-Arab conflict. The author begs leave to give his own opinion on this matter and on the future possibilities as he sees them. The reader may accept or reject them. At least he will know on what these conclusions are based.

The immediate causes of the war of June 1967 could be discussed *ad infinitum*. The study made above, based on documentation available to the author in December of the same year, is of necessity provisional in character. Many facts are still unknown and will come to light only gradually, some no doubt only after a long period has elapsed. The details of crises of this sort, with their inextricable web of political, diplomatic and military manoeuvrings, is always very difficult to unravel. Who was it who initiated such and such a move? Why? What results did he expect to achieve? The disputes continue – for example on the immediate causes of the war of 1914–18. The discussion of the origins of this last conflict is likely to go on for as long and prove as complex. I readily accept that my opinion of the matter may need to be revised in the light of new evidence.

On the other hand it is easy to form a judgement as to the more fundamental causes of the conflict of which this war is only the most recent and the most spectacular manifestation. The pertinent facts are well known and abundantly documented.

The origin of the conflict lies in the settlement of a new population on a territory already occupied by a people unwilling to accept that settlement. This is as undeniable as it is obvious. The settlement may be justified, in whole or in part; but it cannot be denied. Likewise the refusal of the indigenous population to accept it may be thought justifiable, or it may not.

This was, indeed, a new population, radically different from the old. It is true that it claimed to have inhabited Palestinian territory in ancient times, to have formed a state there of which it had been forcibly dispossessed and from which it had been forcibly driven. With certain reservations this is true, as everybody knows. It is generally admitted that a people continues to be such, as a collective entity, however many times its constituents are renewed. In the case of the Jews the number of renewals since Antiquity has certainly been enormous, but this is consequently not a pertinent factor. Moreover while the Jewish people certainly did witness the destruction of their state by force (by the Romans), they were not driven from Palestinian territory except to a very minor extent. More serious is the fact that the Jews, while they incontestably were one people in Antiquity, could later no longer be termed such except in a very special sense. Even in this special sense they lost the characteristic from the time of the emancipation, which differed from country to country. From that time they ceased to be a collective entity, but individuals connected sometimes by ties of religion, sometimes and in some countries by a common but localized culture (so that several distinct 'Jewish peoples' emerged), sometimes simply by the memory of a common ancestry (again only partial). Nonetheless, for the sake of argument and to simplify matters, it may be accepted that those Jews who wished once again to form a Jewish people and a community of the national type, were continuing the Jewish religious community of the Middle Ages, which retained certain national characteristics, and, beyond that community, the Jewish people of Antiquity.

This in no way diminishes the difference. Certainly the Zionist Jews who were 'returning' to Palestine were in some measure anthropologically 'related', in the physical sense, to the Palestinian Arabs. Despite innumerable mixtures of blood they must, in very differing degrees, have included among their ancestors Jews from ancient Palestine, and have retained something of those ancestors in their genetic heritage. Moreover in spite of an equally large number of admixtures, the basis of the Palestinian Arab population, as explained earlier, must likewise have been descendants of these same Jews or Hebrews of Antiquity. But this implies no homogeneity between the two peoples in the sociological sense. What does count, if at all, in the conflicts and compacts between peoples is the identification as a people, or as an ethnic group. The English, the French, the Spaniards, the Germans also have a great number of ancestors in common and are the bearers, in different proportions, of the same genetic heritage. This fact has not in the very least prevented wars between them, nor the desperate assertion of independence of the one on the part of the other, nor a hatred which has often reached a pitch which it would be difficult to exceed.

The same is true of the linguistic relationship, often misleadingly defined by the assertion that both peoples are 'Semites'. This means one thing only, that the Hebrew and Arabic languages are linguistically related, they derive from the same root tongue, they both belong to the linguistic group conventionally termed 'Semitic'. The Hebrew language was the ancient tongue of the Jews, and had become a dead language some centuries before the Christian era. It had been preserved as an erudite, 'holy' tongue, to some extent as a literary language among the Jewish communities, and was resuscitated in the twentieth century by Eliazar Ben Yehuda to serve as a living tongue, common to Jews of different origins called to colonize Palestine. It should be noted in passing that the great majority of Zionists did not know this Semitic tongue, neo-Hebrew, when they first set foot on Palestine soil, although they were shortly to learn it. However, none of this is of the slightest importance. Kinship between languages (often implying some anthropological kinship, in very different degrees, between some at least of those who speak those languages) has never prevented antagonism between peoples. The Spanish and the Portuguese have often been in violent opposition to one another, although Portuguese is only another Iberian dialect. The French of the '*Langue d'oil*' in the north conquered by force the France of the *'Langue d'oc'* in the south, despite the fact that the southern dialects are fairly closely related to those of the north. The Pakistanis and the Indians speak Indo-Aryan languages, sometimes the same ones. Is it necessary to recall the bloody struggles between the Greek city-states? To repeat: what counts is the identification as a special unit or ethnic group.

Palestine therefore was being populated anew. Not only did they have no community of identification, in the sociological sense, with the native inhabitants, their difference was also accentuated by a gross cultural disparity. The great majority of the newcomers spoke a different language from the local population in more senses than one: they had different values, different customs, different modes of behaviour, different attitudes to life. They were altogether of a different world – the European world. Not only were they foreigners, they were also Europeans, that is to say they came from that world which was everywhere known as the world of the colonizers, of peoples who dominated their neighbours by their technical and military power and by their wealth. That they may have been the poorest and most underprivileged of this other world mattered not – they were of it.

The only ones in whom the difference was not so marked were the Oriental or Orientalized Jews, such as already lived in Palestine. But the moving spirits of the Jewish colony and then of the State of Israel regarded them as backward elements, which somehow had to be assimilated. They had to be impregnated with the values of the Western Jews, their social customs and their attitudes would have to be made to conform. The numbers of these Oriental Jews became very great in the years which followed 1948, mainly through the emigration to Israel of Jews from the Arab countries. These were undoubtedly much closer to the Arab population of Palestine. Indeed many of them might, if the problem had followed a different line of development, have become or remained Jewish Arabs; they even spoke various dialects of the same language. However, they were sharply divided from the Muslim and Christian Arabs by communal hostility and a long-standing grudge; as well as this, the Western Jews conducted a vigorous campaign to assimilate them, fearing 'levantinization' of the state more than anything else. Hence these Middle Eastern

Jews tried to model themselves on their Western cousins, whose culture they envied. I should like to quote an example insignificant in itself, but symbolic of what was happening. The Yemeni Jews, who pronounced Hebrew with its ancient Semitic consonants, which appear in the written language and are preserved in their Arabic vernacular, are making strenuous efforts, in Israel, to lose these 'bad habits'. They are learning to repronounce Hebrew in the manner of the European Jews, i.e. leaving out consonants which the latter have forgotten how to pronounce for twenty centuries, confusing others, etc. In other words, they are moving as far as possible away from the standard of the Hebrew once spoken in Palestine in ancient times, and away from the Semitic model which they had partially preserved.

A foreign people had come and imposed itself on a native population. The Arab population of Palestine were native in all the usual senses of that word. Ignorance, sometimes backed up by hypocritical propaganda, has spread a number of misconceptions on this subject, unfortunately very widely held. It has been said that since the Arabs took the country by military conquest in the seventh century, they are occupiers like any others, like the Romans, the Crusaders and the Turks. Why therefore should they be regarded as any more native than the others, and in particular than the Jews, who were native to that country in ancient times, or at least occupiers of longer standing? To the historian the answer is obvious. A small contingent of Arabs from Arabia did indeed conquer the country in the seventh century. But as a result of factors which were briefly outlined in the first chapter of this book, the Palestinian population soon became Arabized under Arab domination, just as earlier it had been Hebraicized, Aramaicized, to some degree even Hellenized. It became Arab in a way that it was never to become latinized or Ottomanized. The invaded melted with the invaders. It is ridiculous to call the English of today invaders and occupiers, on the grounds that England was conquered from Celtic peoples by the Angles, Saxons and Jutes in the fifth and sixth centuries. The population was 'Anglicized' and nobody suggests that the peoples which have more or less preserved the Celtic tongues – the Irish, the Welsh or the Bretons – should be regarded as the true natives of Kent or

Suffolk, with greater titles to these territories than the English who live in those counties.

The native population did not accept the settlement of what must be regarded as foreigners, who, moreover, presented themselves as colonists, as is demonstrated by the titles which they gave to their own institutions. Again, the Arabs have been condemned for this. Without for the moment attempting to assign moral values to the various attitudes which might be taken, it must be made clear that their reaction was entirely understandable. It is certainly true that at other periods alien peoples have succeeded in imposing themselves on a given territory, and that sooner or later custom and law ratified the deed. Usually this was initially effected by force. The best example for present purposes is furnished by the Arabs themselves. The Arabs imposed themselves by force and the native population gave little resistance, then allowed itself to be assimilated by its conquerors. But this native population was already subject to foreign rule, and merely changed masters. Similarly, when Jewish colonization first started, the Palestinians were subjects of the Ottoman Empire, which was dominated by the Turks. Why not accept the new domination which might, as in earlier times, have been followed by assimilation?

This might indeed have happened were it to have taken place some centuries or even some decades earlier. But the Zionists were unlucky. The conscience of the world has developed, and no longer accepted right of conquest, or accepted it more reluctantly. Cultural assimilation between peoples is possible; but each people now tends to cling fiercely to its own identity. This is a fact that nobody can do anything about. Zionism began as a living force in the era of nationalism, of which it was itself a manifestation, and it pursued its career during the era of decolonization. Peoples are no longer willing to accept conquest and will fight to preserve their identity and to keep or win back their independence. Once delivered from Turkish tutelage, the Palestinian Arabs desired domination neither by the British nor by the Zionists. They wished neither to become Englishmen nor Israelis, although they accepted gratefully many elements of that European culture which both brought with them and which the Arabs had slowly been absorbing in small doses for a long time. They wanted to keep their Arab identity, and therefore they wanted to live under the rule of an Arab state. In view of the division of Arab Asia Minor in 1920, they tended to form a Palestinian national community within the framework of the various different Arab national communities, which were pledged to some degree of unity in accordance with certain widely held conceptions. They consequently hoped to see an Arab state in Palestine. Moreover the conscience of the world now supports peoples fighting to defend their identity. It seemed to the Palestinians a flagrant injustice that an exception should be made of them on the sole grounds that the colonists were Jews. The whole world was proclaiming 'Down with colonialism!' They had recently seen many Frenchmen renounce the proviso ' – except for French colonialism' and many Englishmen their proviso ' – except for British colonialism'. All they wanted was to do away with the reservation ' – except for Jewish colonialism'.

The natives had not accepted the foreigners. One point remains to be clarified. The Arab world has frequently accepted foreign settlement on its territory – witness the example of the Armenians, fleeing from Turkish persecution in 1920, who came and settled in the Arab countries. Many had come even earlier than this. As a general rule, they had been accepted. Yet the majority of the refugees, especially those in the latest migration, wanted to preserve their identity as a people, their language, their culture, their own special traditions. It is possible that if this partial refusal to assimilate persists it will one day be the source of conflict. Nonetheless up to the present time, there has been no hostility towards them comparable with that felt towards Zionist immigration. To all appearances this is due to the fact that the Armenians had no intention of constructing an Armenian state in territory populated by Arabs. If they do still harbour any claims of the 'Zionist' type, these relate to territory which is currently Turkish. Similarly no opposition to Jewish settlement existed until Jewish immigration took on its Zionist aspect. Arab opposition manifested itself the moment that the Zionist intention to establish a Jewish State by detaching Palestine territory from the Arab world became clear. This opposition mounted as the true nature of the Zionist project became obvious, and grew more irreconcilable as the Zionists came nearer to success. Therefore the Arabs were not rejecting the foreigners as such; they were rejecting foreign occupation of their territory – whether we choose to classify this phenomenon as colonialism or not.

The conflict therefore appears essentially as the struggle of an indigenous population against the occupation of part of its national territory by foreigners. Of course there are many other sides to the conflict which could be brought out. None of these, however, seems relevant to its basic definition.

I have often been reproached with not taking sufficient account of the millennial Jewish vision of the Return to Zion, the nostalgia for the lost homeland conveyed in Jewish literature and folklore, the settlement by individuals and small groups of Jews in Palestine. In answer it must be said that Zionism has inadmissibly reinterpreted religious aspirations in terms of modern nationalism. These religious aspirations hinged upon a messianic vision of the end of time, when the final Golden Age would unfold in Palestine. As has been explained above, for many years the Zionists had no more implacable enemies than the Jewish rabbis. On the other hand, it is possible that the religious vision itself contained an element of primitive nationalism. Zionism could then be viewed as the secularization of a religious tendency with a partly nationalist content. This proposition would need closer study. Whatever the truth of the matter, it is hard to see how an analysis of these tendencies – with all the sympathy and admiration which some might feel for them – is relevant in defining the basis of the conflict. When a people is subjected to foreign conquest, the moral wound it receives is in no way alleviated by the spiritual tendencies observable within the conquering group, nor by the motives for the conquest or the aspirations which they express.

The same is true of the qualities and defects which may be ascribed to the Jews – even if these qualities and defects were better attested than is generally the case. Again, the same applies to the sufferings of the Jews. Those sufferings might, perhaps, justify the aspirations felt by some Jews to form an independent state. The Arabs cannot be made to see this as sufficient reason why such a state should be formed at their expense. To stretch a point, the idea of the collective guilt of the Germans might be invoked to justify Czech reoccupation of the Sudetenland and the amputation of German territory to the East in favour of Poland. But no collective guilt of this sort attaches to the Arabs for the sufferings undergone by the Jews in Europe. They are perfectly justified in maintaining that if the Europeans feel responsibility for the Jews, it is up to them to provide them with a territory, not to make the Arabs give up some of theirs. Many Arab spokesmen have stated that they are ready to make a contribution to international aid for Jewish victims of persecution if such aid were decided upon, but only on a reasonable *pro rata* basis. They are not willing to pay the full reparation for wrongs committed by others. There can be no possible objection to such a position.

It may be interpolated here that Zionism has not fully achieved its desired objectives. It has, indeed, created a Jewish State. But the creation of that Jewish State was not regarded by the Zionist pioneers as an end in itself, only as a necessary condition for the achievement of other ends. These ends were the regeneration of the Jewish people, supposedly 'alienated' by the Dispersion; and the liquidation of anti-Semitism. However, just as after the 'Zionism' of Zorobabel in the sixth century B.C., the number of Jews remaining outside Israel is much greater than the number which has 'returned'. The creation of Israel has undoubtedly had an effect on their mentality, but this effect has been less uniquely fortunate than foreseen or maintained by the Zionists. As for anti-Semitism, while it has greatly declined in virulence, there is nothing to show that the existence of Israel has had any significant effect on this development. Moreover it concerns only Western Europe and America. In the U.S.S.R. and the People's Democracies at the end of the Stalin era, the Zionist ideology and the creation of Israel were a powerful factor in the resurgence of official and ill-disguised anti-Semitism. In the Arab countries, above all, Zionism has led to an anti-Zionism which could hardly fail, as has been seen, to result in many cases in anti-Semitism. Very many Jews in the Arab countries have discovered this, to their own misfortune. Finally, life in an Israel under continual

military threat hardly seems an ideal alternative to life in the
Dispersion under the threat of a possible rebirth of anti-Semitism.
At all events the Zionist contribution towards solving the 'Jewish
problem' has been ambiguous, to say the least.

In just the same way, the qualities and faults which may be
attributed to the Arabs, and the various judgements which might
be expressed on their political or social structures, have no bearing
on the analysis of the nature of the conflict. It is self-evident that
no-one has the right to make the lordly judgement that a people
or group of peoples has such faults that it deserves to have slices
of its territory forcibly taken away. Pharisaical judgements of this
kind have been made by many conquerors in the past; but they
are repellent to the contemporary conscience. In any case, no
arguments which could be advanced on this level would alter the
fact that the struggle is one between a native population and
foreign occupiers.

Nor is it, as has often been claimed, a struggle for development.
It is indubitable that Israel has brought to the Middle East the
example of a more highly developed society, industrialized or on
the way to becoming so, technically advanced, with a large and
valuable technocracy. Her superiority in this respect over the
surrounding countries is undeniable, and her victories are merely
the manifestation of this fact on the military plane. But the case
is exactly the same as that of the European colonies which did
not eliminate the populations at whose expense they installed
themselves. The technical lessons to be learned from the invader
were in every case accepted, in principle at least. Nevertheless
the local population revolted against the domination or annexation
imposed from outside. The value of Israel's example is diminished
to the extent that the Arabs can take their lessons from many other
sources, from Europe direct or from America, for instance. They
do not need to pay for them by the cession of territory. Moreover
the enemy may be admired, even imitated, as witness France's
attitude towards her conqueror Germany between 1871 and 1914.
This in no way diminishes the hostility and desire for revenge
which the conquered feel towards the victorious conqueror.

Again, the struggle is not a struggle for democracy. It is true
enough that Israel has parliamentary institutions which may be

regarded as models of their kind. This does not mean, any more than it does elsewhere, that the will of the majority of the population and its interests are bound to prevail over the wishes and interests of small but economically or politically powerful pressure-groups. In any case, Israel's political institutions are intimately bound up with her high level of economic development. Once again, there are other examples which the Arabs could turn to, and the value which they might attach to such institutions in no way reduces their hostility. It should be added that given the social, economic and cultural conditions of the Arab nations, the most perfect parliamentary system would only ensure that the most reactionary social groups would be guaranteed power. Parliamentary institutions are not the panacea that the Americans take them to be. This is well illustrated by the case of Egypt between 1923 and 1952. The illiteracy of the masses and the great social power wielded by the large landed proprietors meant that universal suffrage merely underwrote the political power of the latter class. Moreover when the state has to make choices which entail drastic limitations on popular aspirations in order to make the investment necessary to development, it may be said that parliamentary institutions are the enemy of economic development.

Neither does the conflict reside in the struggle between Israeli socialism and the reactionary or Fascist Arab societies, as one version fairly widely accepted in some Left-wing circles would have it. The Zionists settled in Palestine as pioneers of a Jewish State, not as apostles of socialism. I have already given my opinion on the interpretation to be placed on the socialist ideological currents in Israel and on the socialist sector of the Israeli economy. At the very least, it may be said without reservation that Israeli society is not as a whole a socialist society, and that the State of Israel's foreign policy is not directed towards the extension of the socialist system. The Arabs are not opposing the propagation of socialism, but an expansionist encroachment on their national territory. If the Arabs wanted a model, they could find it elsewhere; even if they were to imitate some of Israel's achievements in some respects, this would not weaken their hostility.

The contrary thesis, according to which the struggle is one

between Arab socialism and Israeli colonialism, stands on firmer ground, but is not wholly acceptable nevertheless. It is true that Israel is a colonial phenomenon. But only some of the Arab states have a structure which may, in part, be classified as 'socialist' or are ideologically oriented towards socialism. The others accept the ideology of free enterprise, or ideologies which are older still, and their structure exhibits a mixture of archaic and capitalist features. In their attitude to Israel, however, they all stand united, whether they would or no, at least at times when the problem reaches crisis-point. Their claims are the national claims supported by the Arab people as a whole, which no Arab state dare oppose, whatever its internal social structure. It is true that, on a different level, this struggle can be seen as part of the Third World's struggle against imperialism. I shall return to this point later.

It must be emphasized once again that the conflict cannot be reduced to just another manifestation of anti-Semitism. The prevailing confusion on this latter concept is enormous. The attribution of an evil and diabolical 'essence' to Jews of every kind throughout the ages, which is the fundamental thesis of anti-Semitism, is of course morally and scientifically indefensible and must be vigorously combated. This does not mean that every Jew or group of Jews is automatically protected by taboo. Everyone must be judged according to his merits and his faults, all actions weighed according to their own true value. If these actions harm individuals or groups, those individuals or groups should be allowed to defend their position, their rights, etc., without being denounced as exponents of a doctrine which is repugnant in itself. Any other view would entail either that every Jew or group of Jews can, by definition, only desire and do good, or else that none of their ideas or actions must ever by criticized. Obviously both attitudes are wholly unacceptable, both rationally and ethically.

It is true, conversely, that every action or word directed against the Jews, even though justified, may lead to generalizations which fall within the category of anti-Semitism. Any conflict in which a group of Jews is a protagonist is liable to degenerate in this way. Likewise every war throughout history, though perhaps fought for thoroughly insignificant reasons, has led to abusive generalizations directed against the nature, the very essence, of the opponent. This is what I prefer to term 'war racialism'. Plentiful examples can be found in the 1914–18 war, among others. Among the Allies, it was common to think of the Germans as an accursed race. It was dangerous to point out that certain pure-bred Germans had been moderately competent musicians, for instance, or that others had made some small contribution to Western philosophy. This is a deplorable phenomenon, but apparently inherent in the human species as we know it. It is a particularly dangerous phenomenon in the case of the Jews. It is distressing and dangerous to observe the growth of philosophies which when pressed to extremes have, in the very recent past, led to the massacre of millions. Every effort must be made to combat these pernicious abusive generalizations. We must ask the Arabs to understand, even though the Zionists have done them a great wrong, that this wrong, too, is a normal symptom, not particularly diabolical, of relations between groups of human beings. They must appreciate that they themselves have perpetrated similar wrongs (and are still doing so, in some places) on other peoples. Secondly, they must recognize that this wrong was the doing of the Jewish Zionists, and not of all Jews, past, present and future. Of course as long as the problem created by the Zionists lasts, persuasion is likely to have limited success. It is made still more difficult by the fact that the Zionists freely proclaim that Zionism is the natural outcome of the whole of Jewish history, something which belongs to the very essence of Judaism and to which all the world's Jews owe allegiance. What is more, they have in many cases actually won such allegiance. However understandable these demonstrations of solidarity may be, it should be understood that they contribute towards turning the Arabs' anti-Zionism into anti-Semitism.

In any case, a clear distinction must be drawn between European anti-Semitism, founded on mythical grievances, and Arab anti-Zionism, which has occasionally flared into anti-Semitism. Although some of the criticisms of the Jews made by European anti-Semites might appear to some people to have some small foundation – such as their over-exclusive attachment to certain professions and the character-traits said to result from it – this is only because Christian society had imposed these professions on the Jews. By contrast, in the case of the Israeli-Arab conflict, the first move was a gratuitous act on the part of a group of Jews – namely the project of Zionism. However much one might wish to justify this project, it certainly cannot be claimed that it was imposed by Arab society! The conflict is therefore in no way a new manifestation of congenital Arab anti-Semitism, or of the hostility of Islam towards the Jewish faith. Those Europeans who have been struck by certain similarities in expression between the Arab anti-Zionist struggle and Hitler-type anti-Semitism, concluding that they are the same, are making a serious mistake. As has already been said, they are reducing the problem of the conflict to the categories with which they are familiar. The Muslim faith is certainly hostile to Judaism, but rather less than is Christianity. It allows Judaism some degree of validity, and with few exceptions has not attempted to convert the Jews by force. Many Jews fleeing from Christian persecution have found a refuge in the territory of Islam. The relations between religious communities in the Muslim world were, like relations between the nations, characterized by a finely balanced mixture of hostility and coexistence. The Jews were a minority, defeated and subject community living amongst a Muslim majority which held power. Like the Christians, who shared their status, they were forced into a position of humility and therefore despised. But these conditions, which still held true for the traditional Muslim world, began to change in the course of the nineteenth century. A trend towards a secular society on the European model was beginning to manifest itself. This evolutionary trend was partly stemmed, first by the reaction to the Zionist movement and subsequently by the creation of the State of Israel. Like all similar movements, hostility to Zionism used every weapon that lay to hand. The after-affects of religious hostility to Judaism were exploited, and so were the feelings of contempt for the Jews, a relic of the Middle Ages. However, there can be no doubt that any foreign occupation, Chinese, Katangese, Christian or Buddhist, would have aroused the same hostility.

There is, finally, a popular Zionist theory which regards the conflict as a manifestation of 'pan-Arabism'. It would seem that the reasoning behind this theory accepts that every Arab country should defend its own interests – the Tunisians the interests of Tunisia, the Syrians those of Syria, etc.; but when all the Arab nations unite in the cause of the Arabs of Palestine, that is 'imperialism'. This theory is often accompanied by the rider that if it were only the Palestinians with whom Israel had to deal, nothing would be simpler than to come to some mutually satisfactory agreement – a strange assertion, in view of the fact that the Palestinians are the most fervent and active exponents of the struggle against Israel. More generally, it is also curious to note that the legitimacy of feelings of solidarity among the Arabs should be contested by those who declare that it is the duty of all Jews to stand behind Israel. There have been ties of common history and culture between Arabs of different countries for many centuries, since they have throughout lived in collective groups with significant national characteristics. By contrast, the ties between Jews were very much weaker; they did not even have a common language, the minimum requirement for community of culture. Whether the Arabs unite or remain separate is a matter of indifference to the outside world; there are no possible grounds for condemning either complete or informal union between them, as long as they do not use it for the purpose of conquering other territories. Piedmont was not condemned, during the struggle for Italian unity, for coming to the aid of Lombardy and Venetia, then occupied by Austria-Hungary.

The Arabs of Iraq may be reproached for their recurrent oppressive policy towards the Kurds, the Arabs of north Sudan may be criticized for their policy towards the Negroes of the south. These are not symptoms of pan-Arabism, however; these are no grand schemes for the subjugation of non-Arab countries by the Arab states acting in concert.

It is true that the struggle against Israel may be seen as the conquest of one country by a group of its neighbours, and this is the standpoint from which the great majority of non-Arab governments and peoples view the question. More will be said of this later on. What is certain is that the Arabs reject this point of view, and maintain that their struggle is directed towards retrieving lost Arab territory, taken from them by a process of colonization.

Their 'pan-Arab' solidarity is founded on this basis. No such solidarity has been exhibited when Arab states have put forward claims to non-Arab lands – claims which may always have existed, or at least for a very long time. No support has been found for those who may have wished to Arabize or place under Arab domination various non-Arab peoples. Thus the efforts of the north Sudanese to Arabize the south have not awakened any Arab solidarity; the Iraqis' war against the Kurds has been condemned by Nasser himself; Syria's claims to the Sanjak of Alexandretta (now Iskenderun), with its largely Turkish population, have left the other Arab states cold. The Arabs' astonishing solidarity against Israel is explained by the fact that no Arab can overlook the colonial character of the Jewish occupation of Palestine.

The mechanism of the conflict's development can only be explained if we recognize this fact – that it is a struggle against unaccepted foreign domination.

The Arabs have never, at any stage, accepted the *fait accompli* carried out at their expense and without their agreement by Israeli power, backed up by the support of the European and American world. At every Israeli victory, the most conciliatory of them have resigned themselves to accepting the previous victory but have attempted to reject all the consequences of the latest one. They have always been one war behind, because their protests against the encroachments on what they believe to be their rights have been continuous.

Until 1948 they refused to countenance the seizure of Palestine territory to form a Jewish State. They therefore fought against the Balfour Declaration, which was apparently intended to bring this about (a unilateral act on the part of Great Britain, be it once more noted). At least, this was the interpretation of the Balfour Declaration to which they objected. They directed their efforts towards limiting Jewish immigration, either by appealing to the British, or, as some of them did, by negotiating directly with the Zionists. The object was to prevent immigration from resulting in the formation of a Jewish majority in Palestine, or even in a population numerous enough to provide a basis for the creation of a Jewish State. Their failure to achieve this end was sealed by the U.N. partition plan of November 1947. The international community, dominated by the American and Soviet superpowers, wanted to impose on them a dismemberment of Arab territory. They refused to accept this *Diktat*, and embarked on the guerrilla war of 1947–8, and the war of 1948. They were defeated in the field, and obliged to sign armistice agreements (all except Iraq). From that time on, the Arab states bordering on Palestine recognized Israel's existence, in practice. They still rejected the new boundaries, and refused to accept the Israeli conquests which went beyond the territory granted to Israel by the U.N. They were also outraged at the expulsion of the Palestinians from Israeli territory. They were supported by the U.N. on these two points, but Israel ignored the U.N. decisions and refused to implement them. The general Arab claim was still maintained, and found expression in the competitive militancy of the various states and national movements. This prevented the Arab governments, who were on the whole disposed to do so, from bluntly expressing *de facto* recognition of Israel within the frontiers laid down by the U.N. plan, let alone establishing diplomatic relations with Israel. The Israelis, for their part, provided them with excellent grounds for non-recognition, by refusing to accept the *principle* of a return to the U.N. plan or to implement the Organization's decisions on the refugees and on Jerusalem.

The same process has repeated itself after the conquests of June 1967. Some of the Arab states are now ready to accord *de facto* recognition to the Jewish State within its frontiers of 1948–67, but refuse to endorse its latest conquests. The general Arab claim prevents them from going any further than this.

On the other side, Israel's consistent policy has been to make the Arabs recognize her existence, first of all – itself established by conquest – and secondly the conquests of 1948. These seem to the more moderate Israelis to provide the minimum guarantee for the survival of their state. At the same time, the departure of the refugees, for whatever reasons, seems to them essential if the Jewish character of the state is to be preserved, this being the prime aim and postulate of Zionist ideology. Only a very limited return would be acceptable. The Arab refusal results in a feeling of insecurity which makes any concession extremely difficult. The refusal means that the war is still on, and in no war will either side let go of any part of the advantage it has won.

The activist policy of Ben Gurion and his school is designed to obtain Arab recognition by terror, by the deployment of force. The policy has failed – except possibly for the June war of 1967, on which only the future can pass judgement. However, in Israel no coherent alternative policy is possible. Neither Sharett nor Eshkol and Eban have been able to make any substantial concession on the frontiers or the refugees, given the state of Israeli public opinion. Sharett, who in 1950 went furthest in this direction, met with violent internal opposition. The Israeli Left is just as intransigent on this point as the Right. At most, some are prepared to envisage a conditional return of some of the refugees, which is very far from satisfying the Arabs. Moreover no Israeli is able to point to any clearly stated Arab concession on the formal recognition of the state, or on the renunciation of part, at least, of the Arab claim. They were reduced to making oblique manoeuvres which may, at most and only after a long interval, create a climate more favourable to mutual concessions. But they have not got the time.

The causes of the 1967 crisis seem to lie on the one hand in the weakness of the moderate sector of Israeli public opinion and its representatives in the government, and on the other hand in the internal contradictions which prevent the Arabs from presenting a united front, able to choose a coherent policy and stick to it, and, above all, to offer to Israelis of good will any other programme than their destruction. The good intentions of some Arab leaders have in practice been nullified in any effect that they might have had on the Israelis by the fact that these leaders did not dare to give clear and public expression to them. This has enabled the Israeli activists to persuade the masses that no faith could be placed in them. Moreover, the divisions within the Arab world have meant that some rulers have been in a position to commit acts of war against Israel while others had to take the consequencies. Combinations of circumstances like this occurred on several occasions. It was a rather special chain of events which, on this occasion, led to war, and to its manifold and grave consequences.

In Europe, it is very easy to pass from the observation of facts and the description of the conflict to making moral judgements. Indeed in many cases the moral judgement precedes the mere basic acquisition of a few relevant facts. The judgement should be informed, and the levels of analysis clearly defined. On these conditions, a moral appreciation is legitimate.

There is *some* right on both sides in this affair. But there is no supreme tribunal or court of arbitration equipped with an ethical doctrine to decide questions involving relations between peoples, to grade those rights and draw up a final balance-sheet of blame and praise.

The Israelis have rights, certainly. An abstract judgement would grant them the right to live within the framework of the institutions which they have established. On the credit side, the great works which they have accomplished and the sufferings they have endured may be added to that right. But for one thing, they cannot be said to have a historic right to a piece of territory because some of their ancestors supposedly inhabited it two thousand years ago. For another, they ought to recognize that they have done a considerable wrong to another people, in depriving them of rights at least as great as their own.

The bitterness felt by the people to whom this wrong was done still persists, and as long as it does, the rights of the Israelis will remain purely hypothetical. They can only hope that the Arabs will one day recognize and accept them. Only then will their rights become real.

How are they to make themselves accepted? There is a moral way, which consists in discussion and persuasion. Politically, such a method has more chance of success if accompanied by concessions. There is also an immoral way, by the use of force. Whether or not it is effective has nothing very much to do with ethics. Yet it should be pointed out that the use of force entails very great risks in the case of Israel and her Arab neighbours. A forced acceptance can more easily be called in question by a change of government than a negotiated one. In addition, if recurrent recourse to arms proves necessary for an indefinite period, the force is liable not to remain on the same side for ever.

In any case, it is wrong of Israel to regard its rights as absolute. The good conscience of the Israelis is a sign of their naïvety. How many Israelis, Zionists and pro-Israelis are convinced that the Right is entirely on their side! If the Arabs refuse to recognize this fact, it means that they are morally corrupt, swayed by evil forces, or else the victims of unsavoury conspiracies. The Israelis, on the whole, refuse to accept the fact that *their* right violates other rights which are no less respectable. It is sometimes difficult not to feel more sympathy for the cynicism of the activists, who see the problem simply in terms of the balance of forces, than for this obstinate blindness.

The Arabs, too, have rights. In many respects, they may justifiably be held to be greater than the Israelis'. The Arabs of Palestine used to have the same rights over Palestinian territory as the French exercise in France and the English in England. These rights have been violated without any provocation on their part. There is no evading this simple, incontestable fact. The multiple lesser wrongs which they may have committed, the complex web of circumstance, and the responsibility in detail for specific events cannot alter it.

Neither should it, on the other hand, be made an absolute in turn. If the consequences of pressing a just claim are liable to be calamitous and unjust, and too fraught with practical difficulties, there may be grounds for suggesting that it be renounced. The wrong done to the Arabs by the Israelis is very real. However, it is only too common throughout history. Innumerable violations of rights of this nature have taken place since the beginnings of human society. Sometimes one side, sometimes the other has been the ultimate beneficiary. The Arabs, in their history, have made conquests on an infinitely greater scale and wronged many another nation. Some still behave in an entirely reprehensible manner – towards the Kurds for instance, and the negroes of South Sudan. The conquests of the past have been shrouded by the moral prescript of forgetfulness. The colonists are not monsters in human form, but people responding to reflexes which are unfortunately only too characteristic of social man. No one can without hypocrisy judge himself or his community to be free of such reflexes.

We may therefore plead with the Arabs to accept the *fait accompli*. No oracle can tell us how much time must pass before acceptance becomes the right or advisable thing. In another work I have quoted the somewhat comparable case of Ulster, conquered by force of arms under Cromwell, peopled by English and Scottish Protestants and thus through the establishment of a new population torn away from Catholic Ireland. The expropriations which accompanied the conquest of Ireland and the cruelties of the colonial administration which followed it are well known. When Ireland was granted independence, an exception was made of Ulster. Recognition of the *fait accompli* meant recognizing a violation of right, imposed by force. But at the same time it was a recognition of the right acquired by the Ulstermen to live within their own new national community. This was in 1920. The Irish Republic protested, and solemnly refused to recognize this unjust encroachment of their national territory. This state of affairs lasted for forty-five years. Then, in 1965, came recognition: the President of the Irish Republic made an official visit to Belfast.

The Arabs could, therefore, be asked to accept the *fait accompli*. It is obvious that the request would have a greater chance of being favourably received if it is accompanied with an offer of concessions and inducements. The rest of the world would be happy to see peace established. At the same time, it is quite certain that no-one is so pure as to have the right to *demand* acceptance and condemn the Arabs in the name of universal morality if they continue to refuse.

A case could be made out for giving the Arab cause a near-absolute value. This point of view is held by a section of the international Left, which maintains that Israel is a bastion of imperialism; her very existence is held to be a threat to progress and liberty in the world at large, and in the Arab world in particular.

It is true that because of Israel's colonial birth and the Arab hostility aroused by it, she is forced to rely on the support of the European-American powers which have so far protected her. She is largely financially dependent on the American Jewish community, which is well ensconced in the United States. Her standard of living and advanced technology place her among the highly developed nations. Israel is, therefore, as Herzl would have wished, a bridgehead of the industrialized capitalist world in the heart of the underdeveloped world.

Yet it does not seem that Israel participates to any major extent in the system of exploitation of the Third World by the industrial world. The opportunities for exploitation conferred by her technical superiority are much reduced by the small area of her territory, by the difficulties she has with her immediate neighbours, and by her own economic dependence on the European and American capitalist powers.

Israel's membership of the Western world is more a matter of political choice than of economic structure. The reasons for this choice lie in the factors which have already been enumerated. It makes it very difficult for the socialist countries of the Third World and for progressive elements the world over to take Israel's side in her quarrel with her Arab neighbours. Indeed the Arab masses very much share the aspirations of the Third World to independence and modernization. For fairly obvious reasons, these aspirations drive the masses into resolute opposition to the West's tendencies to economic and political hegemony. Their passionate desire to achieve these ends is so strong that it forces their reluctant governments at least to simulate the same aspirations, and to make some concrete gestures towards their fulfilment. Sometimes it brings to power a government sincerely devoted to fulfilling these aspirations. It is perfectly understandable that the Arab peoples should see in Israel, that colony of the West, politically bound to the West, above all else a bastion of the West, a bastion which must be torn down. It is very difficult for those who share the Arabs' aspirations to oppose them on this matter.

Yet false and over-schematized conceptions of Israel's membership of and dependence on the Western world must be rejected. Such conceptions are very widely held among the Arabs and elsewhere, and are furthermore frequently linked to Marxism. These notions are of a type which was fashionable in the most vulgar ideological Marxism of the Stalin era. The capitalist imperialist enemy of the people's longings for liberty and equality is represented as a kind of legendary monster, with a single head and brain controlling a host of tentacles which unhesitatingly obey the orders of the master mind. The brain is situated somewhere between the Pentagon and Wall Street, and none of the tentacles has any will of its own. Israel is supposed to be one of these, charged with the task of blocking the proletarian and anti-imperialist revolution in the Arab countries. This coarse mythological and pseudo-Marxist construction is obviously false. Israel, with all the limitations which her dependence entails, has a will and a purpose of her own. She does not automatically obey all the injunctions of the United States, nor yet those of that indefinable monster which this over-schematized Marxism calls 'imperialism'. She is primarily interested in survival, which some, but only some, of her politicians wish to ensure through some measure of expansion. The revolution in the Arab countries does not worry her in itself, as long as it is not such as to endanger her survival. Israel only plays the policeman of reaction under certain circumstances, and if it is in her interest.

Besides, nations have no eternal, unchanging essence. Their existence is in a state of constant flux. As has been said, powerful factors have driven Israel into the role which she has assumed up till now. Other factors, however, could just as well drive her in an opposite direction. A different Israel is not an impossibility. If the threat from outside were to disappear for any length of time, the process which has each time begun during periods of respite could acquire very much greater impetus. The reactionary and expansionist parties would find most of their trump cards had disappeared. The internal social struggle could continue on a much healthier basis. The Left-wing parties, no longer suspect of weakening the defences of the fort, would stand a better chance in the political struggle. With the decline of anti-Semitism in Europe and America, Jewish immigration into Israel could be reduced to more modest proportions. Jewish emigration from Israel would grow. Zionism would thus lose much of its force through sheer pressure of circumstances.

Israel would, from that moment, be a Levantine State like any other, and no more a bridgehead of the West, forced by her situation to bear the brunt of the Arab world's hostility and to seek imperialist support. The continual temptation to embark on preventive aggression would likewise be removed. The state ideology would gradually tend to adapt to the new conditions.

The privileges granted to the Jews as such would tend to disappear. Laws with racist or clerical overtones would fall into disuse and eventually be abolished. A considerable proportion of the refugees would be able to return without acting as a Fifth Column. The end-result would be a bi-national state like that dreamed about by the more open-minded and advanced spirits in Mandatory Palestine.

A state of this sort would easily be accepted by the Middle East and could enter on harmonious relations with the neighbouring Arab countries, who would benefit from Israel's technical know-how and aid. This was the dream of King Feisal, and of some courageous Jews in the Palestinian Yishuv. One is inclined to prefer it to the grandiose visions of Herzl and Ben Gurion, and to encourage all men, Israelis and Arabs alike, with the cry first set up by the Viennese journalist: 'If you really desire it, it need no longer be a dream!'

Is there any hope that this optimistic vision will be realized, even in the distant future? The situation could hardly be further from it at the moment. For the moment Israel is Israel, and there is little hope of her changing as long as she is not accepted by the Arabs. Can the Arabs accept her?

The countries which suffered most in the war, Jordan and Egypt, are tempted to accept. Again, their rulers must find a formula which they can present to their peoples without appearing to be offering total capitulation. Otherwise they would soon be overthrown by an indignant population, and nothing would have been gained. On several occasions in the past the Israelis have failed to understand – or else could or would not understand – the need for concessions on their part, which would enable the Arab leaders to win the acquiescence of their peoples. The reason for this failure has usually been their inveterate mistrust of everybody and everything, a mistrust which the intransigence of Arab propaganda, however unreal and unmeant, could only increase. At the moment, the Israelis are victorious, and victory is not conducive to concessions. On the other hand, it will be difficult for Israel to digest all the conquered territories. Indeed, Israel is now truly confronted with the dilemma of victory which I foresaw as

early as 4 June last year.* How is she to keep the conquered territories under her dominion? Either the system becomes democratic, or even remains simply liberal and parliamentary – in
which case the Arabs will very soon be in the majority, and that
will be the end of the dream of a Jewish State for which so many
sacrifices have been made. Or else the Arabs will be treated as
second-class citizens, discrimination will become institutional, a
kind of South African policy will be introduced. This, together
with the necessarily increasingly savage repression of increasingly
bold acts of sabotage and guerrilla warfare, will lose Israel the support of world public opinion, which by its pressure on government
has been Israel's chief prop.

It is therefore possible that Israel will make concessions, which
friendly governments are urging on her. Will these be generous
enough to enable the Arab governments to respond? Will the
concessions of the one party seem to the other a sufficient counterweight to their own? Here lies the crux of the matter.

What if the Arabs once again refuse to follow this course,
whether or not their refusal is justified by intransigence on the
part of Israel? They may adopt the strategy advised by Mao Tse-
Tung, the strategy of revolutionary war. This is the policy which
the Syrian government is tempted to follow, and which some
clandestine groups of Palestinians are already putting into practice,
on a small scale. It is a possible strategic choice, and as has been
stated earlier, one is hardly in a position to make moral strictures,
however terrible the consequences of such a course might turn
out to be. I do think, on the other hand, that those outside the
conflict, who are neither Palestinians nor Arabs, but who spur
the parties on to further bloodshed – these are worthy of moral
condemnation.

It should be emphasized that contrary to the ideas held by a
section of the Arab Left, the revolution does not necessarily
entail revolutionary war. Some Arab countries have been led by
the struggle for independence to carry out extensive nationalization measures, i.e. to the partial adoption of a sort of socialist
economy, in the generally accepted sense. In the absence of a
dynamic and independent-minded class, or of the circumstances

* See article in *Le Monde.*

enabling that class to flourish, this was the only way of giving the economy a self-sufficient base. This was because free enterprise tended to specialize in activities unfavourable to an autonomous economy, and therefore to make the country dependent on Western capitalism. However, it seems that no really far-reaching revolution took place anywhere, making a profound break with the traditions of the past, and placing the controls in the hands of those sectors which have so far been completely denied access to power, prestige, culture and the good life. The deficiencies of the middle sectors of the population which in practice held the reins of power in the so-called 'revolutionary' states – deficiencies which the recent war had cruelly illuminated – reinforced the opinion of those who thought that only more radical revolutions could drag the Arab world out of its backwardness, and truly liberate the underprivileged from the yoke of the traditional hierarchial order.

Some revolutionaries in the Arab world would like to combine a revolution of this type with a popular revolutionary war against Israel. They are right, but only in a sense. A profound internal revolution does not *necessarily* have to be tied to a war against Israel. Certainly the mass of the people in some of the Arab countries would find it difficult to grasp that they were being enrolled in the struggle against imperialism while Israel, to them the most glaring symbol of the imperialist world and the one which touched them most directly, was excluded from the revolution's primary objectives. Yet they understood very well that Syria, for instance, took care not to offer military provocation to Turkey or the United States. Why not take the same attitude to Israel? A policy like Lenin's at Brest-Litovsk is certainly possible, although it demands considerable courage on the part of the rulers applying it.

Conversely, revolutionary war could bring about the revolution. But the circumstances which would attend such a development present a fairly terrifying prospect, and it is by no means certain that the leaders who choose this road are fully aware of them. A revolutionary war against Israel conducted by Palestine commandos supported by some of the Arab states is very possible. It has even begun, on a very small scale. If Israel keeps the territory conquered in June 1967, it is likely to spread. But it is unlikely that the states concerned could both pursue the war and maintain the pretence of neutrality. The situation would resemble that in Vietnam; as a result, the countries directly concerned in supporting the Palestine guerillas would risk the present fate of the Democratic Republic of North Vietnam. Are the Arab peoples concerned capable of facing up to this prospect? The casualties and destruction, in the expert opinion of Mao Tse-Tung, are liable to reach very major proportions over a very long period. If this happens, one of two things could result. There would either be a radical revolution which alone could sustain such a war – if it could; or less revolutionary elements would come to power. Indeed, even highly reactionary forces might take over, no less hostile to Israel in their heart of hearts, but prepared to implement a Brest-Litovsk policy to their own advantage. It would be rash, at this stage, to predict which of these two possibilities is the more likely to prevail.

The Arab countries are numerous; the movements internal to them are even more so. Each will no doubt follow its own path. The result will be a complex compound of the various simple possibilities sketched out here. Israel's intrusion into the historical development of the Middle East has added a further cause of difficulty and distress to all the others which already existed. The outside observer can only hope for an evolution towards freer, less unjust and better-off societies, at less of a disadvantage in the line-up of world forces. He can only hope that this development will take its course with the minimum of tragedy for individuals or social groups. He will understand the protagonists without sharing their passions and their illusions. He will deplore, as others have often and vainly done in the past, the internecine slaughter between men and women equally sincerely inspired by opposing ideologies. But history is cruel, and there is no sign that her thirst for human blood is near to being satisfied. We shall be lucky if these miseries and cruelties at least buy some measure of general progress. Even this is not certain. But we are not excused from fighting against the injustice of today by the prospects of further injustices tomorrow. Let us hope, at least, that the future will see the dubious descendants of the ancient Hebrews delivered from those of their dreams which can only be realized at the expense of their Palestinian cousins. Let us hope that it will see the Middle East delivered from the heaviest of its chains. May this conflict, which in no way serves the cause of humanity, be calmed, and one cause of useless hatred among so many others be eliminated. While the smallest hope of achieving this remains, there can be no excuse for those in whose power it is to contribute towards it and who make no attempt to do so.

I would like to thank G. P. Putnam's Sons for permission to quote the passage from *Golda Meir: Woman with a Cause* by Marie Syrkin. Copyright © 1963 by Marie Syrkin.